CRAZY & OBSESSED

THE COMPLETE COLLECTION

LENA MA

CONTENTS

CRAZY & OBSESSED

#OBSESSED

THE UGLY TRUTH

Crazy & Obsessed
The Complete Collection

© 2021

Cover Design by EmCat Designs

CRAZY & OBSESSED
ADDICTED TO RELATIONSHIPS

A Crazy & Obsessed Series (Book 1)

FOREWORD

The purpose of my personal love story is, not to advocate for out-of-the-ordinary, abnormal, self-destructive, and, sometimes, abusive, behaviors, but to provide insight into how and why people engage in these behaviors.

I believe there are still standards to be upheld when it comes to engaging in a relationship with another person, and that there will always be consequences when certain behaviors go awry, so I am, by no means, advocating for any of the actions that people engage in.

The purpose of my story is two-fold:

To help people see that they are not alone in the actions they partake in when they are heartbroken and in pain, and,

To minimize the stigma of pain as something to be ashamed of, and to allow people to recognize that the actions they make when they are in pain are due to sporadic and uncontrollable emotions, not personalities, and should not be used to define them as people.

We need to take a stand against having to feel "normal" and "sane" after a traumatic experience, such as the loss of someone we loved and trusted. We need to speak out against shaming people when they are only acting out of natural instincts.

It is easy for us to point blame and criticize when we are not the ones deep in the throes of those emotions, but we also need to realize that everyone eventually falls victim to feelings.

Here is my story.

PROLOGUE
MY TRAGIC LOVE LIFE

Me: "I love you so much, and I will never leave your side. These rings will stay on both your finger and mine until the end of time because I've known, from the first day I met you, that I want to marry you."

Him: "I love you too! I'm so glad you're in my life, and I promise to love you and grow old with you until the day I die."

The next afternoon

Him (via text): "We're done."

Me (dumbfounded): "Wait. What!?"

Him (frustrated and annoyed): "I said we're over. We. Are. Done. Do NOT message me or talk to me anymore. We are done."

Me: "Wait, what the fuck is going on?! What the hell changed since last night?! Talk to me about what's going on!"

Silence

Me: "Are you there?!??"

Silence

Me: "Fucking answer me! You can't ignore me like this!"

Silence

Me: "Talk to me!! What the hell happened!? You promised to marry me, and now you're dumping me!??! We've been together for six fucking years!!"

Silence

Me (thinking): Maybe he's working or too busy to realize that I'm texting him. I should call him. That'll get him to talk to me.

Calls

Voicemail

Calls again

Voicemail

Calls ten more times

Voicemail

Me (via text): "Please pick up your fucking phone!"

No answer

Me (via text): "Please pick up your phone and talk to me about this! I love you so much!"

Silence

Me: "Can I come over, and we can talk about this?

Silence

Me (tears running down my face): "I can fake sick and leave work right now, and we can talk!"

Silence

Me: "If you don't pick up, I am going to mix a bottle of vodka with a shit ton of Tylenol tonight. PAY ATTENTION TO ME!!"

Silence

Me (thinking, heart pounding rapidly): This can't be happening. What the hell did I do? Is he seeing someone else? Did I say something wrong last night? Were any parts of our relationship real? What the fuck is going on? What the FUCK is going on?! Did I just threaten to kill myself? That was messed up. He knows I'm just messing around anyway, right? Not like he fucking cares what happens to me. He's probably not even reading any of this. He FUCKING BLOCKED me, didn't he? Fuck it. I'm going to go cry myself to sleep. I hate my life! I hate my STUPID LIFE!

Later that day back at the apartment, the police show up.

Police: "Excuse me, miss. You're going to have to come with us. We have reason to believe that you are a danger to yourself and possibly others."

Me (feigning ignorance and faking a smile): "What!? I'm fine! I have no idea what you're talking about. See, perfectly happy and normal!"

Police: "Come with us, miss."

Me: "Why? There is nothing wrong with me. I just got back from work. I don't have thoughts about harming myself or others. I don't know where you're getting this information from!"

Police: "We received an anonymous call informing us that you are going to hurt yourself tonight, and we need to bring you into the hospital to keep you safe."

Me: "What the fuck!? Who the fuck called you?"

Police: "Miss, please come with us. Please don't make us utilize physical force."

Me: "God fucking damn it. FINE!!"

Inside the lobby of a psychiatric institute, after three hours of waiting and four hours of nonstop interrogation...

Nurse: "Excuse me, miss. We have evidence to believe that you are a danger to yourself. Someone sent over text messages that you had plans of harming yourself with a bottle of vodka and some Tylenol pills tonight. You need to voluntarily sign yourself in for a 72-hour minimum treatment by order of the law and your job. You are not allowed to return to work until we can successfully determine that you are no longer a danger to yourself. If you do not consent, we will be held liable for your safety, and we will be forced to take you to court on accounts of mental insanity. We will need to hold possession of your belongings: phone, keys, wallet, and any other objects except for the clothing on your back. Please sit tight in this solitary room until we can find you a bed upstairs."

Me (thinking): That fucking asshole! First, he proposes to me. Then, he breaks up with me through text and ignores my 350 messages. Now, he throws me into a FUCKING LOONY BIN!?!! FUCKING SOCIOPATH!! Who the hell does he think he is!?! I'm a person! Not a fucking doll!!! I FUCKING HATE HIM!! I love him, but I HATE HIM!!!

Me (angry, in tears, and shouting): "I'm not crazy! I'm just hurt and pissed off! And how the fuck am I supposed to hurt myself with money!? Really!?"

Silence
Quiet
Darkness
Emptiness
Loneliness
Silence

Sixteen hours later...

Nurse: "Alright, miss. Come with us. We need to have you examined by a psychotherapist before we can assign you to your room."

Me: "Can you please stop calling me "miss"? I have a name. It's on that board you won't take your eyes off of."

Silence
Me (annoyed): "Really? Okay, MISS, you have me on lock-

down with 24/7 supervision. What am I supposed to do, NOT BREATHE TO DEATH?"

Nurse: "Miss, please behave, or I will be forced to have you restrained."

Me: "I'm not even doing anyt…"

Nurse: "I said, BEHAVE!"

Restrained and in the therapist's office (or rather, a dark and empty crapshack conference room)…

Psychotherapist: "So, how are you feeling right now?"

Me: "Why do you guys always ask that as a starter question?"

Psychotherapist: "We find that patients tend to respond better to questions and statements that show we care."

Me: "Do you really care though? Or are you just following a script so you can go home after your shift?"

Psychotherapist: "So, how are you feeling right now?"

Me: "You totally dodged my question! What happened to, "showing that we care"?!"

Psychotherapist: "Please just answer the question."

Me: "For fuck's sake. Fine, I feel like crap. Are you fucking happy now!?"

Psychotherapist: "I am always happy, and you can be too. Also, crap is not a feeling."

Me (chuckling): "Wait, wait. You're ALWAYS happy??! I call bullshit, mainly because you totally have resting bitch face right now."

Psychotherapist: "Please watch your language. I am here to help you because I understand what you are going through, and I want to help you get out of here as soon as possible. Now, please, tell me how you are feeling."

Me: "You don't give a shit about me! If you do, you would focus on what I'm saying and my tone of voice rather than focusing on writing, whatever the hell you're writing, on that clipboard! Also, watch my language?!?!? Does it fucking look like we're in church?!? Oh no, save me, Jesus! I can't wait to get out of here so I can cut myself with A DOLLAR BILL!"

Security guard (holding my arms down): "PLEASE STOP RESISTING AND COMPLY!"

Me: "Damn, dude. Chill the fuck out. Fine, I'll fucking behave."

Psychotherapist: "Let's try this one more time. How are you feeling right now?"

Me: "Like crap."

Psychotherapist: "Like I said, crap is not a feeling."

Me: "Okay. Like pissed-off crap."

Psychotherapist: "Why are you pissed off?"

Me: "Wouldn't you be pissed off if your son-of-a-bitch fiancé broke up with you for no reason and with no explanation, through FUCKING TEXT of all things, after promising to love you forever, ignores you all day, and then gets you locked up in the loony bin without answering your 60 phone calls? We were together for SIX FUCKING YEARS! He didn't think I deserved a little more respect than silence after being together for six years?!"

Psychotherapist: "Okay, and how does that make you feel?"

Me: "Really, bitch? You asked that already. LIKE PISSED-OFF CRAP!!!"

Psychotherapist: "I am afraid you will have to stay here for a few days. You seem very hostile, and I fear that you will harm yourself or someone else, particularly your fiancé, if I let you leave here tonight untreated."

Me (thinking): Wait, hold the fucking phone. Back up about a mile here. First, what the fuck do you mean by "untreated"? What kind of fucking treatment are you planning on doing to me!? You better not overdose me with a shit ton of pills, that you don't even know works or not, and then use that as an excuse to keep me in here longer! Second, you asked the same question twice, both times which I answered, and suddenly I'm the crazy one? Third, since when does feeling angry because of a terrible situation equate to being suicidal and homicidal? I can't express my emotions without being deemed a psychotic murderer? Were you even listening to anything I said, or were you deliberately trying to piss me off on purpose so you can use that as an excuse to keep me here!? What the fuck is wrong with you people!? I am a fucking human being, not some doll that you can throw around from place to place just because I'm currently a little erratic!

Psychotherapist: "Are you okay? You haven't said anything in a while."

Me (thinking): It was ten seconds, bitch. Get off my back. Besides, the more I say, the more you can use what I say against me to fucking LOCK ME UP EVEN LONGER!

Me (mumbling): "Yeah. I'm okay."

Psychotherapist: "Alright then. Let me show you to your room."

Me: "Can I just make one phone call? It's important! Just one!"

Psychotherapist: "I'm sorry, miss. It's after hours. The other residents need to sleep. You can use the phone tomorrow."

Me: "I'M NOT FUCKING CRAZY AND STOP CALLING ME "MISS"!!"

The doors close.
I remain alone.
In a dark, damp room.
Locked up.
In solitary confinement.

CHAPTER 1
I AM NOT CRAZY

"To be crazy is to possess the mindset of craziness. Only by acknowledging that the acts we create are flawed, will they be flawed." ℒ

I AM sure I am not the only one who has been through crazy and psychotic messes after a terrible breakup, a breakup that feels like betrayal, from someone I once loved deeply and thought returned the same feelings. It is completely natural to feel like we are going insane when we fall from the very top of the positive emotions' spectrum to the very bottom.

You probably thought, or still think, that you are crazy for becoming obsessive over someone you love who will not love you back, and there is good reason for that because, for so long, everyone around you has told you that certain types of behavior either resemble that of a stalker or that of a serial killer.

But just because we act out in response to the pain we feel, does not make us psychotic or evil. If these actions persisted for months and months, then that is a different story, but feeling hurt does not have to equate to being ashamed of the way we feel in response to traumatic situations.

We want to love so badly that, when we are let down or when we are betrayed, we revert to childlike states and act out impulsively and wildly as a coping mechanism. We have been given one knowledge of information for so long, to meet someone, fall in love, and get married, that when that suddenly changes, we become confused and lost in our ways, unsure of which actions to engage in next.

We lose our conscience and our logic because the person we have fallen in love with and trusted has betrayed us, putting a dent in our knowledge of information without the option of another path.

What my synopsis above did not cover was, my 6-year relationship was not always full of love, promises, and fancy rings. About five months into the dating phase, my now ex-fiancé cheated on me. Inexperienced with long-term relationships at the time, my emotions started fucking around with me, telling me both to leave and to stay, to find someone new and to try to make it work.

But he was a charmer, and he was manipulative. He fed me lies and bullshit excuses of how he thought I was his soulmate and the other woman was just a mistake. He sucked me back in, and I became entrapped for the next six years.

Looking back now, it was obvious that he did not love me, or at least not enough to remain loyal. The cheating did not stop; it just became sneakier, and soon after, he stopped trying to hide it altogether. Woman after woman, bra after bra, excuse after excuse, but I still could not get out. It felt like I could not see the reality of what was going on.

I thought the cheating meant that I had to prove that I was good enough to be with him, like it was some sort of competition. I hated myself because he enjoyed being with other women more than he enjoyed being with me. I gave him everything I could to try to get him to stop cheating, including buying him everything he wanted, paying for his car, and paying rent I could not afford alone when he stopped working for five years. I had become his slave and caretaker, but he still did not stop.

Then the abuse came, first mental, then physical, and eventually, both simultaneously. I was called "bitch," "idiot," "stupid," "whore," "cunt," and everything in between. When I tried to defend myself, I was beat, first purely out of rage, and then daily. I went to work several times with a black eye, and I hid my bruises from my family. I told everyone around me that my relationship was amazing, and I could not be more in love.

But inside, I was dying. I wanted out, but at the same time, I felt guilty for leaving after having invested so much time and energy into the toxic relationship. There had been a few times, 298 to be exact, where he had broken up with me, giving me the out that I wanted, but I did not take it. Instead, I chased him and begged for him to come back, making impossible promises I could not uphold, and losing more and more of myself each time.

Soon, I was trapped in an infinite loop where it felt almost instinctual to chase after him whenever he leaves, even when I consciously knew I should not. I started to feel like I was doing something wrong, with anxiety kicking in when I WAS NOT begging for him to come back.

Pretty fucked up, right?

But, like all addictions, love included, realization usually does not set in until AFTER hitting ROCK-BOTTOM. Being locked up in a psychiatric institute for six weeks, yes, six weeks! (the 72-hour voluntary stay they make you sign is a bullshit excuse for them to get you through the doors), was my rock-bottom.

Maybe I just needed space away from him to realize that I did not need him.

Maybe I needed an external physical force to keep me away from him and snap me out of my behaviors.

Maybe I just needed time alone to reminisce on all the pain that I had endured when I was with him.

Maybe part of me will always love him and want to be with him.

Who knows?

I just know that I am out, and I do not want to go back in.

Why did I continue to stay in my toxic relationship after the FIRST time he cheated on me, or even after the second? Why do a lot of people continue to stay in terrible and abusive relationships?

Because of a little thing called "false hope."

When we enter new relationships, we become so infatuated by the charm of other people, seeing only the positive and putting them on pedestals. So, when they make the switch and begin to show their true colors, despite how malicious, we still try to reason with ourselves that they are just having an off-day, and that things will go back to normal if we have a little patience and wait around for them to recuperate.

The problem is, nobody has an off-day for six years straight! I did not know then what my tiny brain knows now. Maybe it was loneliness, maybe it was desperation, or maybe it was a combination of both, but I forced myself to hold on regardless of how much I was hurting.

I forced myself to continue loving a manipulative and

abusive cheater. I believed that if I fought through the physical abuse and the infidelity, then maybe, FINALLY, I would have proven my love to him.

I realize the shit I have been through are not normal behaviors in relationships. But what I have learned is that, as messed up as the actions I engaged in were, those actions are much more common than we like to believe.

Crazy behaviors are what we tend to hide from the world to show others that nothing is wrong, or could ever be wrong, with us. Another moral I have learned is that, this whole time, I was fighting a battle with myself, not my ex, during and after the relationship.

The biggest demon I was facing was my emotions, and the more I tried to fight it, the more I lost. Part of me knew that calling out suicidal threats and staying with a man who beat me were out-of-the-ordinary behaviors.

However, I felt so hurt, alone, and sad that crying for help and staying in the comforting behaviors I have been so used to seemed to be the only ways, at the time, to relieve myself from those burdening emotions. I hated dealing with how I was feeling.

Emotions can pull us toward the highest highs and the lowest lows, and I just wanted them to disappear completely. We try so hard to keep ourselves together, blocking out all unpleasant emotions, that we leave ourselves feeling numb.

We would rather experience apathy and emptiness than experience pain, because pain means pain while apathy and emptiness mean lack of pain. Unfortunately, because I tried to numb myself, I also felt alone for years, unable to see past the darkness that I was consumed in, unable to escape the shit-hole life I was living in, and isolating myself from everyone I cared about. My biggest enemy was myself, and I could not see past the paradigm of loving someone I hated and hating someone I was supposed to love.

The crazy acts that I engaged in during my relationships

and my breakups, the crazy acts we all engage in during our relationships and our breakups, come from a place of love and care rather than a place of insanity and psychosis. We expend so much energy and effort on someone, or something, because we cannot imagine what it would feel like to not have that person, or that thing, in our lives anymore.

Being emotional DOES NOT mean being a PSYCHOPATH. We deal with so many emotions at once that we become unsure of whether to give up or to persist, to accept or deny, to live or let live. When we are in relationships where we do not allow pain to affect us, we become numb to love, making it more difficult to give love back to ourselves.

Let me be the one to drill this into your head! You are NOT crazy!

We are NOT crazy!

Emotions can destroy the best of us and drive even the most level-headed person up the wall! It does NOT mean that we deserve to be sent to mental institutions; it means that we are experiencing feelings that are too overwhelming for us to handle in our current states of mind.

These feelings can be old or new; it DOES NOT MATTER. When the heart breaks, it breaks, and it takes the rest of the body down with it.

Embrace that we are emotional creatures. The more we try to hide that we have feelings, the longer it takes for us to heal. Each relationship and each breakup did not teach me something about that specific person and what I should and should not be looking for in a partner.

Instead, each experience taught me something about myself and how I experience and handle emotions. Unless these emotions are suicidal or homicidal, why not just let them roam free?

CHAPTER 2
WHAT IS WRONG WITH US?

"We have become so hated by society that we even begin to hate ourselves. Our obedience is our Achilles' heel." ℒ

LOVE.

Dating.

Soulmates.

Promises.

What do these words all have in common?

The first words that come to mind are "false beliefs." We all want that special someone to share our lives with, to share the good times and the bad, to have that shoulder to cry on, and to have hands to hold when we feel joyful.

We have longed for these moments from when we first experienced affection toward someone, whether it was our first crush in elementary school or our first kiss in high school. We reveled in being able to love someone, but with that naivety, our hearts were also shattered when those relationships ended.

Maybe some of you are the lucky ones who marry the first person you felt a connection with. The rest of us know, all too well, how it feels to open our hearts and our lives to one single person, to put so much power into the hands of that person, just to have him/her rip our hearts out from inside our chests and walk away. Many people still believe that there are levels of severity for which you are allowed to feel heartbroken.

Marriage > long-term relationships > short-term relationships > casual partners > friends with benefits > crushes

But this is not the case at all, and the more we try to tell ourselves that it is and believe that other people's heartbreaks are more "severe" than ours because of the length of their relationships, the more we end up hurting ourselves.

We need to stop lying to ourselves that we are not in pain.

We need to stop trying to quickly heal ourselves from losing the ones we love by having mindless sex with or serially dating other people.

We need to stop covering our true pain with fake smiles so others think we are okay.

We need to stop pretending that we are okay when we are not.

Even more so, we need to stop obsessing over the ones we have lost and bombarding them with every thought that pops into our heads. That may have been alright to do at one point IN THE RELATIONSHIP, but when someone wants out of a relationship, for any reason, valid or invalid, stupid or not, we need to learn to accept that and let that person go.

I am not innocent or logical when it comes to breakups, and my impulsivity can turn me from a sweet and caring girlfriend to a crazy and psychotic bitch who does not know how to accept rejection and move on.

I go back and forth with hating my exes.

Loving them.

Apologizing for actions I have not committed.

Begging for forgiveness and second chances.

Accepting responsibility for all faults of the relationships.

Telling myself that I am better off without them.

Denying the reality of the situations.

Attempting to move on by dating the next person I run into.

Becoming angry and hostile when pleads to my exes do not work.

Becoming depressed and borderline.

Sitting in my apartment for months, drinking, binging, and hating the world.

Completely losing myself.

Being desperate and heartbroken make us ignore what is going on. We become addicted to reaching out to our exes and the idea of our exes rather than wanting to be with them. Our addictions blind us from what we want and keep us focused on one goal: TO GET THEM BACK.

We think that by making dumb compromises and promises we do not believe in, they will come running back to us and pleading to be with us.

But when does that ever happen? The more dumb compromises and fake promises that we make, the more we drive them away, and we know that, BUT WE STILL DO THEM ANYWAY. This is life, and life likes to fuck with us by giving us what we do not want and taking away the things we love most.

Haven't you ever realized that when your ex-partner, the same ex-partner you have spent months, or even years, crying miserably over, comes back to you ONLY when you are NO LONGER OBSESSING over him/her, you feel instantly turned off, regardless of whether you have met someone new or not, and you no longer want that ex-partner back?

We think we love someone now and that this is the greatest person out there, and in some cases, that may be true, but the person we painfully chase and destroy ourselves over will most likely not be the person we end up with.

Persistence does not equate to love. 99% of us do not end up with our first lovers or the "perfect person." Instead, we end up settling for those who actually stick around, those who love us enough to NOT HURT us. Not even once.

If they are capable of hurting us once, they are capable of hurting us again.

When someone leaves us, we expend all our energy on him/her until we are drained. We then become tired of chasing "the one" and settle for those who treat us like we matter. We do not marry the ones we fall for at first sight, the ones we connect with immediately and have amazing sex with; we marry the ones who treat us the way we deserve to be treated, and we eventually learn to love them.

I firmly believe that, if a relationship does not work out the first time, then it will never be the same the second time around despite how hard we work at it. It may work out in the sense of fewer arguments and more compromises, but the spark, passion, and trust that drove two people together in the first place will never be recovered.

Once a traitor, always a traitor.

When we commit ourselves to long-term relationships, or when we have learned to trust someone so immensely, we fear letting that go.

We fear not being able to find someone else who understands us and loves us.

We fear starting over.

We fear the idea of trusting someone new because we do not want to be betrayed again.

We fear acknowledging that we have made decisions that ended in failure.

We fear failure.

We all desperately want to love that we generate thoughts we do not believe in like, "we should change for someone else," "this is the best it is going to get," and "it will definitely work out this time!" Human beings crave love and affection. We fall head-over-heels when the ones we love promise to never forsake us or promise to give us the world.

These "promises" strike our core desires so intensely that, from that moment on, we place those people on our pedestals. We become attached to the words of those people rather than the people themselves. We lose ourselves in those relationships as we try to make those partners happy, and we lose ourselves when those relationships are over as we try to get those partners back.

We no longer know who we are.

We are all strong and independent people who had lives of our own before we fell in love, and we strive to continue to have lives even when that love is taken away. However, when heartbreak hits, our hearts drop to the ground, our brains turn into mush, and we become the people we ridicule in romantic movies. When we are heartbroken, we can only focus on trying to get our exes back. We do not take the time to reflect on whether having them back is what we truly want, and we do not know if we still love them. We only know that we want them because we no longer have them.

We want what we cannot have. We need that challenge, and our exes thrive on that. We give them power when we chase after them, and they hold onto that power when they refuse to acknowledge us. They know that as soon as they answer us or hint that they want us back, we stop chasing, and ALL EXES LOVE BEING CHASED.

This is also why exes always come back AS SOON AS we stop chasing. Like I said, human beings want what they cannot have, and they will go crazy until they get it.

Why is it difficult for people to form faithful relationships without craving infidelity or drama?

Why is it difficult for people to compromise without maintaining stubbornness?

Why is it difficult for people to stop fucking with our emotions so they can feel satisfied and powerful?

Why is it difficult for people to stop expecting us to prove our love to them daily?

Why is it difficult for people to stop manipulating others into romantic love?

CHAPTER 3

IF RELATIONSHIPS ARE FORCED, THEY ARE NOT BASED ON LOVE

"People can only love us if they want to love us. If we attempt to control opinionated minds, they will eventually rebel and destroy us." ℒ

HAVE you ever tried to force someone to love you?
    Of course!
    Has it ever worked?
    Hell no!
    Why not?

Because love cannot be forced, and no one wants to love, nor be loved, solely out of obligation and pity.

I am guilty of trying to force my exes to stay with me after my breakups. I get anxious that I would lose them forever if I let the breakups run their course. However, forcing someone to love us only drives them away.

If it is meant to be, set them free, and they will come back.

If they truly care about you, they know how to find you.

If they do not, then they do not deserve to be in your life.

Do not waste the best years of your life on someone who is wasting theirs on someone else.

Do you want that?

Do you want to throw away your peak years on someone who barely knows you exist?

When people break up with you, say they need "space," say their feelings for you are gone, or say they no longer see a future with you, BELIEVE THEM! Take the three weeks that you need to spit out every word vomit of pain you have toward them (in the solitude of your own home), but when those subside, just let them go.

FOR THE LOVE OF GOD, DO NOT CHASE SOMEONE WHO TELLS YOU THAT THERE IS NO FUTURE.

Do what you need to get all the shit you have out of your system, but do not, I repeat, DO NOT, let your exes know that you have been miserable without them! If you do not already look pathetic in their minds, you DEFINITELY WILL if you tell them that you have been locked up in your basement for the past three weeks, crying about how much you miss them while listening to Taylor Swift and how much you wish you could see them.

KEEP IT TOGETHER! Please DO NOT be that person who obsessively emails, texts, calls, or shows up at your ex's home or work unannounced!

I have been there.

I have done all of that.

I have locked my phone in a safe to avoid texting, just to break open the latch ten minutes later.

I have forced a friend to take my phone, just to fight her into giving it back.

I have traveled four hours to sit in the parking lot of my ex's workplace, just to be ignored.

I have skipped work to sit outside my ex's apartment until he came home from vacation, just to have him walk right by me.

I have frantically texted my ex's family to try to relay my messages to him through them.

I have smashed my phone to prevent the urge to call my exes. (And no, deleting numbers never work because we always manage to find them, either through billing statements, mutual friends, social media, or work, school, and city directories, and we memorize them to the point where it becomes the only number we can recite.)

I have done it all.

Trust me.

You do not want to go there.

It feels like shit, and it makes you want to crawl into a hole and die!

You are beautiful!

DO NOT die on me!

DO NOT become the stalker who makes your exes proud of their decisions to walk away.

Be the person who is STRONG enough to walk away.

Make your exes regret leaving you!

When they do regret it, DO NOT take them back!

Anyone who can crush us once, can always crush us again.

What happens when the people we desperately want back find other romantic partners to replace us and move on? What is the point of going "no contact" in hopes of getting them back when they are happy with other people?

This is especially true for short-term relationships that have only lasted a few short months. To us, these short-term exes feel like the loves of our lives, and we would do anything to get them back. But to them, we are just another "fling" on their journey toward finding suitable long-term partners.

This truth is hard to swallow. The relationship JUST ended, and they are already posting selfies with someone else while we are still plotting ways to get them back, begging, compromising, and sending them gifts in hopes that they will see the mistakes they have made.

Sadly, but unsurprisingly, they do not give a rat's ass about any of it. They do not care if we feel like hell or if we are miserable and depressed without them.

If you have only been dating someone for a few weeks and have not stopped harassing that person with calls and text messages since the breakup, that person will most likely shut you out of his/her life, completely forgetting who you are after a few months.

When people decide to leave us, there is nothing we can do to GENUINELY make them change their mind.

CHAPTER 4
TIME TO LET GO

"Why hold onto something that is broken when it slowly dissolves in our palm with every passing second? If we set the dust free, maybe one day, it will find its way home." £

IF SOMEONE WALKS into your life, deceives and lies, and then wants to walk into the arms of someone else, just let go.

Chasing after someone who does not want us is one of the most crushing experiences we can deal with because we lose all value in both our eyes and theirs. We end up destroying our own lives for someone who is still going to move on regardless of how miserable we are.

It does not matter how great the relationship was, perfect or flawed, successful or failing, if someone's mind is already made up about leaving, it is going to happen, and anything we try to do to prevent that will only catalyze the process.

As much as I still care for the people who have walked in and out of my life, I have learned, the hard way, that even if we care about some people, they are not worth pursuing if we sacrifice our own mental well-beings in the process. If people truly cared for us, they would be preventing, not instigating, our sufferings.

They would make it a priority to NOT hurt us and to NOT leave us (and none of that crap where they come back after being away for six months, and we suddenly believe that they love us again).

Exes usually only come back because they have tried to find someone else and failed, or because they crave the chase and attention we shower them with. They say all the right things and make us feel like the most special people in the world so we will take them back. They call us every night (for a few weeks) and tell us how they cannot wait to spend their futures with us, making us fall in love all over again.

Then, they take it all away and pretend like we are nonexistent again. We are not idiots; we are successful scientists, doctors, lawyers, entrepreneurs, and leaders of the world, but for some reason, we become incredibly dumb and ignorant when it comes to love.

Is love worth chasing?

Yes.

Just not love from those who have already taken it away from us.

I am not advertising dating every seemingly nice and unattractive person in attempts to find the one you are destined to marry.

I am also not advertising proposing to the next person who offers you a slice a pizza, although that certainly makes it easier.

I am not even advertising that you NEED a partner in order to find love.

We all crave the idea of love, but what is love? How do we find love? We hear influencers and advocates say, "We must love ourselves before we can love others or before we can expect others to love us."

However, many people misinterpret this saying. TRULY LOVING OURSELVES does not mean buying five Prada handbags, getting brand-new faces, or acting like egotistical assholes who do not have time to be decent human beings because we are too busy "loving ourselves." Truly loving means figuring out WHAT love means to us.

Love is a subjective term, and the more time we spend defining love under the generic definition of "being with our soulmates and living happily ever after," the more time we take away from discovering what it means to US.

Love can have many meanings, from loyalty and acceptance to non-judgmental thoughts and honesty to friendship and humor. We cannot rush what love means because it will appear when we ALLOW it to appear. There are many people, especially those in their late 20s to early 40s, who believe they MUST FIND LOVE NOW, or they will end up old and alone.

How can we let love in if we hyper-focus on PRETENDING to be in "love" with people we have only known for two weeks?

How can we decide whether people are right for us and propose marriage based on a couple of months?

Why do we automatically assume people are not right for us as soon as complications occur?

We like to judge relationships based on feelings. If we feel positive emotions toward someone, we stay. If not, we leave.

Simple, right? Not at all, and we need to stop destroying relationships and the lives of others based solely on how we feel.

Seriously, just stop.

Feelings change all the time based on what is going on in our lives at specific moments. Stress makes us hate everyone while joy makes us love. Stop making impulsive decisions to break up with our partners because we are mad at them for being late or because their choices do not currently align with ours.

"My feelings for you have changed." A classic breakup line. Just because we are not in the honeymoon phase anymore and our infatuations have turned to content, does not mean that it is time to throw in the towel and call it quits. We cannot be head-over-heels for someone all the time, and there will always be obstacles that change how we feel toward the other person at any given moment.

We cannot judge how a relationship is going after only a couple of months. How can we be so sure that the relationship will not work out when we are only starting to get to know a person?

Most relationships need at least six months before two people can figure out each other's likes and dislikes, and determine if they can compromise with each other on issues that could potentially arise.

Sadly, when our feelings begin to fade, the person we crush on also fades, and we move onto finding someone else. It is a shallow perception, but in the moment, we make up excuses as to why we do it, and we justify breaking off what could potentially turn out to be great before giving it a chance to get there.

We tell ourselves that what we feel in specific moments is what we will feel forever toward that person, and we run before giving the relationship a chance to play out.

When our minds become congested with opposing feelings and overwhelming anxiety, we train ourselves to narrow our focus toward one dichotomous aspect: to give or not to give.

We refuse to compromise when our feelings take over, and we become stubborn to any ideas that go against our own. Relationships are hard, but unfortunately, many still believe that if it is not easy during the beginning stages, then the person is not worth pursuing at all.

This mentality causes us to hurt people because we blindsight them. We lead them to believe that they mean everything to us, and that we are completely happy with them, while holding back our true feelings.

Maybe it is due to the fear of trusting someone and potentially getting hurt.

Maybe it is due to the fear of hurting someone's feelings.

Maybe we are just not ready.

Not being completely honest and open from the start does more harm than good. If there are doubts early on, speak up! If there is no spark, say something! Let the other person know whether changes can be made to improve the relationship or if it is time to end it. Trust me, it hurts far less to be honest than to lead someone on when you clearly know that there is no future.

We lie and ghost people because we are afraid of dealing with their pain.

We feel guilty when our actions hurt someone.

We find it easier to deal with hurting someone by removing ourselves from them rather than acknowledging their pain.

We ghost, we block, and we completely ignore people we used to care so deeply for because we are not strong enough to carry their sufferings.

We fail to realize that we can relieve a lot of their pain with simple honesty.

Share every part of who you are.

Share all your thoughts, your doubts, your issues, your likes, and your burdens.

If someone is meant to be in your life, they will accept you for who you are despite your baggage.

Why hide parts of who you are?

Why be ashamed of showing your true self just because you think you are different?

Why change the person you were born to be just to please the selfish needs of others?

Relationships based on lies and secrets never last. If we expose ourselves completely, we can filter those who will stick around from those who will eventually break our spirits. Although heartbreak is inevitable, we can still avoid regret when a relationship, long or short, ends because we know that the end was based on incompatibility rather than something we controlled.

We cannot control or change the actions of others.

We can only express how we are affected by their actions.

We can only control our own actions in response to others.

We cannot force others to love us, but we can force ourselves to love us.

People walk in and out of our lives every day for all different reasons. Even compassionate people have their moments and can surprise us by leaving.

A good friend once told me that you must be prepared for anything and everything.

We should not put ourselves in positions where we feel vulnerable to another person and give them so much power over us that, when they betray us, we completely crumble. Even if it feels comfortable and familiar to depend on someone other than ourselves, NO ONE SHOULD HAVE THAT KIND OF CONTROL over our lives.

We are the only ones we can trust completely. Even our family and friends can forsake us and leave us dry. Spouses leave all the time despite committed vows. We can spend 60+

years with people, commit to sharing every part of our lives with them, and STILL RISK them walking away.

Even if they are still physically present, mental separation hurts just as much when we realize there is almost nothing we can say or do to bring them back. It kills us to know that the people who used to say "I love you" to us are now secretly hating every part of our existences, but, just as we chase people who leave us, we also chase people who resent us. The desire to want love and connection can feel so strong that we often put up with abuse and neglect.

Note: FEELING like we are still with someone is NOT the same as BEING with someone.

We refuse to accept that the people we love can actively choose to remove themselves from our lives, and we hold onto the fantasy of what used to be and let those memories drive us toward physical and emotional abuse.

Memories of the "happier times" and thoughts of "what could have been" force us to ignore reality and put abusers on pedestals when they do not deserve it. We fault and blame ourselves for causing others to hurt us, and we take full responsibility for our sufferings regardless of who is at fault.

We cannot blame ourselves for feeling hurt, and we cannot blame ourselves for being emotional.

As human beings, we naturally feel pain. Just because there are certain societal standards on how we SHOULD feel and react after someone breaks our hearts, does not mean that we are obligated to follow them. No one has the right to tell us how to feel nor do we have the right to tell others how to feel.

We question whether we have done everything "right" during the relationship.

We question if we could have done more.

We question whether the relationship ended because of us.

We usually believe that it did.

We question what we could do now to redeem ourselves.

We question if the relationship is a lost cause.

We question our self-worth and whether we deserve happiness.

We question if anyone will ever love us again.

Why is it so easy for us to obsess over, chase, and give our worlds to others, but so difficult for us to do the same to ourselves?

Why do we believe that it is selfish to obsess over our own happiness by splurging on ourselves?

Why do we frown upon taking ourselves out on dates?

Why is it only socially acceptable to go out on dates with partners?

Why do we hurt ourselves when someone else is already doing it?

Why do we become stubborn and childish when someone does not want to be with us?

It is because we LOVE too much.

We fight for people and for relationships that we care about even if the fight destroys us. We deceive ourselves into believing that chasing after someone is a sign of love, compassion, and strength, but doing so only implies weakness and narcissism.

We become so hurt by the relationship that we try to compensate by acting like saints, professing our love and affection when the other person just wants out. The only way we can truly be "saints" is if we let go.

As hard as it is to not reach out to someone we love, it is the only non-selfish act we can do.

Keep in mind that I DO NOT mean not reaching out for the sake of manipulation. I mean not reaching out for the sake of letting go and letting those we love make their own decisions, letting those we love choose who they want to be with, and not forcing them to love us when they can barely look at us.

I need to let him go.

We all need to let them go.

Stop torturing ourselves by loving someone who refuses to love us back.

They might come back.

They might not.

But we cannot hold onto the belief that they will.

That belief will tear our lives apart.

That belief will take away our sanity, happiness, and youth.

We should not be hoping that our days end quicker so we can bypass our no contact periods.

We should not be living for others.

We had lives before we fell in love.

We still have lives when love dies.

As challenging as it is to not feel angry, miserable, depressed, or suicidal after the loss of someone, we must.

We must continue living.

Do not give anyone else the power to control our lives.

If we do, we will always regret it.

Trust me.

YOU WILL REGRET IT.

CHAPTER 5
WE ARE ALL AFFECTED

"We need to stop believing that we will never be flawed, stop believing that we will never encounter problems, stop believing that we will never be pained by what pains others. Beliefs are no match for the wrath of life." £

As HUMANS, our emotions change all the time. The sadness that comes from heartbreak can quickly turn into happiness from finding new love, which can quickly turn into depression from the loss of a parent, which can quickly turn into excitement from traveling somewhere new.

We are emotional creatures, and therefore, we can never predict how we will behave in different situations. We may call ourselves "calm," "patient," and "collected," and we may have even discovered a pattern in our reactions based on various experiences, but every circumstance is different, every day is different, and every time we interact with a situation, similar setting or not, we are presented with a new challenge.

Our emotional presence, the relationships we have with those around us, our current living situations, and our current satisfaction with life all dictate how we react to specific situations that occur at specific moments.

Many of us have been dumped, yet many of us get back together. Hell, many of us cycle through on-and-off relationships so much that we struggle with getting out when we want to. However, the reason we are stuck is because the problems that caused the relationships to initially fail never get resolved. Therefore, we become crazy, devastated, and heartbroken, and we swear to ourselves that we will never look back.

But we go back anyway.

We fight.

We break up.

We become crazy, devastated, and heartbroken once again.

Until we are fed up.

And we begin obsessing over someone else.

The cycle continues.

Until we finally meet someone who will stay.

Someone who will love us.

Someone who will always be there.

The someone we have been searching for all these years.

And we leave.

Because we struggle with our own happiness.

Someone is always the victim.

Someone always loses.

Even mutual splits are never actually mutual.

One person always feels more than the other.

One person always moves on quicker than the other.

We are victims in some relationships.

We are heartbreakers in others.

Emotions are messy.

No one can truly know what they want or who they want.

Some of us still confuse love with infatuation.

Some of us cheat on those we love because of moments of weakness.

We crave acceptance and companionship all the time.

When we cannot get them from the ones we are currently with, we seek them out in others.

Friends.

Colleagues.

Exes.

Strangers.

Anyone.

We become obsessed with our new "loves" because we believe they are everything that our current partners are not. We base our entire relationships on a few bad moments and use them as excuses to be unfaithful. We fall in "love" with people we have just met because we compare their positives to our partners' negatives. But, when the new "relationship" falls apart, we blame them for not being as good.

We do not know what the fuck we want.

New relationships never thrive when we are stuck in the old. We end up becoming too attached too soon, and we scare them away. We start comparing them to our pasts, and we fault them when they do not measure up.

If you ever wonder why you are still single, see if you notice a pattern when it comes to meeting new people.

I know I am not alone when I say I would rather throw my phone into a lake and crawl into a hole than face another 96-hour day staring at my phone with no messages from my ex and more pictures of him with his new catch. IT HAS ONLY BEEN TWO DAYS! Every minute of every day becomes a debilitating struggle when the one person we need is the only person we cannot have, and it makes us doubt every word, every action, and every decision we have ever made when we were with that person.

We meticulously reflect on all the mistakes we could have avoided to prevent that person from leaving, and we blame every second of bad choices on ourselves. We hate ourselves for letting the "perfect" person walk away, and we hate ourselves for continuing to engage in acts that keep them away.

If he cared, he would have stayed.

If he loved me, he would try to compromise.

He was not right for me.

There was nothing I could have done to make him stay if he wanted out.

If I must change how I am for someone, he is not worth my time.

But we do not believe in these clichés' sayings, do we? When we are in a state of grief and resentment, nothing can pull us out, and it is draining! What used to make us happy no longer do, and depression begins to close in behind.

The people we used to call our "friends" and "family" are now seen as a nuisance when they try to help.

The world around us becomes our enemy.

We become bitter and angry when we see others in love.

We slap on fake smiles to hide our miseries.

We are dying from the inside out.

Heartbreak destroys lives and perceptions become clouded.

We begin to hate when we used to love.

We become selfish and angry when we used to be sweet and kind.

We become crazy and obsessive when we used to be independent and strong.

Our entire world flips, and we no longer recognize who we are.

Whether we are male or female, whether we fit society's standards of attraction and intelligence, whether we are the "dumper" or the "dumpee," whether the relationship was long or short, and whether we were in love or just pretending, heartbreak cripples all of us equally.

We all experience the same devastating shatter in our hearts when a lost occurs.

It pains us when the people we used to call our "lights" now become our enemies.

It pains us when we no longer have the support system we have had for years.

It pains us when the people we used to love now see us as strangers.

How do we deal with this pain?

How do we breathe when our minds cannot fathom reality?

How do we wake up every morning when the depression weighs us down?

How do we "get over it and move on"?

We are told to love ourselves instead, but how do we do that?

What if we no longer know what it means to love ourselves because we have spent all our time loving others?

What if our overwhelming fears make us incapable of ever loving again?

We look at others and wonder how they get over heartbreak. We envy those who seem to heal by the snap of a finger. But are they healed? Are they really over their heartbreaks, or are they just that good at hiding their pain? We live in a world where we must pretend to be strong, where we must pretend to be resilient in the face of obstacles, and where we must walk outside with our shits held together and the biggest smiles slapped on our faces or risk being judged for having problems. God forbid that humans beings have problems!

We all have issues in our lives, but we still judge those around us for having the same issues. We are hypocrites. We hold others to double standards. We are intelligent enough to know the consequences of our actions, but we are also too proud to admit our flaws. We believe that by meddling in the lives of others and giving them advice that we do not believe in, then we can pretend that our own struggles do not exist.

We trick ourselves into believing that we are "perfect" while everyone else is flawed. We run and hide from ourselves all the time. We run from our therapists by withholding full disclosure. We say just enough to be medicated but not enough to be hospitalized.

We lie to everyone around us.

We lie to ourselves.

We do not know how to be honest with ourselves. The ones who say they do are only admitting the parts that they want to admit, and the ones who embark on "spiritual journeys" to "find themselves" only do so for bragging rights. We do not need to spend $4,000 in India on a yoga retreat to gain "honesty within," and we do not need to hike across the country or strand ourselves in the middle of the woods to "find ourselves."

Just.

Stop.

Running.

Only by admitting that we are crazy, stupid, obsessive, impulsive, manipulative, and psychotic can we finally begin to move forward with our lives, away from fear. We may not want to admit our flaws to other people, but what harm is there by admitting the truth to ourselves? We cannot possibly judge ourselves more than we already do.

We are already our own worst enemies so we have nothing more to lose. But we still hold back! We are so afraid of ourselves and our thoughts that we cannot even admit to ourselves what nobody else needs to know!

What is wrong with us?

Why are we so afraid of our negative sides?

We try so hard to become the qualities that are "favorable" and "attractive" while shoving everything else inside a box.

And that, my friends, is why we drink.

That is why we let pain and anger unleash the dark sides of us.

Because we will then have something to blame other than ourselves.

We let our emotions and external factors speak what we cannot communicate through words.

CHAPTER 6
SOCIETY DOOMS US ALL

"We cannot call ourselves 'independent' when we abide by the rules of others; it is an oxymoron." ℒ

EVERY SINGLE ONE of us is a scared, timid, and angry child, afraid of rejection, loneliness, pain, and anxiety, who pretends to be mature adults with our lives put together because then, and only then, will we be accepted as functional members of society rather than social outcasts. We reject those who do not fit in with the norm.

For example, on dating apps, no one chooses to like and

connect with those who are disabled and uneducated. We swipe left on those who do not meet our standard of attractiveness because they do not meet society's standard of attractiveness, and by dating them, we, by default, also become rejected by society.

We cast aside those who do not fit the mold, and we ignore how we may have just hurt people we really liked just because everyone else refused to accept them, and because of that, we do not apologize, we do not acknowledge, and we do not communicate; we just block.

The rules of dating and love that others have set for us make us lose control of our own minds. We believe that we are in control of ourselves and that we are the "pilot of our own lives," but when we blindly follow what we are SUPPOSED to do rather than what we WANT to do, we give up that control, and we allow those around us to dictate who we love, who we can accept into our lives, and who we can talk to.

We let society tell us that we can no longer acknowledge that our exes, despite how long the relationships were, ever existed. We force ourselves to treat someone we used to love as strangers because it is not socially acceptable to keep in contact with an ex-partner as it prevents us from healing and moving on.

While it is true that keeping in constant contact with someone who we can no longer love prolongs our pain and keeps us from moving on, it becomes cruel and unnecessary to just shut them out completely.

How would you like it if someone did that to you?

We do not have to talk to them every day, like we used to in the relationships, but we also do not have to actively ignore them and block them either. We try to manipulate people's feelings by enforcing the dumb "No Contact Rule," deleting their numbers, ignoring them, blocking them, and doing everything we possibly can to remove them from our lives, that we fail to realize that we are still hurting human beings.

When we are hurt or angry, we can only focus on ourselves.

We only want to focus on ourselves.

We fail to notice the feelings of the people on the other end of our pain when we are trying to repair ourselves.

We fail to realize that we are actively bringing down the confidence levels and self-esteem of others just so we can bring them up in ourselves.

We only realize how much we are hurting the people we care about AFTER the damage has already been done.

CHAPTER 7
WE NEVER GET OVER IT

"We can run away all we want, as much as we want. I did, but if we never address what we are running from, we are only pulling it along for the journey." ℒ

IMAGINE a couple of months after the breakup, where we actually do say "fuck you" to everything and start feeling okay again. We start feeling like we can finally walk outside with confidence and go entire days without thinking about our exes. We learn how to enjoy a cup of coffee or a nice dinner out alone, without the company of another person.

Then we find out our exes are dating again, and all hell breaks loose. To make it worse, they have the audacity to TELL US about their new dating life.

What the fuck do they expect from us by telling us that? Are we supposed to say, "Congratulations on finding my replacement and completely forgetting the fucking life we had together!"? It is hard enough when people move on, and it is okay that they do, but when they decide to drag us along for the ride, making us suffer even more as they move on, that is just deceitful.

Decent human beings cut off contact with their exes when they start dating new people, to not offend the new and to not mess with the old. Narcissistic people, on the other hand, intentionally tell everyone about what they are doing because they know it will hurt, and narcissists thrive on the misery of others.

Narcissists want attention. They know EXACTLY what to say to piss us off and get the reactions they want out of us. ANY reaction we give them, even saying "fuck you," will only fuel them because that shows them that we still care enough to respond. The only thing that can hurt a narcissist is complete silence. As much anger, sadness, pain, and hate we have toward them, do not let them know!

And what do we do?

We have one moment of weakness, and WE LET THEM KNOW.

That is when they have us hooked.

When we let people in, we leave our vulnerabilities open and allow them to hurt us.

When we welcome the chance to love and trust others, we also welcome the chance to become physically and emotionally crushed.

Humans are resilient.

Believe it or not.

It feels like shit when someone leaves.

It feels like shit when someone decides we are no longer worth it.

It feels like shit when we invest so much of ourselves into something, just to watch it all fall apart.

But feeling like shit is just an emotion.

Just like feeling in love is just an emotion.

Emotions are always changing.

One minute, we can be in love.

The next minute, we can decide that we hate our partners.

That is why divorce is so common. We trick ourselves into believing that we are in love even when we are not. We do not realize that this feeling of "love" is simply a fleeting emotion that can change just as quickly as we change our clothes. When we FEEL in love, we get married. But just as easily, when we FEEL angry or hatred, we get divorced, walk away, or become unfaithful.

We are impulsive creatures, and we take major actions based on fleeting feelings. However, the lesson here is, emotions and feelings come and go! Even if we feel like we do not want to live anymore after the end of a relationship, or if we feel like we will never get over the pain, we will, because we all eventually do!

Whether we find love in someone else or something else, we WILL move past the heartbreak, and years down the line, we will look back at our painful moments and realize how much of our lives we have wasted on JUST a feeling.

Note: I am not saying this is time wasted on the relationship or time wasted on the person. I am saying time wasted on a FEELING, something that we create and can easily remove, something that is a part of us, but does not define us.

CHAPTER 8
IDENTITY CRISIS

"Sometimes I wonder what life would be like if I was perfect, if I made no mistakes, if I was just like everyone else, and if I did not possess one single flaw. Then I realize, I would be a robot." £

WE LET OUR PAIN, our guilt, our fear, our happiness and sadness, our anger, and our anxiety drive our lives, and we begin to define ourselves based on how we feel rather than who we are. When someone asks us who we are as people, most of us tend to say, "I am a wife," "I am an optimist," "I am a forgiver," "I am a risk-taker," etc. These labels all stem from our emotions.

We say we are someone's spouse or partner because we FEEL loved. We say we are an optimist because our lives are currently going well, and we FEEL happy as a result of it. We say we live to forgive because we are either lying and want to give off the appearance that we are good people, or because we FEEL tremendous amounts of guilt when we do not forgive those who hurt us.

We say we are risk-takers, not because we are not afraid of dying, which is a common misconception with risk-takers, but because we are afraid of not living. We skydive, swim with sharks, climb Mount Everest, camp out in the woods for months with minimal supplies, and backpack to the most dangerous cities in the world, not because we are brave and fearless, but because we fear the idea of dying without having lived a full life.

We risk our lives for adventure and excitement, whether by jumping off a plane or having an affair, because we FEEL afraid that the monotonous lives we are currently living will be how we live until we die, and that is SCARY!

We overcome obstacles because we fear being dull and boring, not because we are courageous and adventurous. We live in a constant state of comparison, where we feel like we must be "different" even though we are all doing the same things to achieve that difference. Who are we trying to please? Our parents? Our friends? Social media? Who are they to say that our lives now are not enough?

NOBODY!

But we try anyway! We literally die trying to live up to the standards of "living life to the fullest." We freeze on top of mountains because we believe we "must climb to avoid failure." We plummet to our deaths by jumping off planes because, for some oxymoronic reason, we associate near-death with living life.

I am guilty of falling for these gimmicks myself, and I have tried to convince myself that these are my unique wants and desires even though they are the same as everybody else's. That does not make me unique! That makes me just as gullible as everyone else, but I still do not stop.

I continue falling for the lies of needing to put my life at risk in order to live. I continue falling for the lies of terrible decisions being fantastic ideas because that is the mentality I am forced to acknowledge.

This is what relationships are. As I mentioned before, human beings are intelligent creatures, far more intelligent than we give ourselves credit for, but human beings are also very gullible, and because of that, we become very stupid. Deep down, we know we must work on our own lives and figure out our own issues before we can even think about bringing a partner into our mess. We know that, when a relationship is terrible and it makes us feel depressed, then it means it is time to walk away.

We know that there is only so much we can do in a relationship before realizing that it just is not going to work. But, the more we realize the emotionally dangerous situations that we put ourselves in, the more we try to avoid facing them.

Why? Two reasons. We avoid acknowledging that our terrible relationships are terrible, and we avoid getting out of them because we are SCARED and/or STUBBORN.

We do not want to admit that we have failed in something we invested so much of our lives in.

We are afraid that no one else will love us so we would rather stay in a failed relationship than no relationship at all.

We are too proud to face our friends and family because they will flaunt in our faces how they told us the relationship was not right, but we decided to pursue it anyway.

We are scared of being left behind when everyone our age is moving forward, getting married, and having babies while we are still stuck in our parents' basement, eating cookie dough out of a tube in our pajamas, so we snatch and settle for the first, potentially abusive, suitor for face value, to show that we are adults and not a 10-year-old inside a 35-year old's body.

We lie to ourselves and everyone else that we are okay with physical and mental abuse from our partners because we are "in love," and "love overcomes everything."

While love can overcome petty fights, stress, financial struggles, and in some cases, infidelity, how many of us can stick by this belief when we are:

Lying, half-dead, in a hospital bed,

Ripping our hairs out until we create bald patches,

Driving aimlessly in the middle of the night, afraid to go home because we might get beat,

Forcing ourselves to look and feel ugly just to ease our lovers' insecurities, while damaging our own confidences,

Hating ourselves when we look in the mirror,

Or, taking a gun to our heads but afraid to shoot because we feel guilty for acting selfishly?

I, like many others who have been in abusive relationships, have had these thoughts once or twice before.

We struggle between hating and loving our partners.

We struggle between leaving and staying.

Those of us who fear for our lives still contemplate this decision.

We go back and forth so many times that we eventually drive ourselves insane.

We give up trying.

We stay in the relationships.

We become depressed.

CHAPTER 9
INNOCENT ABUSERS

"Do not chastise them for being themselves; they do not know the pain they cause." ℒ

SOMETIMES, the abusers are innocent. Yes, I said it. There are some abusers who are aware of what they are doing with no intention of stopping; these are usually the physical abusers. Then we have the emotional abusers, the more common type, where the question of whether they are guilty or innocent falls more in the grey area than the dichotomous black and white.

Because we are each our own individuals, we have different upbringings, personalities, culture, values, beliefs, standards, and definitions of what it means to be in a relationship. Hence, while our words and actions may not seem offensive and abusive to us, they can to someone else.

Think of it in terms of a culture shock. Norms in the western part of the world are seen as insults in the eastern part of the world. For example, it is customary to tip the waiter after service in most western countries, but when that is done in eastern countries, waiters become offended, and they literally chase you down to give you your money back.

In healthy relationships, those who feel triggered or offended by their partners' words or actions often speak up and let their partners know, and thus, the partners stop. However, this can become abusive when we either refuse to speak out due to shame and embarrassment, or we do speak out but the other person dismisses us because our values do not align with theirs.

The more people dismiss our feelings, the more we need to speak out and let them know; otherwise, they keep repeating the action because we keep letting them.

People can be incredibly slow and terrible listeners, and this is not an excuse for them, but when we encounter these situations, mentioning only once or twice that our feelings have been hurt and then failing to remain consistent, this only portrays the idea that we were never serious or hurt in the first place.

Ladies! Gentlemen! We need our voices and our feelings to be heard! No one can speak our souls for us, and no one will ever understand us unless we make ourselves be known. And no, none of the bullshit, "It must be true love because he/she understands me in a way that no one else ever has."

No! Unless this person has telekinesis, or is a troll living inside your brain and your heart, the only person who will ever understand you more than you is YOU!

You are probably thinking, "How can I understand me more than me if I am me? This is a paradox!" Maybe it is. Maybe this is a dream and none of the words you are reading exist. Or maybe, as stated previously, human beings are complex creatures. We are in constant discovery of ourselves and of the world.

Every day we are learning:

Learning about our likes and our dislikes as we experience new encounters,

Learning about how we react to different people in different situations,

Learning about how others react to us based on our specific behaviors,

Learning about why some people like us while others dislike us,

Learning about why we like some people and dislike others,

And, learning about how we are compatible with everyone and but also compatible with no one.

We never fully establish who we are or what we want from others. We are so spontaneous and unpredictable that it is rare that we find people who want the same things or behave the same ways their entire lives. Breakups and divorces do not happen because two people hate each other; they happen because one person in the relationship has changed their wants. This change can happen within years, months, or even days.

From personal experience, I have been with someone who went from worshipping the ground I step on to wanting absolutely nothing to do with me within a span of two hours. Although I did not know his thoughts and perceptions of me during the short month we have been together, I do know that his feelings have changed, whether sudden or not.

From his perspective, his thoughts and actions may make complete sense, but I am speaking from my perspective:

The perspective of those on the receiving end,

The perspective of those who blame themselves because of the rejection and confusion other people have caused,

The perspective of those who never receive an explanation or closure from the end of relationships,

And, the perspective that ultimately leads people to end their lives because heartbreak can literally kill us, mentally and physically.

Feelings change sporadically due to faults of no one, but we do not see the change. Instead, we see the result and blame ourselves for being the cause.

How many times have we said or heard someone else say,

"Losing you makes me feel so depressed and miserable that I no longer have a reason to live,"

"I will never feel happy again without you,"

And, "Without you, I feel like I am nothing."

These are all feelings caused by the pain of breakups or divorces, not necessarily due to anyone's fault since this can arise even from mutual breakups, which is a topic in its own league that I will touch upon later, but we always try to rationalize where these painful feelings come from. We can never truly understand that we can feel different emotions because our brains are wired to do so, and feelings can be triggered by even the smallest of things.

We can never just say, "I feel like shit right now, but it is just a feeling, and tomorrow I may have a different feeling." We rationalize our feelings, in that if we cannot blame the feeling on something or someone, then we should not be feeling it because it is "not acceptable."

In our society, we are only allowed positivity and optimism. We must be happy all the time or there is something "wrong" with us. Millions seek out therapy because we trick ourselves into believing that any ounce of sadness or pain that we experience is a problem that must be treated.

We cannot fix something that is a natural part of us, and

attempting to do so will only cause unnecessary stress, anxiety, guilt, regret, and, ultimately, more pain.

Unfortunately, on the flip side, feeling too happy and too optimistic can also be seen as "problems." If we seem too happy, we are either defined as "manic" or "abnormal." If we seem too optimistic, we are either defined as "sheltered" or "privileged."

Even if we are the "normal" amount of happy, this can still be problematic depending on the people surrounding us. Some may see it as still too much while others may see it as not enough. Either way, we cannot win.

This is the unwritten rule: Be the right amount of enthusiasm and positivity, catering to every person's needs at the same time, and never show any other emotion because any emotion other than happy is frowned upon.

Simple enough.

Right?

CHAPTER 10
THE DEMISE OF XY

"Women justify equal rights when they try to take from men what they believe was taken from them. In reality, they are only stealing."

ℒ

MANY OF US have been told that only women are held to high standards. However, men deal with the same pressure as women do because women and men are equally mean and cruel, just as we are both are equally vulnerable to pain and rejection.

We like to categorize men as "dogs," "pigs," and the 50

other animals we call men after they break our hearts. Yes, men lie, cheat, run, and abuse, both verbally and physically, but so do women. In fact, women can sometimes be worse because we usually do not associate domestic abuse with women.

Women are still seen as "weak," "frail," and "victims." Even if a woman repeatedly kicks a man's genitalia, we still defend her by saying she must have been provoked.

Women are just as terrible as men, but do we see movies, magazines, and books catered toward men outlining,

"10 Ways to Find Your Inner Masculinity Again After a Breakup,"

"You are a Beautiful and Independent Angel Without a Woman,"

"Be the Unforgettable Man,"

"Discover your Spiritual Manhood," or

"The Penis Monologues"?

CHAPTER 11
HAPPY WIFE, HAPPY LIFE

"Can true happiness really be dependent on one quote, one word, one person? We are all looking out for ourselves; no one cares if you perish." £

THIS PHRASE IS the epitome of men being brainwashed into taking abuse from women. Most men are willing to bow over for the women they love, despite what it takes, until they reach their breaking points.

But men, try this: leave. As soon as you decide to end a relationship, the women suddenly switch personalities, lose power, and her insecurities begin to show. It does not matter how strong, confident, demanding, or un-gettable someone appears to be.

Everyone is only human, and the only reason these seemingly powerful people got to where they are is because everyone around them enables their behaviors, and the men/women who shower these powerful people with attention, gifts, blood, and tears are only screwing themselves over. It is a common misunderstanding that the more we give to make someone happy, the more likely the other person is to return the favor.

You are laughing too, right?

What really happens is that the more we give and are willing to give, the more others take. Catering to people to make them "happy" only fuels their selfishness. However, because one of the biggest strengths and flaws in human beings is fear, in that fear motivates us to reach for the impossible but also cripples us to hold onto tragic pasts, we are also gullible enough to willingly give up our own lives and our own happiness in hopes that our sacrifices will be rewarded.

Unfortunately, this reward is not the reward of our partners loving us back or the reward of them making sacrifices for our benefits; this reward is the fake lifetime promise of "forever." So, we give up everything we have for each relationship because we fall for these false promises of forever EVERY SINGLE TIME. We search, we drain ourselves, we settle, we resent, we leave, we find someone else, and the entire cycle starts over again until we reach the point where mediocre is good enough.

While finding our soulmates is a great dream to chase, it is not reality. Neither is compatibility. No two people are "meant to be together" because we all have our own opinions, our own ways of living, being, and feeling, and it becomes near impossible to find someone who meets ALL the desires and personalities we look for.

Love exists; I am not against it. I fully believe in finding someone we want to share and dedicate the rest of our lives to. What I do not believe, however, is giving up our own lives solely to benefit the lives of others and failing to see how detrimental it is to do so.

As much as it sucks to say, and sucks even more to believe, people are flakes. It is in our nature to run away from our problems because we are taught to seek out happiness and avoid every other emotion. Therefore, we relish in the happy moments in our relationships, feeling on top of the world, but once life starts to get hard and reality kicks in, we bolt as if Godzilla is chasing us.

We are not wired to deal with hardships. We have been so sheltered and/or privileged that we expect our lives to transition smoothly from one stage to another. We would much rather destroy the life of someone else than face our own insecurities and our unwanted emotions. Epinephrine skyrockets in situations of fear, which in this case is the fear of being unhappy, and we run.

It is rare that we fight for our relationships, and I mean fight in cases like a partner loses his/her job and files for bankruptcy, accidental pregnancy with lack of preparation, or moving to a different country when a partner finds a new job, not in cases like getting mad at our partners for buying us Snickers instead of Milky Way.

Note: If your partner cheats on you in any way, shape, or form, he/she is not worth fighting for.

Humans beings are selfish. We hate compromises, and we hate opinions that do not align with our own. We would much rather leave someone we love than admit that we are wrong. This is why on-and-off relationships are so common. We leave when we are stressed out, angry, or sad, cool down, and then realize how petty we were and how much we love the other person, and beg for him/her to take us back.

Why leave it up to chance? Why throw everything away

based on one emotion in hopes that the other person is patient, stupid, or lonely enough to want us back after we turn into assholes and walk away?

Unfortunately, cliché gifts and a slew of false promises are usually enough to win people over even after we crush their hearts. When we want out, we put the other person through hell and make damn sure that he/she never wants a future with us. When we want in, we become sly enough to manipulate the other person into not being able to imagine a future without us, and we literally become a "knight in shining armor" or an "angel sent from heaven."

We are manipulative, and this is one of the greatest strengths of mankind throughout history.

Machiavellianism has existed in our repertoires for as long as we can remember. Even as kids, before we could even come close to pronouncing this ungodly long word, we have manipulated others for the purpose of our own selfish needs.

We pretend to cry and throw tantrums so our parents would buy us toys and pay attention to us.

We form cliques, selectively bribing those we want in our circles, for the purpose of building up our own reputations and finding reason to exclude those we dislike.

However, by doing this, we only hurt ourselves. We selectively deprive ourselves from the good that people have to offer us, and we write our own tragic endings. We obliviously train ourselves to believe that we know ourselves better than anyone else can know us, but in truth, we are the ones who know the least about ourselves even though we have the most potential to because we struggle to see ourselves outside of our relations to others.

Therefore, we attach quickly to our partners and significant others. When we are in a relationship, we sacrifice a huge part of ourselves to that other person, in a sense, we give ourselves to that other person, and they become the person who knows us best. So, when the relationship ends, we lose that part of ourselves and literally fall apart when they walk out of our lives.

Ultimately, so many of us become debilitated and depressed when we lose our partners. Every ounce of trust that we had put in that other person is now gone. The person we used to rely on to learn about ourselves and believe in ourselves is now gone.

CHAPTER 12
MUTUAL BREAKUPS ARE A HOAX

"As kids, we only shared when we expected something in return. As adults, we are not much different." 𝓛

MUTUAL BREAKUPS, despite how much of a unanimous decision both parties say it is, are never mutual. There is no such thing as two people, who shared so much together, who can part ways without some sort of resentment, especially when one person moves on, and even more especially when one person moves on quickly.

We begin to self-doubt and question all the things that went wrong, all our flaws, things we could have done better, and the reasons for our ex-partners choosing other people over us. Even if we know that the relationship was terrible and toxic for us, we place blame on ourselves because, when someone chooses not to be in our lives and chooses to be in someone else's instead, we start to believe that there is something inherently wrong with us, and we begin to dwell on our mistakes.

There is a saying I heard recently on the Internet, no surprise there, that when someone chooses to leave us or cheat on us when we have not already done the same, it reflects who THEY are, NOT who WE are. When people leave or cheat on decent partners, they are leaving and cheating themselves out of the good and happiness that come with having partners who care about them and are willing to do anything for them.

Remember, people leave and cheat because of their feelings AT THE TIME, not necessarily because of the situation or something that we did. People walk away from good partners because they selfishly expect more and believe they deserve more. Casting people aside to chase that rollercoaster dream of deservingness is never the answer.

CHAPTER 13
THE BROKEN HEART

"The heart can only be taken away when we relinquish ourselves to others. If we never expose ourselves, we will never be broken; however, we will also never learn to become whole." ℒ

I ONCE DATED someone who left me out of the blue because he said he feared commitment. This was the breakup that made me question my entire existence (I know, a little dramatic on my end), and made me hate myself and the world for months, only to find out that THIS SAME PERSON BETROTHED two months later. Fear of commitment, my ass!

I used to reflect on what his action said about me, but now I know that this reflects who THAT person was. Whether he lied or had been cheating on me the entire time we were together, all this did was show me how shitty other people can really be, and how we should not look at their actions as a reflection of our own humanities. I still believe that person had a good heart and is still one of the most amazing people I have ever met, but his actions reflected issues and problems that manifested in his own life, something that was outside of my knowledge and control.

People without trust and attachment issues do not get married after two months of knowing someone unless they are:

Actively trying to avoid turning back to their exes,

Actively trying to forget and distract themselves from past traumas,

Actively trying to commit to anyone they find because they are desperate to find "love,"

Actively trying to hurt someone,

Actively trying to uphold an image or,

Literally has such low self-esteem and self-worth that they would cheat themselves from the chance of getting to know someone before settling.

We do not cheat on people or date multiple people at once unless we are searching for something within ourselves vicariously through other partners. We are not satisfied with how we feel about ourselves, and we do not feel fulfilled in our own lives, so we believe we can find ourselves in others.

We bounce from person to person because we falsely believe that there is someone out there who can make us feel whole about ourselves, who can give us the desires and needs we have dreamt about, who have unconditional acceptance of all our flaws and our nonsensical thoughts, and who can love us when it seems like no one else will ever love us again.

But that person is not someone we can meet on a dating app or in a bar.

That person is someone we come face to face with every day.

That person is someone who has been by our sides since the day we were born.

That person is our family, our friend, our confidant, and our partner through thick and thin.

That person is us.

Despite how hard we search and how many partners we go through, we will never find the person we truly are looking for until we have accepted the fact that we, ourselves, are the only ones who can complete us. All this endless searching and sleeping around only distract us from loving and accepting ourselves.

We fight against ourselves because we are terrified of not being able to rely on something we can see with our eyes that is not a reflection. We do not trust ourselves because we do not love ourselves.

It is far easier to love something else or someone else because we can choose to only love the good and fake blind to the ugly. But with ourselves, we are forced to accept our flaws, flaws that we do not want to acknowledge are there, flaws that make us question why anyone would ever love us, and flaws that make us run from reality.

How can we turn the culture we live in from a culture of self-doubt, self-hate, and shame to a culture of self-acceptance and self-love, and see flaws as a part of existence and uniqueness rather than reasons to cast someone aside?

How can we stop selecting partners and friends based on external beauty and wealth, and focus on internal beauty and personality?

How can we learn to be happy for someone else's success rather than secretly hating them and cursing at them silently, hoping failure will soon fall upon them?

How can we learn to love, not only in a romantic way, but in an accepting way?

CHAPTER 14
GET OVER IT ALREADY

"Holding onto the past only makes it easier to forget about the present." ℒ

WE ALL KNOW THE PATTERN.

Boy meets girl.

Boy and girl fall in love.

Boy and girl break up.

Boy and girl avoid each other like a plague.

Boy and girl post Instagram pictures of their new catch to make each other jealous.

This is nothing new.

We all do this.

We all know people who do this.

We all pretend that we can walk away from romantic love as civil and mature people, but who are we kidding? The adults in us try to reason that our exes were not the right ones for us and that there are others far more suiting. The children in us think that our exes were assholes, that there is something wrong with us, and that we must stalk our exes and their new partners to find out why they chose them over us.

Naturally, our "id" forces us to behave in more childlike states and overpowers the "ego." Age does not play a role in which side we act more on. Whether we are 20 or 60, when we feel hurt, our raw emotions unleash, overtaking our logic, and we become the people that we judge.

How is it that, despite the numerous times we try to reason that our exes were not right for us, or that they just want different things at this point in time, we still fault ourselves? Whenever our hearts feel broken or betrayed, we revert to our adolescent states, where we religiously believe that the only possible reason that people do not want us is because we are not good enough as lovers or as people, and that we are flawed and unworthy of any connections. We let our emotions hurt us and turn us into a statistic.

Saying that we should stop letting breakups or divorces tear apart our lives is much easier than living that to fruition. It has been shown that when people emotionally feel a broken heart, their hearts LITERALLY BREAK. This is known as "Broken Heart Syndrome," and its symptoms mimic that of an actual heart attack.

When we feel hurt from separation, we experience immense stress in our hearts, chest pains, and shortness of breath. Therefore, many of us feel like we are unable to breathe when someone we love leaves us.

Contrary to what our friends and family say, this feeling is not an exaggeration. We are not being dramatic. The feeling is REAL. The pain is real and unless someone has experienced this first-hand, he/she will always continue to believe that we can just "heal" and "get over it." When we experience this, we believe that the ONLY person who can help us is the person who walked away from us.

We stalk, beg, and threaten suicide not because we are psychologically sick and disturbed, but because we are trying to HEAL OURSELVES. What our exes and bystanders see as us being "psychotic" are our broken hearts and minds attempting to heal.

Believe it or not, stalking is MEDICINE!

Begging is THERAPY!

It sounds insane to someone not going through it, but to those who are in it or have been through it, these behaviors are completely normal and justified. These crazy attempts we engage in to win someone back are our minds' attempts to heal our bodies from the physical pain we find unbearable.

Even when we know that the people we chase are not good for us, we chase after them anyway because we perceive these people as the only ones who can relieve our sufferings at the time.

These people do not even have to be alive. It is the ACTION of actively trying to win someone back that gives us the relief.

Similar to how addicts feel the rush from the ACT OF OBTAINING drugs rather than having the actual drugs, we feel the rush from knowing that we are taking the steps toward getting someone back despite whether we actually succeed.

We find satisfaction in mapping out our daily routes so we can "accidentally" run into our exes.

We find joy in writing out long and elaborate love letters, dreaming about how these letters are the perfect weapon in making our exes fall in love with us again.

We bask in the idea of what it would feel like to reunite with someone rather than the actual reunion.

How many of you have ever spent months trying to win someone back, but when that person does come back and want to be with you, you no longer want them?

I have.

This is because we are addicted to the chase.

The chase is our medicine.

We expend all our efforts on the JOURNEY that, when the destination finally arrives, we are already relieved from the physical pain and no longer want anything to do with our exes.

So, what is the lesson here?

To the victims of our crazy behaviors, understand that we are only trying to heal ourselves, and we are not as psychotic as you may think.

To those we call "crazy," check in with yourself.

Is this a constant pattern in your life after the end of a relationship?

Is this how you really want to be portrayed?

In your mind, your crazy behaviors are justified.

In someone else's mind, you may be branded as the "crazy ex."

As much as we want people to understand that we are only messed up because we need to heal, mental medicine is still not as understandable as physical medicine.

CHAPTER 15

YOU ARE CRAZY. DEAL WITH IT!

"I would rather be seen as "crazy" than be seen as "ordinary." ℒ

BE the crazy that you are.

Embrace the crazy that you have.

We are all crazy.

Hell, shout from the top of a building and EXPRESS YOUR CRAZINESS!

There is NOTHING WRONG with SHARING our emotions, EXPRESSING our anger, and UNLEASHING the painful feelings that we so often keep hidden.

Unfortunately, we also do not want to risk losing ourselves and our self-respects, and we especially want to avoid letting those who hurt us take away our identities.

So, what is the solution?

Unleash all the craziness in private?

Stalk cardboard cutouts of our exes instead of the actual people?

Scream into a bag?

The truth is, there is no solution.

The very thing that provides immediate relief for our pain is also the very thing that can bring us to our own demise.

Do we risk appearing insane to allow our minds and souls to heal?

Do we maintain our sanities and succumb our hearts to internal damage?

Do we choose to protect ourselves from ourselves or choose to protect ourselves from others?

We all know the saying, "We are our own worst enemies." Suicide rates soar with each passing year. Every twelve minutes, someone commits suicide in the United States, with 120 suicides every day and close to 45,000 suicides every year. Knowing these statistics, ask yourself again, would you risk your mental health to protect your mental pride?

Would you hold in your life-threatening emotions to protect yourself from how the shallow and misunderstood world sees you?

At the end of the day, you are left alone with yourself.

Would you rather be left alone with the "you who accepts who you are," or would you rather be locked up alone with the "you who regrets the choices that you have made"?

CHAPTER 16
WHO THE HELL ARE YOU?!

"If you look in the mirror and do not recognize yourself, smash it, and unleash your inner soul." £

WHO ARE we outside of a relationship?

    Are we just seen as people in relation to those around us?

    Our mother's daughter.

    Our husband's wife.

    Our child's mother.

    Are we just seen as important due to our labels?

    A writer.

An actress.

A motivational speaker.

Can we ever be someone of value without an association?

We live in a world where being alone is "pathetic," and we are taught to be ashamed of it.

Because of this, we have become afraid of being lonely and would rather settle for abusive relationships.

We form partnerships with people we cannot stand just so we can tell others that we have someone significant in our lives.

We blatantly ignore the people we are with 364 days of the year so we can find a reason to celebrate Valentine's Day.

We plaster our "happiness" and "love" all over social media to give others the illusion of our newly formed connections and lack of loneliness, when in reality, we are dying from internal loneliness.

Internal loneliness does not stem from physical loneliness.

Internal loneliness stems from the lack of satisfaction with ourselves.

Even when we are surrounded by people, we can still feel alone.

When we are not satisfied with ourselves, our lives, and the choices we make, what we have and who we are with have no meaning. We can lie to others by pretending to be happy, but we can never lie to ourselves. Many have tried, zero have succeeded. Even if we do plaster on that fake smile every day and tell ourselves that our lives are good, our minds and hearts know the truth. If we are not happy with the choices we have made, our bodies will tell us.

Depression will kick in.

Anxiety will creep up.

We will catapult from being fine one minute to having a mental breakdown the next.

We will always be lonely if we remain dishonest with ourselves.

Infinite number of Instagram followers and Facebook friends mean nothing if we are not friends with ourselves.

We can walk away from friends, relationships, people we find incredibly intolerable, family, colleagues, even our religions, but we cannot walk away from ourselves.

Even if we change our identities and develop an entirely new personality, we will still be forced to deal with the guilt and shame of doing so, eventually developing a fear or intense hatred toward our new selves.

The only way to truly run away from ourselves is death.

Learning to love ourselves is one of the hardest things we have to do in life, as silly as it may seem. But this is something that we must learn to do if we ever want to stop running.

I ran from myself for years, turning to addictions to distract myself from myself.

I ran across the world to try to get away from my own thoughts of self-hatred and denial.

Running only makes it worse.

Running only delays the process of healing and self-acceptance.

Running builds upon the shit that we are already facing.

Would you rather deal with one piece of shit now or deal with piles of shit later?

We cannot run.

We cannot hide.

Stand up.

Look in the mirror.

Acknowledge that you exist.

Smile.

Tell yourself that you deserve to be okay.

Tell yourself that you deserve to be loved.

CHAPTER 17
STRANGER DANGER

"The stranger sitting across from you, winking at you while you avoid eye contact, can very well be your next spouse." ℒ

JUST AS ABUSE from a loved one can cause us to shut ourselves out from our friends and family, abuse from a stranger can also have the same effect. At least 80% of the world participate in some sort of dating app, whether it is Tinder, OkCupid, POF, Match, you name it. We all know that being hurt by loved ones can tear our souls apart. However, being hurt by strangers can also leave us incapacitated.

A stranger can walk into our lives, change everything for the better, and then walk out just as quickly as they came in.

A stranger can walk into our lives, destroy us, decide to stay, AND WE LET THEM!

Earlier, I had mentioned how short-term relationships can hurt just as equally, if not more, than long-term relationships due to how we only see "perfection" in short-term partners rather than the flaws they hide from us.

However, imagine meeting the perfect person, infinite common interests, nonstop sparks, pretty much the person of your dreams one minute, and the next, they give you the cold shoulder, tell you that they do not want a relationship, that they do not want you, or even worse, that they are already taken.

Crushed, right???

You become devastated and overwhelmed with so much pain and agony that you either attempt to convince that person to love you, like a crazy person, or you give up on love and vow to die alone. As dramatic and immature as this may seem, we know EXACTLY how this feels, regardless of age and life-experiences.

Human beings are fragile and our emotions tend to override who we are as people. In cases of love and romantic relationships, we turn to extremes. We either completely shut off our emotions, for the fear of further experiencing pain and heartbreak, or we allow our emotions to become vulnerable. We are often told that when it comes to romantic companions, we need to use our common sense and give when we need to give, but also hold back when giving becomes too much. However, this is more viable in theory than in reality.

Love is a drug and, many times, we cannot control how we behave when it comes to love. The phrase "head over heels" exists because, when we fall, we fall hard. This is especially the case for those who feel lonely and still affected by the betrayal of previous endeavors.

Loneliness and pain drive us to use our hearts rather than our heads because, similar to drugs, the craving overpowers the logic. This makes us vulnerable to the manipulation of strangers we meet. We fall for strangers quickly because they represent freedom from loneliness and freedom from pain. We channel our vulnerable emotions toward people we do not know for two reasons:

Emotional support from strangers comes with the benefit of non-judgments because they do not know who we are or where we have come from and,

Strangers provide distraction from the current bullshit in our lives and distraction from having to face the reality of living with ourselves.

What does this all lead to?

Abuse.

From strangers.

Disgust.

For ourselves.

At one point or another in our lives, most of us have allowed strangers to take advantage of us when we were at our worst, ranging from going on dates with people we did not find attractive to one-night stands and sexual assaults. Looking back, from the logical standpoint, we know the stupidity that comes with allowing strangers to take advantage of us. We blame ourselves because, on some level, we were probably too distraught and sad to remember that we gave consent to our Tinder dates to take our pants off.

This is a clear difference from rape, unfortunately. When we are sober but still fail to tell the other person to stop, or when we freeze up when someone is trying to have sex with us, allowing it to happen, we can no longer consider this rape. We can become so emotionally vulnerable that a single human touch can drive away our logical thoughts.

How many of you have ever felt numb or regret DURING sex but FAILED to say anything to stop it and instead, closed your eyes and prayed that it was OVER soon?

This is the work of our emotions. When we do not know what we want and when our emotions become overwhelming, we freeze, and we become paralyzed. We lose our words, and we pray the night away, pushing off the consequences until the next day.

So, how do we stop these overwhelming feelings and numbness?

How do we stop letting strangers take advantage of us?

How do we stop relinquishing our power and control to those who abuse them?

Even though it is easier said than done, we MUST acknowledge before going into any kind of situation with strangers whether we are going into it because we ACTU-ALLY like them or because we feel LONELY and HEART-BROKEN. I struggle with this all the time, and I still struggle with this. I let my anger from seeing an ex, or someone I once loved, with someone else turn into meaningless sex with the first person interested in me. I realize why I do this, and I realize the consequences from doing this, but I still do it anyway.

Anger and jealousy are some of the most difficult emotions to overcome. Similarly, when we are starving, we will eat anything, and we will take all the necessary actions to do so until we are full. These are called the "Deadly Sins" for a reason. They drive us toward one goal, stopping only when we have achieved it, regardless of what and who we destroy along the way.

CHAPTER 18
SOCIETAL RULES SHALL DIE

"Our lives are not based on reality; our lives are based on what we perceive as reality." ℒ

WE GREW up in a society where the idea of a relationship is commonly related to the idea of sacrificing our own lives for the benefit of someone else's, where we must give up our one chance for happiness to make someone else happy.

Wait.

WHAT??!?!

Who the hell decided that this was the standard to live by? Better yet, who the hell decided to follow these rules?!?

The phrases "happy wife, happy life" and "life ends with marriage" are two of the most nonsensical phrases that people have chosen to use as their mantras. Although we most often associate these phrases with men who give up their freedom and souls for women, women also often give up their lives for the sake of relationships. Men and women equally give up their dreams, their family, their friends, their hobbies, and even their careers for relationships and marriages.

When we fall in love, we make sacrifices so that others will stay and continue to love us. We give and give to other people, catering to their needs, such as giving up friends of the opposite sex to avoid relationship conflicts or giving up our homes to move across the country for our partners' job relocations, until we have nothing left to give.

Why should we give up our chances at happy lives to support our spouses who, keep in mind, are full-grown adults?

Or, why are we not able to support them and STILL live our own lives?

I believe that the reason we hold to heart these beliefs of one-way sacrifices is because we fall for people who only look out for themselves, people who take from us until we have nothing left so we must abide by their demands. We become so afraid of losing these people that we convince ourselves to give up our chances at happiness because, if these people are happy, then we are "happy."

Our friends and family tell us that we deserve better, but we do not say anything nor do we acknowledge them because we have already fallen for the trap of loving people who do not love us back.

We have this list of what it means to find the "perfect" partner, and we are willing to give up true love for the image of being with someone "perfect." Stop holding onto expectations that we MUST be with someone wealthy and beautiful in order to have a happy life and a happy marriage.

We live in the 21st Century! We do not need some white-collared pimp to take care of us because we are independent and successful human beings who can take care of ourselves, and we do not need to have beautiful babies with Victoria Secret models because beauty is subjective!

JUST.

STOP.

Everyone is beautiful, and everyone deserves a chance at life. The term "ugly baby" is sickening because those who truly think that babies can be ugly, that innocent and helpless infants can be disgusting, should be punched in the face. We need to fall in love with and marry those who will be by our sides no matter what.

What happens when we lose our jobs and stop bringing home luxurious gifts every night?

What happens when we lose our muscles and replace them with fat?

Will our partners leave us because we are no longer rich and fit?

Should we even give a shit if our disgustingly shallow partners leave us?

We are worth so much more than our paychecks and our looks!

If our partners decide to leave us for someone wealthier or prettier, will we still be able to look at ourselves in the mirror at the end of the day?

We need to know that we are worth loving just as we are, not because we are rich, smart, pretty, or whatever other "positive" terms that people seem to value.

We need to stop trying to impress people who walk in and out of our lives quicker than we can say "fucked up."

When we let the values of others define who we are, we lose ourselves.

We are not defined by others, and our lives should not be put in their hands.

What makes them more deserving than us?

What gives them the power to dictate whether we move on or lie deep in depression?

We need to find partners who love us for everything we are: crazy, stupid, the face we are without a pound of makeup, the value we are worth if we lose our jobs, and everything else in between.

We need to find partners who support us to be the best that WE can be, not the best that they want us to be.

We need to find partners who, despite all obstacles, will always find a way to make the relationships work.

We need to stop the endless patterns of infidelity and divorce by choosing people who care for us, not people we HOPE can care for us.

When we are forced to try even a little, and I mean a micro amount, to get others to love us and want to be with us, they are no longer worth the effort.

Love is not something we need to chase after.

Love is something that finds us.

Having partners who truly love us means having partners who will NEVER make us work for them.

Human beings are not meant to chase after one another. We are not supposed to subject ourselves to that level of worthlessness, where we allow other human beings to treat us as less deserving.

I do not give a fuck how rich, how hot, or how Ryan Gosling this other person is; no man or woman is worth CHASING after, and no man or woman is worth our submission.

We need to stop being afraid of ending up alone, and we need to stop giving people chances they do not deserve because we are afraid of losing them. When we find the right people, the people who are MEANT to be in our lives, not the people we WANT in our lives, we TAKE our lives back. We GAIN ourselves back because we REPLACE toxicity with the support of those who genuinely want to see us succeed.

Until then, do not be afraid of waiting. Stop pouting and bitching about how you are going to end up alone when you are only 30. The average age of millennials getting married is 35, but even then, so what?

Why rush into marriage if it is just going to add more stress, burden, and pain to the hardships that already exist?

What is the benefit of marrying someone who is completely wrong for us and raising a family for reason of status?

Nothing!

It is much less anxiety provoking to WAIT and LIVE our lives the way we WANT than endure years of pain and suffering just to end up in divorce, or even worse, in marriages that make us want to jump out a window. When we stop being so afraid of living on our own, when we stop trying to search for love via ten different dating apps and start finding love within, we start realizing that others are only added bonuses to what we already possess, not sole necessities. The purpose of finding a partner is to share with someone the happiness that we already have in our own lives, not to achieve happiness.

When we start respecting others more than we respect ourselves, we need to hop on a plane, go live on a mountain, and figure out what the fuck went wrong with our sense of logic.

Okay, maybe not to that extreme, but we do need to force ourselves to have a reality check and realize that we are worth so much more than our labels as "belongings." We are not labeled as "someone's spouse"; we are labeled as "I."

We are NOBODY WITHOUT OURSELVES!

Stop trying to find purpose through others and learn to find purpose WITHIN.

Being ALIVE, even if we are alone, is enough to be meaningful in this world.

STOP taking shit from those who think they are more valuable than we are!

CHAPTER 19

SERIOUSLY, WE DO NOT KNOW WHAT THE FUCK WE WANT

"Those who have everything are those who feel lost in emptiness." ℒ

WE TELL ourselves that we just want to love.

We tell ourselves that we just want to find someone kind and honest who will love us back.

We fantasize about finding a partner who is patient, understanding, and accepting of all that we are.

So, why do we deceive ourselves into accepting anything less than that?

We are so afraid of being alone that we settle way too

much, and we would rather be miserable than alone at the age of 30. How often do we hear horror stories of couples divorcing, especially those who anointed their marriages in their 20s? Our fears overpower our abilities to see beyond the consequences of present moments. We cannot logically see past our immediate fears and into future consequences, in that, marrying people we do not love will only end in misery and migraines.

We let our emotionally-charged selves and our irrational fears dictate our love lives and force us to "love" the first person willing to love us back. We deceive ourselves into believing that we are truly in love because we become so paranoid that if we do not marry the person who somewhat tolerates our flaws, then we will never find someone who will.

How many times have you walked out of a relationship and back into the dating scene, just to reminisce about your ex and how much you miss him/her?

When we have a FEW bad experiences with a FEW new people, we either want to give up on love completely, or we turn back to our exes because of the familiarity.

Dramatic, right?

GROW A PAIR!

We have the tendency to turn back to our pasts, not necessarily because we love them, but because with time, we forget their flaws and zoom in on their positive qualities, qualities that made us fall for them in the first place, rather than qualities that made us walk out.

We tell ourselves, "Our exes were sweet, loving, generous, funny, and patient," but we forget to tell ourselves that our exes were also abusive, unfaithful, deceitful, lazy, and manipulative.

We ignore the reasons for our previous relationships ending and revert to them when we fail to make other connections within a month or two of dating. 99% of the time, this does not mean that we want to be with our exes; we may still love them, and we may always love them because they were a huge presence in our lives, but we may not actually want to be with them. We only think we do because we lack the patience to wait for our next partners.

Dating shortly after a breakup usually ends in a disaster. We compare new people to the old, and we set the bar so high that we deprive new potential partners of any chance if they do not meet the EXACT qualities that we are looking for. We also date with hopes that the next person we meet is the person we marry.

When that does not go as planned, and most of the time it does not, we attempt to rekindle relationships from our pasts, believing that we may have made a mistake in letting our potential spouses leave.

We hate waiting. We would much rather jump from person to person, from relationship to relationship, than deal with being single for more than a couple of months.

We HATE the idea of being SINGLE.

When we are single in our mid-20s to early-40s, while the rest of our friends are married with kids, we feel like losers.

We feel like no one will ever want to be with us if they have not already by now.

We believe that we are unlovable and too crazy to be with.

We begin to hate couples, relationships, and all things related to love.

We do endless research on statistics of failed relationships and annoy everyone with that information.

We become miserable, and we want everyone around us to be miserable as well.

Why do we do this?

Why do we become anti-love venoms when we feel like we are the only ones alone?

We associate relationships as hallmarks of personal success and happiness.

False.

Relationships only serve to ENHANCE our personal success and happiness.

WE are the HALLMARKS of our own personal success and happiness.

We struggle to acknowledge how much power we have because, ever since we were kids, we have been told that we should aim to find a wife/husband who can make us happy, start a family, and have kids so they can carry on our legacies. Some people spend their entire lives dedicated solely to finding their spouses.

Imagine this:

One chance in life.

One goal.

Find a spouse.

Sole dedication.

Lifetime of misery.

Never-ending.

Death.

Sounds pretty terrible, right?

Unfortunately, some people are STILL okay with that. They still believe that finding the "perfect" person is the ULTIMATE GOAL in life.

We are strong and capable of so much.

Why dedicate all that POTENTIAL to another person?

We have the skills of climbing Mount Everest,

Winning Olympic medals,

Running with bulls,

Traveling around the world,

Creating artificial intelligence,

Building empires out of nothing,

Hiking across entire countries,

And SO MUCH MORE!

We have been able to ACCOMPLISH these goals on our

OWN for decades because we never needed a partner by our sides to prove our strength and motivation!

So why do we need one now!?

That was a rhetorical question.

Do not answer it.

Seriously, shut up.

Take a lesson from those who are single AND happy. These are not people who are against relationships because they are anti-commitment.

These are people who ENJOY being with themselves rather than running away from themselves.

These are people who do not rush from relationship to relationship because they know that finding someone who is not right for them will only end in self-destruction.

These are people who enjoy their own companies.

Instead of calling themselves "losers" for being single, they acknowledge that even though they are not in the company of another person, they can still enjoy life independently.

We all must learn how to live outside of a relationship. We may feel alone without a romantic partner, but we are never truly alone. We have friends, family, colleagues, pets and, most importantly, ourselves, to lift our spirits and support us when we have fallen.

Even if we are dating or in a relationship, we can still be alone. We cannot stick like glue to our partners forever. People have their own activities and commitments and sometimes, believe it or not, they DO NOT involve us.

We cannot follow someone 24/7 because we will look PSYCHOTIC if we do. We cannot sit around, do nothing, and wait for someone to come back because we will look PATHETIC. We are already learning how to be alone when we are IN a relationship, so let us channel that to when we are NOT in a relationship?

Is it because we miss having someone to rely on and communicate with daily?

We can still have that!

Pick up the phone and call your parents once in a while! You know they need it!

Is it because we miss having someone to talk to and trust?

Friends are called "friends" for a reason, and if they are truly our friends, they will be the "hand of trust" for us regardless of how busy they are. However, friends can also sit in the grey area. If our friends are too "busy" for us or too "in a relationship" for us, then they were never truly our friends. There are billions of people in this world with kind and decent hearts who will jump over lava to offer a helping hand. Shitty friends can be replaced.

Is it because we miss the feeling of human touch and affection?

Although this is much more difficult to find when we are single, we can still provide affection for ourselves.

Why not give yourself a hug?

You may look stupid while doing it, but why not try hugging yourself once or twice a day, and saying "I love you" in the mirror?

It can be an eye-opening experience to know that we can physically and emotionally love ourselves.

If that is not enough, get a dog.

Dogs will give us more affection than we will ever want, and better yet, without strings attached.

We do not have to make promises to dogs or buy them anything to receive affection. Dogs will give us affection even when we are mad at them.

Dogs are fucking amazing.

Get a dog.

Okay, so we know about the people who serially enter new relationships to avoid being alone, but what about the flip side? What about the people who never want to be in relationships and only serially date, going from one person to the next after 1-2 dates? Whether this applies to us or someone we know, when someone is so resistant to enter a relationship, they tend to use these common excuses (hint: watch for red flags!):

"I am too busy to dedicate time to a relationship."

"I get bored when I spend too much time with one person."

"I do not like commitments because I tend to flake on them."

"My family takes up all my time."

Here is my personal favorite:

"I am not relationship material."

Fuck you too, dude!

While there are SOME truths to these excuses, they all stem from one internal reason: FEAR.

The fear of being hurt or the fear of hurting.

Let us first explore the fear of being hurt, which has already been touched upon earlier.

Whatever the reason, past trauma, paranoia, or indirect experiences from relationships with others, we all have deep fears of getting hurt, refusing to give others the power to control our feelings. We become overly independent, not because we love ourselves, but because we know that we can CONTROL ourselves. We trust no one because anyone can have the motive and desire to hurt us.

When we take trust away from others, family included, we prevent ourselves from getting burned. However, we also devoid ourselves from the love that comes from trusting someone else. Nothing is a necessity in life, relationships included, and we can choose to have one or not. But there is also a difference between wanting to be alone and not serially dating versus wanting to be alone and serially dating.

When we serially date and never settle, we crave the feeling of being with someone, but we still fear getting hurt, so once we start feeling a sense of commitment, we bail. When we serially date, we are not okay with being alone. We want to be with someone, but we do not allow ourselves to do so.

On the flip side, sometimes we resist entering new relationships because we fear hurting others. We may still be hung up on those from our pasts, or we are too afraid to let those we are not interested in down, aka the creation of "ghosting." We continue seeing people we do not see futures with while also dating others because we are too afraid to let anyone down.

Regardless of the reason, when we make an effort to avoid hurting even just one person, we end up hurting everyone, including ourselves.

CHAPTER 20
TAKING OUR LIVES BACK

*"Carve your own future by fighting for your present. The winner
shall be deemed victorious of your life."* ℒ

I WANT to stress how important it is to take a breather when
you feel like your face is about to explode.

Breathe in.

Pause.

Breathe Out.

Pause.

Repeat.

When we find ourselves excessively texting and calling someone who wants nothing to do with us, we are only hurting ourselves.

When we find ourselves obsessively thinking about someone who refuses to love us, we are only delaying the time it takes for us to move on.

When people refuse to be in our lives, nothing in the world will make them change their minds unless THEY want to change their minds.

Contacting them nonstop will NOT make them want to answer us.

Camping outside their front doors will only make them call the cops.

Serenading them from the top of a building, surrounded by doves, will only force them to turn the other way.

We can be as loving, as affectionate, as compassionate, and as passionate as we want, but when someone wants to ignore us, we are GOING TO BE IGNORED!

I have been kicked and slapped (by myself) in the face for continuing to obsess over people not worth obsessing over. I keep trying to remind myself that if Mr. Loser and Sir Unavailable still wanted to be with me, they would. They have my number. They know where to find me.

BUT THEY DO NOT COME!

BECAUSE THEY DO NOT FUCKING CARE!

AND NEITHER SHOULD I!

NEITHER SHOULD WE!

We are all INTELLIGENT people who know DAMN WELL that we should not waste our time on toxic people, but WE DO IT ANYWAY. The romantic side of us continue to hold onto the hope that one day the ones we loved will come back.

We dream about this.

We lose sleep over this.

This idea consumes our minds day and night because we once had something amazing who are now strangers.

We pray that they will still come running back.

Unfortunately, people usually only run back to us in movies. In real life, people leave, and they just leave. There is no regret, no compassion, and no sorrow. They know we are suffering, and they thrive on it. Even the most selfless people can become cold and selfish when people refuse to accept their decisions.

We need to stop losing our values and dignities over unrequited love.

We need to forgive those who hurt us and move on.

Even if we still love them, letting go is the most loving and selfless act we can do.

If we wanted to leave, and someone was incessantly trying to hold us back, we would become angry and distant also.

Let them go.

They might come back.

They might not.

That is an inevitable risk that we must take if we want to stop being depressed and learn to love again.

Holding onto false hope only makes us feel worse.

Sure, sending that text and waiting optimistically for them to maybe respond can be uplifting and thrilling in the moment.

But what happens when they do not respond?

Our hearts sink.

We react toward their silence by continuing to send messages, and we eventually spiral out of control, leaving us feeling worse than before.

This is how patterns form.

We like to believe that one innocent, "how are you?" can do no harm, but that one innocent text soon becomes, "I fucking hate you for ignoring me! Please answer me! Please come back to me! I love you, and I cannot live another day without you because every minute without you makes me miserable, and I am so depressed that I cannot focus on life anymore!."

It is CRAZY how that switch can happen within a time span of ten minutes, but we all know how familiar this sounds and how often we use variations of these same exact words. BEGGING is NOT attractive, and it further PUSHES people away.

However, if there is still a sliver of hope that begging can cause people to have a change of heart, we grab onto that hope and act on it. Soon, it becomes comfortable to beg, plead, and cry until we are left rotting in our torn pajamas and trash-filled apartment for months.

No one can love us if we do not have self-respect and self-love.

CHAPTER 21
WE CAN HEAL

"The words 'can' and 'cannot' are only words; they only take form of the meanings we provide to them." L

WE CAN ALL HEAL because we are all victims despite our roles in breakups.

> We all get hurt.
> We all feel guilty.
> We all have regrets.
> We all have pain in our hearts.

We all need comfort and closure.

We all need people to confide in.

Most importantly, we all need to forgive so we can heal.

Forgive the ones who walk away from us.

Forgive the ones who tell us we are not worth staying loyal to.

Forgive the ones who drive us to our breaking points.

Forgive the ones who force us to walk away for our own sanities.

Forgive the ones who deceive us into forming relationships with them.

Forgive the ones who betray our trusts.

Forgive the ones who cheat on us.

Forgive everyone who has ever hurt us and let go of grudges.

While it may seem therapeutic to hate those who hurt us and swear to never have anything to do with them again, when we continue to hate people with such passion long after heartbreak, it is because we hate ourselves. Most of us do not love ourselves enough to stop our hateful thinking. We falsely believe that we love ourselves so we do everything we can to have others also believe that we love ourselves. We join meditation retreats, take ourselves out on dates, and write "#iloveme!" on our mirrors to deceive ourselves into believing that we have self-love.

Do we though?

Our actions and thoughts when we are in our worst moments truly reflect how we think of ourselves.

We are not our hashtags.

We are far from who we present to the world.

It is okay to not love ourselves as much as we should.

It is okay to smile at the world while dying on the inside.

It is okay to feel negative emotions toward other people.

The only thing that is not okay is lying about it,

pretending that we are happy and full of life when all we want to do is say "fuck you."

The guilt that comes from knowing that we are living a lie eventually tears us apart.

We can try to pretend that we are not living in a lie, but the truth will always be there.

Shoving it under a rug will only cause further detriment to ourselves.

To self-love is to self-discover. We need to get to the core of who we are and what we are capable of before we can contribute to the lives of others. Think about it, how on earth are we supposed to dedicate our lives and time to other people when we, ourselves, are a mess? There is not enough of us to go around!

Other people are living, soulful creatures, just like us, and if we dive into their lives and interfere with their journeys when we are not prepared, we are only going to fuck them over even more, and that is not love. Unless we only want partners for the sake of manipulating and using them for our own benefits, without giving a damn about them, we cannot be with others until we can learn to love and accept being alone.

If we truly love the ones we claim to love, we would never want to do anything to hurt them, and by trying to be with them before we are ready to do so, we are actively beginning the journey toward their pain.

Even though the journey toward self-discovery is a never-ending path, we need to still reach the point where, if someone we love leaves us, we do not result in complete meltdowns, a feat that proves challenging for many.

We need to accept that we cannot force everyone to love us, that openly expressing love to someone does not always mean it will be returned, and that the only person we can count on to love us, is us.

Our own lives are the only ones we can control.

We cannot change love, and we cannot stop love from changing.

When we choose to love, we choose to accept the pain that inevitably comes with it.

No relationship is without pain.

No marriage is without agony.

The difference between what keeps people together and what tears them apart is their resiliency as individuals, how capable they are at tackling and solving challenges that arise, and how willing they are to keep going despite all odds.

Such as those who can keep going and maintain a positive attitude after a relationship ends versus those who lock themselves away for days and turn to drugs and rebound sex as distractions.

None of us have it all figured out, not in life, not in relationships, not in family, and not in our careers. Most of us are only doing our best to survive and make it through each day while the rest of us reject these responsibilities and deny that they exist. I want to believe that we are all doing the best that we are capable of.

I want to believe that the reason life fails on us is because our best is just not good enough in some circumstances, which is okay, and not because some of us are too selfish and lackadaisical to put in the effort.

However, even with my naïve thinking, I know that most of us fall within the latter group. Because we have been taught to fend for ourselves and look out for our own happiness before anyone else's, we somehow translate that into self-absorption, resulting in taking from others rather than learning to give.

These are the people who use others to satisfy themselves. These are the leeches who suck other people dry, draining them of their energy just to temporarily feel happier.

I am not innocent of this. I have used people, and I have also been used. We train our brains to become selfish, to take for self-survival, and to push down anyone who gets in our ways. We follow the norms and take all means necessary to reach conventional goals that we may or may not want.

CHAPTER 22
MY OBSESSION

"I cannot remember the exact moment when I became addicted to love. Perhaps I never will. All I know is that I am, and I cannot stop." ℒ

MY OBSESSION with men and the idea of "fantasy love" started when I was five. I sat next to this boy who I fantasized about spending my life with ever since he gave me a Christmas card featuring two teddy bears hugging each other. I thought this meant he was in love with me, whether he was or not, and I fell in love with him IMMEDIATELY.

This obsession lasted for the next eight years. I was a shy and timid child so I never had the nerve to say anything to him; I just avoided him as much as I could and spent those eight years journaling, in detail, about how we were going to spend the rest of our lives together.

To this day, I still do not know how he felt about me.

I wish I knew.

I wish I had said something.

Instead, every time he dated other girls, I psycho-stalked them, meticulously researching what they had that made them "better" than me.

Nothing!

Other than a little confidence and sluttiness.

Nothing!

During my sophomore year of high school, I somehow fell in love, yes somehow, with another boy whom I had turned down in middle school. I thought he was more disgusting than rotten cheese, and I made every effort to let him know that.

But, when he started dating and fucking someone other chick, someone whom I have hated since the day I met her because I thought she was trying to steal my personality, I felt the competition, and I suddenly wanted the man I had previously turned down.

I made every effort to be as platonic as possible, but when his girlfriend started seeing me as a threat for being his friend (I have known this kid since I was four!), she did everything she could, even threatened to self-harm, to get him to stop talking to me. And boy, did her methods work! He stopped talking to me.

GUESS WHAT?!

This drove me INSANE! So, I BECAME INSANE. I did everything I could to try to get him to speak to me, including creating a fake alias and lying about how I had Leukemia.

Yes, I am aware that my methods of trying to get someone to speak to me are a little unconventional.

Yes, I am also aware that I will never be the right person, in any way, shape, or form, to give anyone relationship advice.

Fast forward a couple of years, I start dating my first boyfriend, my first relationship that was not a fantasy. This relationship started off great, taking my mind off the mess that I had dealt with thus far, making me feel like I can be "normal" for a change.

That did not last long.

For some reason, reason even I could not understand, I deliberately tried to sabotage the relationship by bringing up problems that did not exist and stirred up jealousy at every corner I turned.

I did not want the relationship to end.

I just wanted the attention.

I craved the feeling of someone pining over me, chasing me, and expressing how much he cared about me, so much that I created drama just for that self-assurance.

I had such low self-esteem that I felt the need to destroy the emotions of others to build up my own.

I sought out arguments because I wanted more attention than what I was already getting.

I threw tantrums because I wanted someone to tell me that I was special when I was incapable of doing it myself.

Finally, it got to the point where he grew tired of all the drama I was creating and broke up with me…via text, taking us back to the synopsis shown at the very beginning of this book.

I repeat, I am not crazy.

Crazy actions do not make crazy people.

Crazy actions create emotional beings.

Between my first and second relationships, the whole three months, I wish I could say that I took time off for myself to recover and recuperate, the right way to deal with a difficult breakup.

Instead, I found myself writing over 100 sappy love letters to my ex (AND ACTUALLY MAILING THEM!), flirting with as many people as I could find from over four different dating apps, and getting drunk/hooking up with random guys I had just met.

I was a mess.

I even hooked up with someone I met in a psychiatric ward, falling head-over-heels for him while also hating everything he was, writing a five-page love letter to him expressing how I felt, all after only knowing him for three weeks!!

I found myself "in love" with everyone who gave me the time of day, and I fantasized about my future with men after only the first date, including dates that did not even go well!

I was running away from myself.

I did not want to deal with the reality of my breakup.

I did not want to accept that it was over.

I could not get out of my own head.

The world felt like it revolved around me, and I could not objectively see how my actions were affecting others.

My second relationship did not stabilize my craziness as my first one did. In fact, it made it SO MUCH WORSE. I dove, head first, into my second relationship from day one, throwing myself at him sexually just to give him a reason to want to see me again.

I have regretted it ever since.

However, at the time, I did not care.

I wanted someone to pay attention to me again.

I missed the feeling of constant love and affection.

I was going to do everything I could to get it.

Even if it meant abusing myself.

Unfortunately, my grand scheme of manipulation only works with pushovers, not those who have stubborn minds of their own. Acting the way that I had in my previous relationship only got me into a bigger mess than I had anticipated. After a month of dating, he broke up with me.

Naturally, I refused to accept that.

Let us keep in mind that I only knew this kid for a month, seeing each other twice a week, and I was already cyber-stalking AND physically stalking him.

I even stalked and continuously messaged his FAMILY AND FRIENDS, trying to convince them to get him to talk to me after he HAD ALREADY BLOCKED ME.

When people block us, via phone AND social media, it is usually a sign that they want us gone.

Nope!

I saw it as a motivator to try even harder to get his attention.

I skipped out on work early, just to take the bus to his apartment and knock on his door until he answered, because my anxiety took over.

I sent him gift and food deliveries with stupid little messages because I knew he would open his door for strangers when he did not open it for me.

That worked.

Once.

Until he stopped answering everyone altogether.

Fuck.

Long story short, I was able to get him to talk to me, and we eventually got back together...for three weeks, until he broke up with me again.

Of course, again, I refused to accept rejection so I pursued him.

This cycle became an on-and-off relationship with over 250 breakups!

Yes, I counted.

It was not love.

It was no longer my goal.

It was miserable.

After a certain point, I did not even love him anymore.

In fact, I do not even think I ever loved him in the first place!

I just loved the attention and the affection.

But I pursued.

And I stayed.

And I vowed, to both him and myself, to keep this relationship alive despite whatever happened.

He cheated on me.

I begged for forgiveness.

He hit me.

I justified that I deserved it.

He stole from me.

I looked the other way.

You are probably wondering the same thing that I had been: what the fuck is wrong with me?!

I could make up some sob story about fear and only staying because I was too afraid to be alone, but instead, I only stayed because…honestly, I have no idea why I stayed.

At the time, it just felt more comfortable staying, continuing to live in misery and pain, than leaving.

Day and night, I contemplated leaving. I imagined what life could be like with someone who respected me and did not abuse me. Then I think about how much effort I had put into getting my ex back, how shameful it would feel to throw it all away, and how much of a failure I would be if I could not hold onto a relationship even after sacrificing my self-respect.

I stayed with my abusive ex because, at the time, that pursuit was the only aspect in my life that I felt I could control. Somewhere in the mess of my on-and-off relationship, I had mentally shifted from obsessively being in "love" and obsessively wanting affection and attention to obsessively craving power.

You feel a certain sense of power when you can change a person's mind and manipulate situations so they are in your favor. Just like being in control of whether a relationship continues or ends gives power temporarily to one person over the other, being able to alter people's decisions and convince them to go against their original desires provides the same satisfaction.

We all want to feel powerful in at least one aspect of our lives whether it is in:

Relationships:

Through physical and emotional abuse

Making breadwinner choices

Engaging in temper tantrums and silent treatments when things do not go certain ways

Withholding pleasures until deeds are done

Jobs:

Snitching and stepping on the toes of others

Throwing coworkers under the bus to get ahead

Indulging in power trips

Our own bodies:

Constructing rigid diet and exercise plans to sculpt that "perfect" image of ourselves

Taking toxic diet pills and risking death just to stay thin

Throwing millions away on liposuction and plastic surgery

Power is fun. It gives us control over our lives when we feel we are losing it to others. But so many people get the wrong idea of what "control" really means. Control means taking BACK control of our OWN lives, NOT controlling the lives of OTHERS. We have this false perception that by controlling others and manipulating their feelings, we become in control of our own lives.

We believe "taking back power" means destroying the lives of others before they can destroy ours first.

As much as we all want to believe that relationships are about equal amounts of love and respect, they are really about who has more control over the other. Think about it:

ONE person always chooses the restaurant, ONE person always feels too "sick" to work, ONE person always decides on outings, and ONE person always chooses who the other can and cannot be friends with.

I am sure there are couples who do have equal balance in shared interests and opinions, but in most relationships, one person usually feels less in control and demeaned. Power and competition are inherent instincts that people possess.

We all want to feel strong.

No matter how hard we try to ignore this instinct, the moment we get the chance to order someone around and make that person bow down to our feet, we go for it.

Before I get carried away with my tangent, let me continue my story about my reckless cycle of obsession and insanity when it comes to men. After my seemingly never-ending breakup/makeup cycle with my second ex, the relationship FINALLY came to an end, to no one's surprise. And you know what? For the FIRST time, and probably the ONLY time in my series of dating adventures so far, I felt FREE and RELIEVED to not be in a relationship. I was HAPPY that he was no longer in my life. I did not even feel the need to TEXT HIM!

Of course, like the end of any kind of relationship, I still wondered about him, thought about him, and maybe occasionally stalked his Facebook five times a day, but remind you, I WAS RELIEVED and NOT AT ALL OBSESSED.

But habit is habit, right?

Can we really turn it off?

It is like breathing.

When we go too long without engaging in the habits that we have been used to for so long, we become strangers to ourselves.

Our usual behaviors now become nonexistent, and we are left experiencing an out-of-body feeling with our minds floating around, confused and lost.

The concrete schedule that we had of:

Texting every hour

Stalking every two hours

Nonstop Google searches of "How to Win Back Your Ex"

Constant thoughts of "Is he seeing someone else?"

Piles of books on "How Can I Get Him to Pay Attention to Me?," and

Endless nightmares of "How the FUCK can he be dating SOMEONE ELSE ALREADY?!"

When my previous relationships ended, I obsessed over these thoughts and resources constantly. I did not want to move on, and I could not get over the breakups. I meticulously researched every book and every blog on how to win back exes and how to manipulate them into getting back together with me. I tried everything, from constant texting so they would not forget about me to not texting at all as per the dumb "No Contact Rule."

I wrote love letters, pouring my heart out in every metaphor and poem I could think of, begged for forgiveness and made false promises to change when I had no intention to, and sent hate messages to every girl who commented on their pages (despite whether they were family).

I did not care.

You might think that by doing all this, I had already lost myself, lost sight of the independent person I was born to be and turned into an obsessive monster who spent hours Googling biased blog posts on "How to Win Him Back When He No Longer Wants You."

I could literally take all the resources I found, slap them together, and create an entire library on this one topic alone.

I was very invested.

However, I did not lose myself.

Because I never knew who I was in the first place.

So, by doing this, I was at least able to throw myself into a scenario where I felt both grounded and distracted from the spirals inside my head.

However, this was much more than just a surface desire, much more than just a "I need a distraction," a "I want him back," or a "I need to fuck someone new and move on."

This was about my struggles.

My demons.

My insecurities.

My desperate need to break something that was already broken.

When people end relationships, they grieve, they hate, but then they move on.

I struggled with that.

Instead, I begged, threatened suicide, threw tantrums, manipulated, ruined the lives of innocent people, and got myself into dangerous situations because "if it is not sketchy AF, then it is not enough of a distraction."

What is wrong with me?

No, really?

Why do I put myself through situations where it is literally life or death?

Why do I put myself in scenarios where I feel so out of touch with myself, and I only begin to feel a sense of satisfaction AFTER I have latched myself onto someone I do not even know?

I fall "in love" with the first boy who winks at me.

IN LOVE!?!!!

My self-esteem is so low that I am willing to settle and love literally anyone who walks by me.

A random boy waves, my heart sinks.

Someone smiles at me, I dream of a fairytale wedding with him.

I struggle with distinguishing between feeling love and feeling infatuation.

I cannot separate how I ACTUALLY feel from how I WANT to feel.

Is this a problem that only I seem to have, where I believe every first date automatically warrants into a relationship?

Am I the only one who thinks I am actually FALLING IN LOVE after ONE DATE?

I mean, I know I am not actually falling in love, but it feels like it when we become so desperate to be with someone.

We see happy couples all around us.

We hear our family and friends criticize how we are still single at 30, making us just want to snag a beau of our own to shut them all up!

So, am I crazy?

Or have the influences that surrounded me turned me into the monster I am today?

CHAPTER 23
STOP JUDGING US BASED ON OUR PASTS!

"We all have scars, visible or not. Take your eyes off mine and focus on your own." 𝓛

SIGMUND FREUD BELIEVED that childhood trauma influences and shapes who we become later in adulthood. He may have had a point. My obsession with men developed very early in my childhood. I was masturbating by the age of three and dreaming of detailed weddings with random boys in my classes by the age of five.

Does that mean I am crazy though?

Or does that mean the lack of romance and love between my parents drove me to find romance and love on my own, through any means possible?

Growing up around two people who constantly bickered and fought drove me away from them and straight into the arms of strangers. Having a father who was never available or attentive drove me to search for men who were. I fell for men who listened and were present despite whether I was attracted to them. I chased after assholes because they payed attention to me despite their incentives behind it. I convinced myself that anger and abuse from men mean passion and love. The more I was hated and emotionally abused, the more I felt loved.

What the fuck, right!?

Who does this?

Who says this?

Who equates getting punched in the eye with love?

Growing up, my family expressed care and concern through yelling and hitting. Those were their ways of showing my brother and I that they cared and loved us enough to put in the effort to punish us. They reasoned that, if they did not love us, then they would not waste the time and energy to punish us.

As a little girl, I believed them. From the age of two until the age of eighteen, whenever I was beat with a broom or with a chair, I told myself it was out of love. Whenever I was screamed at ferociously, I told myself that I deserved it.

In short:

Anger = Love

Abuse = Passion

Raise of Voice = Care and Attention

Those are the connections I am used to.

Those are the mantras I live my life by.

Those are the rules that I cannot stop following, no matter how hard I try.

I let people run over my life because I see control and manipulation as love, and therefore, I use the same methods on others.

It is disgusting.

It takes a terrible toll on the human psyche, and it drives insanity to devour minds. Humans are not meant to be controlled and manipulated because we are animals at heart.

We want the chance to roam free, make mistakes, and fall on our own accord.

We want our thoughts to feel like they can expand.

We want to feel limitless rather than feel locked in a cage.

When someone ignores or rejects us, they are in control.

We give them permission to grab hold of our lives and twist them into whatever they want.

We allow others to run the controller on how we can feel and how we should behave.

When they ignore us, we feel sad.

When they text us, we feel ecstatic.

When they leave us, we become devastated.

We need to stop giving others so much power where they become our puppeteer.

We are not puppets; we should not be controlled by someone we have just met.

We have known ourselves our entire lives, yet we let strangers waltz in and screw us over in a split second!

Some people actually commit suicide because of breakups.

From an outsider's perspective, we assume that these people have more internal psychotic issues going on than just a simple breakup.

That is a false perception.

Breakups can be fatal.

They mess with every emotion and feeling that we have, translating into physical symptoms. As I mentioned before, when people experience heartbreak, their hearts can literally break. They can feel like they are dying, their arteries feel like they are clogging up, and they find it difficult to breathe. Their stomachs sink and their chests begin to compress, similar to symptoms of heart attacks.

When people say that they would rather die than continue to experience the pain of a breakup, they mean it.

They are not just being overdramatic.

The feelings that come with heartbreak can become so severe that even death seems like the better alternative.

Feeling suicidal after a breakup is not limited to a certain demographic. Anyone can experience it, despite the color of our skin, despite our financial status, despite the family we grew up in, despite our intelligence, and despite our relationship history.

We like to joke about people who have "crazy eyes" and how that is seen as a red flag. We steer clear of certain people based on appearances, and we judge others without giving them the chance to tell their stories or explain their situations.

Sometimes the ones we judge are the ones we need in our lives.

Sure, they have had rough pasts but so has everyone.

Some people are just more open and honest about their pasts than others.

Some people hide their crazy until AFTER they have locked us in, only unleashing it when we have already invested.

Others show their crazy early on but end up being the ones who are caring and kindhearted.

Terrible situations can turn any person into a mental case.

Just because someone has had a rough past does not mean they deserve a rough future.

Just because someone has a history of suicide does not mean he/she is going to act on it.

Just because someone has had a terrible relationship and has made mistakes in the past, does not mean the same sequence of events will repeat again.

We do not know where people come from, therefore, we should not assume the worst. If we do, everyone would be single. Scars make people beautiful, and if we reject people based on those scars, we deserve to be alone.

The reason I want to share this little insight on suicidal behaviors after devastating situations is because I know, all too well, how difficult it is to not want to pull the trigger when all we feel, day and night, is immense pain. I was not a sane or clear-headed person during my intense periods of heartbreak, where all I wanted to do was die. I was not in a place where I could respectfully give myself to someone else.

I was a mess, and my mind was cluttered; it all felt too unbearable to carry on. I do not go into relationships PLAN-NING to unleash my craziness, manipulate people, and make their lives miserable. I care about people. I am loving, patient, and I am an extreme people pleaser, but when I get hurt, I get angry, and that is when the switch happens.

Some may call it "bipolar," but I call it, "you-fucking-hurt-me-so-I-am-allowed-to-be-angry."

Pain is expressed in so many ways; it does not just involve crying and shutting others out. Those are what caused the pain to happen in the first place when all we wanted was to be heard.

Suicide is a cry for attention, a drastic measure to get people to listen to us and see that we need help.

Unfortunately, many of us still see suicide as a coward's way out, a selfish act of giving up and leaving loved ones behind to deal with the mess.

CHAPTER 24

ARE WE JUST NOT GOOD ENOUGH?

"We can only stand tall and proud if we allow ourselves to fall and crumble. Most days we will feel like shit, but all we need is one moment to prove our greatness." ℒ

No MATTER how hard and how much we try to distract ourselves from the feelings and emotions that rush over us when we remember all the pain and agony we have endured while in the state of "love" and constant obsession, we will ALWAYS be pulled back.

Accept it.

We will experience times where we seem fine, enjoying the things we love alone, regardless of what others think, but one second can lead to the next, and we find ourselves, once again, in constant turmoil and anxiety over people who make plans for dates and ghost us instead.

We text and we call.

We try to be respectful.

We try confrontation.

We try demanding answers.

We even try patience.

But patience can only last so long when "busy" equates to leaving us dry for three weeks and counting.

We live in an era where everyone is glued to their phones, whether they like to admit it or not. When we text people, regardless of how busy they are, they usually respond within twenty-four hours of receiving it, that is, if they wanted to respond.

I will admit it.

I have done this.

I have read texts and blatantly ignored them just because I did not feel like talking.

However, being on the other side makes you realize how much it hurts.

When someone texts us, it is usually because they genuinely want to talk to us, see how we are doing, connect, and find out more about us, except for maybe the occasional "DTF?."

It takes effort and courage to pick up that phone, choose our names out of the contact list, and type out the message, which can sometimes be deep, personal, and embarrassing. When we ignore them, it leaves them with many lingering thoughts.

"Why are they not responding to me?"

"What could they possibly be so busy with that they cannot send back a simple reply?"

"Did I do something to piss them off?"

"Did I do something to hurt them?"

"What the fuck did I do?"

"Are they over me already?"

"Are they talking to someone else?"

"I bet they are fucking talking to a bunch of other fuck-tards right now."

"What the fuck is wrong with me?!"

"Do they hate me that much that they cannot even give me the decency and respect of TELLING me that they are not interested?"

"WHAT THE FUCK DID I DO!?!"

It hurts fifty times WORSE to NOT say anything than to let people know that we are not interested. Yes, rejection hurts, but we believe that if the rejections are not direct, then we spare others of hurt feelings, and that by ghosting people, it slowly weans them off us and eventually both parties move on and neither side remembers any of it.

NO!

What REALLY HAPPENS when we ghost someone is that, although we may feel nothing, or we may feel free and capable of moving on, the person who was ghosted becomes stuck in constant anxiety. Regardless of how long two people have known each other and regardless of the status of the relationship, not knowing what is going on is one of the worse cycles of emotions anyone can go through. It is not cut and dry, where the person being rejected immediately gets the hint and moves on. It is a never-ending constant mind battle.

Regardless of how strong and independent we are, we still struggle with the demon of the "what ifs."

The person who rejected us did not just reject us.

They left us feeling unworthy, unloved, and undeserving of respect as if our lives did not matter.

We begin to doubt our self-confidence.

We begin to wonder whether we are good enough to be respected at all.

We begin to wonder what we have done to deserve this type of treatment.

Why is it so common for people to do this?

Has there been evidence in their pasts that makes them believe that ghosting is the best plan of action?

Are they that cowardly that they cannot even send one text?

People are literally hiding behind their phones.

What is the worst that can happen?

They send a rejection text, and the person being rejected leaps through his/her phone and poltergeist out from the other side?

At least send the text and immediately proceed to blocking to avoid confrontation.

It is still a terrible thing to do, but at least the other person gets closure.

It will hurt, but at least it will hurt less.

Sometimes, even this is too much for people.

So, where does that leave us? Some still ponder and obsess over "the one who got away" or "the one who could have been." Others fall back into own habits, settling for people they do not even like and crumbling into pieces when they eventually get rejected, letting the power of others destroy them.

How is it that someone, whom we have only known for a short period of time, can change our entire lives, alter our perspectives of love and ourselves, and leave us feeling empty and unfulfilled so quickly and so easily?

I once knew an actor, very responsive, great personality, and what seemed like a deep connection. The first date ended well. We made plans, went our separate ways, and ended the night with promising conversation.

Then it all fell apart.

No answer, no responses, no more of the daily conversations we used to exchange back and forth.

So, naturally, I thought:

"What the fuck is going on?"

"How can someone who seemed to like me ignore me so quickly?

"Did he die?"

"Did I say something wrong?"

"Was there something in my teeth?"

I then proceeded to ask him:

"Hey, haven't heard back from you."

"Did I do something wrong?"

"Did I scare you away?"

"Do you not want to talk anymore?"

"Are you ghosting me?"

"If you do not like me, can you at least tell me?"

While this all seem like normal conversational behaviors for the victims of ghosting, they apparently appear as a crazy act of obsession for the ghoster.

No answer.

For SEVEN days.

Then, a response.

"Not ghosting you. I'm overwhelmed by the texting. You can still text me, but if I don't respond IMMEDIATELY, don't FREAK out."

"Okay, first, there is a HUGE GAP between texting back IMMEDIATELY and texting back ONE WEEK LATER. I know you have your phone on you because I have STALKED you enough to know your social media activity so do not even dare pin this on me."

That was what I should have said.

But, being the timid person that I am, I responded with, "Of course! Take all the time you need! I'm patient! Please let me know if you need anything! Good luck at your acting conference!"

I said that over three weeks ago...

Now, I know I am not an actor, so I do not know the exact glitz and details of what the life of an actor looks like (mind you, not even a Hollywood actor, just some local dude trying to act like a big shot), but I need to know, IS THREE WEEKS THE DEFINITION OF "NOT IMME-DIATELY"???

I get that you do not want to be overwhelmed with text messages, but I have not sent one in four days!

Two sentences a day, three days a week, are too much!?

I know I call myself "crazy," but I really tried for this guy.

Normally, after one week, I would have blown up his phone with psychotic messages demanding answers until he proceeded to block me, but this time I waited.

Waited.

And waited.

And waited.

And waited....

Oh, but do not worry, the crazy did not go away just because I liked him; the crazy became stronger BECAUSE I liked him, so I tried replacing him any way I could. I tried to get him out of my head by talking to twenty other people, hoping one of them could replace him. I hooked up with as many people as I could, but that only left me feeling disgusted with myself.

It is often the ones who walk over our lives the least that leave the biggest marks.

We strive for answers because we are innately curious. We want what we cannot have, what we cannot know and, for some of us, we chase this fantasy that we must know every thought of every person we encounter.

We meet someone new, get married, have a family, grow old, and still, we are left with this feeling of wanting to know why our past lovers rejected us, what was wrong with us, whether the person we are with now is just someone we have settled for, and what our lives would have looked like if we had ended up with our exes instead?

Would that have made us happy?

Would anything have made us happy?

We will always have this itch in our hearts that make us doubt every decision we have ever made. The life we are living right now has been decided by a chain of events that led us up to this very moment.

Feelings are ever-changing.

We think we can be happy if only we had this "person," if only we were "married," or if only we had what everyone else "has."

These are only transient materialistic "things" that can never truly justify happiness for us because we do not know what will make us happy. We see others "happy," and we assume it is because of the things they have, but people are also fantastic at hiding their true emotions and their problems.

When my ex broke up with me, the only thing I could focus on was getting him back, how happy I would be if he was in my life again, and how everything would be perfect if I can just see him again. But that was just my mind clouded with what I wanted AT THAT MOMENT.

And I got that moment.

I got him back.

I believed my life was perfect again... for a whole two weeks until it wasn't, and I became more miserable than I was before because I made promises I did not believe in to get back something I did not want.

I got what I wanted.

But I was still miserable.

We all try so hard to recover, so hard to take back our lives, until asshole number six comes along and ruins it for us all over again.

We spend thousands of dollars on therapy and meditation

classes to try and detox from the obsessions and negativities of toxic relationships.

We give ourselves positive affirmations daily to boost our self-esteem.

We date ourselves and attempt to meet only decent people rather than players.

We spend more time with friends and family to distract ourselves from overbearing loneliness.

We travel around the world to fall in love with our surroundings rather than rely on others.

We develop new hobbies, make career changes, and move to new cities to start over.

We delete social media and completely stop dating so we can piece ourselves back together.

But then he comes along.

With his perfect smile, gorgeous body, dazzling personality, and just like that, all our hard work goes straight into the trash.

We fall back into pretentious and non-existing love.

He breaks our hearts into a million pieces.

He throws us back into the dump we just picked ourselves out of.

We pretend we are fine, brush ourselves off, and try to keep it together.

We tell ourselves that we WILL NOT engage in our obsessive behaviors.

We write reminders on our mirrors.

We carve them into our skins.

We deny that the craziness is still inside us.

We crack.

We rejoin social media.

We pull out our stalking resources.

We pop in a chick flick.

We go to town.

Scrolling through "Mr. Perfect's" Instagram page, wondering what the girl in his arm has that we do not.

Thinking:

"I just spent the past five years of my life improving all the qualities I can possibly improve and constructing myself into a "perfect" being, and I am STILL being rejected?!"

"What the hell?"

"What the hell did I do this time?"

"What is wrong with me now!??"

"That is it."

"I give up."

"I will never get the guy."

"I will be a loser for the rest of my life because I suck."

"Nothing I do will ever be good enough."

"What the fuck does she have that I do not?!"

Truly, but unfortunately, this thought process rings all too well for most of us. It sucks to swallow the fact that, most of the time, two people are just not meant to be. The sparks are just not there, and the people we want may just have better connections with others than they do with us regardless of appearances or intelligence.

Not everyone we want is going to want us back, just like we do not want everyone who wants us.

There are going to be people who reject us just like there are going to be people we reject. But it does NOT mean that we are worthless. It does NOT mean that we are not perfect because perfection lies in our subjective perceptions of ourselves. It does NOT mean that our last five years were a waste of life because we learn and grow with each terrible dating experience.

We may not realize it in the moment, but with each rejection, we slowly learn how to recover with less pain. We cannot compare ourselves with the ones chosen over us because, in the end, it may have just not been the right fit, and it is better that we realize it sooner than later.

Somewhere on the other end, some people are wishing that they are us, just as we are wishing that we are not.

When the right people come along, we become perfect in their eyes no matter what we do. But we are to blame for the assholes we let in. We choose who we let in, and we choose who we keep out. For most of us, attractiveness and intelligence drive us toward certain people, i.e., the assholes and the bitches. We want people who look like models despite their moral characters because

We believe that being with gorgeous people will make us gorgeous by default and,

We believe that if we do not date people "up to standard" physically, then we would be judged for having low standard.

There has always been an unwritten criterion in terms of the types of partners we should have: men should be physically strong and fit to play the role of the breadwinner while women should be petite and pretty to play the role of the loyal housewife and caretaker.

We have taken this socially-constructed idea of the body type we SHOULD be looking for while casting aside everyone else.

We have replaced objective eyes with a checklist that we mark off as different people enter and leave our lives.

We tell ourselves and others that we want someone with a kind and caring heart rather than a pretty shell, but time after time, we continue to chase based on our shallow desires.

Despite knowing the truth, we still falsely believe that we only want deep and sincere connections. When we are rejected or endure a broken heart, we play victim, in that we "never saw it coming," when we knowingly choose partners with higher risks of leaving.

We pretend we are the innocently-rejected because we do not want to admit that we fucked up again by choosing Prince Charming over the Pauper.

We want others to feel sorry for us and hate all the other

prince charmings because it makes us feel better for our poor decisions.

We want others to NOT have Prince Charming because we hate the idea of our friends having "Mr. Hottie" while we settle for "Mr. Mediocre."

We secretly want everyone to be as miserable as we are, and we hate the idea of someone else having what we do not.

We should be happy for others because they are happy, not only when we are happy also.

Jealousy and hate exude more power than gratitude.

CHAPTER 25
WE ARE ALL CLOSET SOCIOPATHS

"We are all sociopaths. Some of us are more honest about it. Some of us deny it by exuding all opposite behaviors. We can only keep the truth hidden for so long before it all comes spilling out." ℒ

TAKE single women in their 40s, for example. They find joy in drinking wine and bitching about how all the men they have dated suck, and how women who marry in their 20s will have rude awakenings when their men leave them in ten years for younger chicks.

*Note: I am only using "single women in their 40s" as an

example. This can apply to all ages, genders, and relationship status.

The purpose of "bitch-speak" is to make people feel less ashamed of themselves. However, "bitch-speak" also forms a bond between people. Hating a specific type of people or a specific relationship status is what brings people together. It is very rare that human beings connect through positivity and sincere joy for each other; it is often a connection based on a common hatred for others. We struggle with being sincerely happy for other people because we are competitive by nature.

When we are happy, we want to be happier than everyone else.

When we are sad, we want others to be more miserable than us.

We even go as far as manipulating others into feeling terrible about themselves and lying about what their partners do in attempts to break them up.

We are not proud of it.

But it works.

Because the end goal is to make ourselves feel better, despite what it takes and, most of the time, we accomplish that, even if we consciously ruin the lives of others.

Friendships form tighter when two newly single people come together rather than when two people in separate relationships come together.

When I was in the midst of one of my obsessive chases over men, I hated it when people I knew were happy in relationships. I Facebook stalked one of my exes, found out that he was in a serious relationship, and contacted him, not having spoken to him for over two years and fully knowing that he still had feelings for me. I played it off as "just wanting to catch up" but really, I wanted him to see me, realize how much he still loved me, cheat on his current girlfriend with me, and break up with her for me, just so I can

REJECT HIM and FEED MY EGO by knowing I was still wanted.

I knew what I was doing was manipulative and pure evil, but I did it anyway because how I felt at that moment was much stronger than any moral compass buried inside my head.

At that moment, it felt like THE ONLY THING THAT WOULD MAKE ME FEEL BETTER WAS TO BREAK THEM UP.

At that moment, all I wanted to do was make someone else feel worse than I did despite what it took.

At that moment, I wanted to destroy all love, and because I had the power to do so, I went for it.

At that moment, I found joy in telling his girlfriend that he cheated on her while playing it off as an act of humanitarianism.

At that moment, I knew there was definitely something wrong with me, but I just DID NOT CARE.

At that moment, I felt guilty but proceeded anyway.

At that moment, I was flawed.

At that moment, I was broken.

We never want to admit our flaws because that would mean that we are flawed.

We find it difficult to accept that there is nothing wrong with being a little different, making mistakes, and occasionally falling.

CHAPTER 26
PICK YOURSELF UP!

"Do you really want your ex to see you lying on the sidewalk, dirty, sad, and pathetic? Who cares if you feel like crap? Pick yourself off the disgusting ground, slap a smile on your face, and pretend that you own the world!" $\mathcal{L}$

WE OVERSEE how we deal with failure, how we deal with imperfections, and how we bounce back after tragedies.

No one will ever go through life without falling.

We are all flawed, and we are all going to make mistakes whether big or small.

We can either choose to mope in our failures and let our lives be controlled by them, or we can choose to acknowledge that we are all messed up and do something about it.

We can choose to break the patterns that we are living, as hard as that may be.

We can choose to be the person that we strive to be rather than just pretending that we are.

We may not be able to stop obsessing over and craving attention from whoever we can find, but we can start by putting the phone down.

Download that app, flirt with as many people as you want, but put the phone down when the urge comes up to either go out on that date with that person you do not even like (because you know you will just end up fucking him/her and getting too attached), or to nonstop message someone you do like just because he/she has not responded in a few days.

The latter is very controversial. Depending on who we are, some of us get worried when people do not respond within a day, and for others, we are perfectly fine with not hearing from people for two weeks.

TWO WEEKS??!!

Do you know what you can do in two weeks??!

You can quit your job!

In all seriousness, two weeks is the right amount of time to begin forgetting about people and move on, especially if we are on apps where we are chatting up multiple people at a time. If people do not respond to our messages within two weeks, they are either dead or clearly not interested. We know which of the two I am.

Ask yourself why you are talking to these people, why you are considering meeting up with them, whether you only swiped right because you are lonely or because you actually like them, whether you are only talking to them to forget about a recent breakup, and what intentions you have going into these dates.

We may be crazy and obsessive, but we are also resilient.

We may not know the right time to fight versus the right time to quit, but we do know how to bounce back after seemingly endless failures.

We FEEL like we will never recover.

We FEEL like we want our lives to be over when the person we are currently crushing on refuses to return our texts.

We FEEL like we will never love again after someone breaks out hearts.

We FEEL like we want to give up and are not strong enough to continue.

But our feelings can be WRONG.

Our feelings can deceive and manipulate our thoughts and actions in ways we can never imagine.

And we let them.

Feelings are strongest when we are most vulnerable, so we engage in behaviors that would be insane to us otherwise. We are all intelligent people who know that our feelings do not define us, yet when we are broken, that logic no longer exists.

But what if these "feelings" did not exist?

What if, instead of becoming emotional over heartbreaks or other tragic incidents, we become fully logical?

What if we experience a painful breakup, and instead of breaking down in tears and anger, we simply acknowledge it and move on?

However, there are also complications and consequences for turning off our feelings. People actively choose to become indifferent, apathetic, and unemotional after breakups. There are classes, clubs, organizations, and self-help books and videos on how to remove emotional pain IMMEDIATELY post-breakup.

They challenge people to numb themselves, prepare for the worse at the very START of the relationship, expect everything to go wrong until proven otherwise, and if the relationship falters, they would have already been prepared, well-equipped to deal with and cease any pain that comes with heartbreak.

But is this what we want?

Pain is painful, yes, it is in the word, but with pain, also comes a soul, a person, and a unique life. We think we want to forget and become numb to avoid feeling pain. We think forgetting and not caring will make us able to move on quicker and skip the five stages of breakups that almost all people go through.

But what do the five stages of grieving after a breakup mean? Denial, anger, bargaining, depression, and acceptance are all critical stages in learning and building ourselves whole again after being torn down. Most people look at these stages, dread the first four, and quickly want to move onto acceptance.

But moving onto acceptance right away takes away our chances to learn from our mistakes, to learn the types of people that we can and cannot get along with to avoid making the same mistakes, and to learn more about what we want in a person as opposed to our physical impulses and external attractions.

So, what are the consequences of turning off our feelings rather than just letting them flow through us?

When we turn off our emotions and how we feel toward situations, we experience a lack of emotional and physical pain that can prove as life-saving. Normally, when we experience mental pain such as heartbreak, our minds and bodies take in this information and learn from it:

The types of triggers that cause us to react emotionally,

How quickly or slowly our bodies react to different situations and,

How our bodies recover and the time it takes to do so.

We subconsciously store information based on each inter-action or relationship with people, so when we enter back into the dating world, we actively screen out those who remind us of our pasts. We avoid people who have similari-ties to those who have hurt us, and we gravitate toward people who have similarities to those who have loved us.

When we remove the pain, we are no longer able to recog-nize and screen out the people who will hurt us. We put ourselves in a place of high risk and danger because we can no longer recognize signs that our pasts have given us.

When we train ourselves to become emotionless and stop feeling, we lose the quality that makes us human: empathy. When we stop feeling, we also stop caring, and we end up turning off our emotions toward everyone around us, good and bad, and we become soulless. Turning off our emotions means we are telling ourselves and others that we do not care and do not want to care.

CHAPTER 27
THE FACE BEHIND THE MASK

"Behind every smile is a tear. Behind every dollar is debt. Behind every story is a lie. Behind every person is another person crying for help." ℒ

IT IS common to see suicidal ideations and behaviors as signs of weakness because we tend to see them as signs of giving up and selfishly leaving behind loved ones to deal with OUR MESS. Even though we will never know the true story behind those who go through with suicide, those who have been at their breaking points and have come down from the ledge know what it means to truly become the heroes of their own lives.

Wanting to die is a result of absolute pain and an influx of overwhelming feelings that are no longer able to be controlled. Wanting to die is the last resort from dealing with pain because the means to cope are no longer present.

Suicide can be a result of many reasons, but one of the main reasons why suicide happens too often is because those around us have either chosen to cease their brains from experiencing painful emotions or are actively hiding their own pain and thus, lose that empathetic connection with us where they are no longer able to understand why people can feel suicidal, turn to judgment instead of empathy, and make us feel even more isolated and unsupported.

When we are at the brink of suicide and decide to choose life instead, that is a sign of turning off these powerful emotions.

When we recover from a painful breakup without having to get under someone else, that is a sign of turning off these powerful emotions.

When we stop our tears midway through crying, brush ourselves off, and walk out the door to deal with life, we are turning off these powerful emotions.

When we are finally able to wake up, still feel incredibly overwhelmed with pain and NOT climb back into bed, we are turning off these powerful emotions.

For those who have experienced many, or even one, powerful breakup(s), how do we know if the next person we meet is right for us? There can be pieces of them that resonate with our long list of desires, or they can even check off our entire list, but how do we TRULY KNOW? Just because someone seems right, feels right, and is, hypothetically, everything we have always wanted, does not guarantee that he/she is not like those who have hurt us in our pasts.

How do we know when we are no longer confusing love with infatuation? How do we know when we have found the ones we want to be with and are not just blinded by desperation? This is the problem with having a brain that never stops adapting and changing.

We never truly know what we want.

We know what we want based on the knowledge of what we DO NOT WANT. When we experience a situation or a person that has hurt us, we know we do not want to go back to that.

But is this enough?

Is screening out the negatives enough to see the positives?

The process of elimination only works if we have exhausted every possible option of pain that has ever existed or will exist. We cannot choose who our next partner(s) will be based on who we think we do not want.

For example, everyone behaves differently during the first date, exaggerating the positives and shadowing the negatives. We want to show off our best qualities and hide the worst. We make up white lies to enhance our portfolios, and we shove everything else inside a box and chuck it into the river, making us seem like the "perfect specimen" rather than the "average Joe." We do this again, and again, and again, and again, only showing our true selves AFTER years of dating.

By then, our brains have become so adapted to the lies that others have shown that we become blinded when their flaws begin to appear. We can be burning in fire but still only see the flowers we have been given on day one. We can never know if the next person we meet is right for us because we do not know when someone is lying and when they are not, especially when they are good at it. We do not know if the "good" impressions that they make are really who they are.

We cannot trust the words of anyone unless their actions continue to prove them true. Everyone can be a liar. Some people still lie forty years into a marriage, and it is something that can or cannot be controlled by the liars themselves.

When we love someone or want to impress someone, we cannot help but subconsciously exaggerate who we are based on who we want to be or who we think the other person wants us to be.

CHAPTER 28
BLIND LOVE

"If we never open our eyes, we never see the ugly truth of what we cannot have. Our perceptions only exist if our minds become weak enough to allow it." ℒ

I RECENTLY MET someone who I thought I really wanted to be with. We seemed perfect together. Everything felt right, similar interests and personalities, and I wanted to say and do everything I could to impress him. When he ended date number one on a high note and ignored me indefinitely, I continued to pine over and chase after him.

When he scheduled date number two, five months later, I still thought we had a chance. When he texted back after nine weeks of hiatus, I believed I loved him. When he kept postponing our third date for an additional eight months, using work as an excuse and running off to a concert in Canada with another girl when he deemed "too busy," I FINALLY realized what I was doing.

I was chasing after "blind love."

Blind love is when we become so infatuated with strangers that we feel like we are "in love" even though we have just met them and know nothing about them. Blind love is when we intensely want to be with and love someone despite any red flags or negative consequences. Blind love is when we fantasize about spending the rest of our lives with someone after only the first date.

However, blind love is not necessarily a bad thing. Blind love can be dangerous, but blind love can also mean passion. When we fall in love with our instincts rather than our logic, we prevent ourselves from checking qualities and people off a checklist. We follow what we FEEL we want rather than what we SHOULD want.

We block out external judgments and reasoning that may prevent us from loving freely. Unfortunately, blind love is only passionate if we DO NOT cross the border over into obsessive love. We can blindly fall in love with someone at first sight, but DO NOT let the other person know because then it can become fatal.

We can fall in love with someone, but then STEP BACK and monitor the signs to ensure that is what we want. We can wear our hearts on our sleeves, but BE SMART enough to not give ourselves to just anyone. We can fall in love at first sight, but when they reject us, know that we were at least passionate enough to take that RISK in the first place.

CHAPTER 29
WHAT IS JEALOUSY?

"Jealousy is wanting what we already have, loving what we already hate, living what we already dream." ℒ

FOR MOST, jealousy is "insecurities manifesting into selfish acts that tear apart happy relationships." Jealousy is not selective to certain groups of people; jealousy hits everyone, and when it does, it hits us hard. Even the most confident and secure deal with the anxiety that is jealousy when it comes to someone they love.

Jealousy can creep in at all angles; men tend to be more

jealous of physical connections with a third party while women tend to be more jealous of emotional connections with a third party.

Although jealousy has been shown to be a healthy emotional dynamic for people in serious relationships, jealousy is not commonly seen as a healthy expression. For example, when two people are "in love," and by that, I mean with completely healthy and balanced levels of communication and understanding, jealousy is a healthy emotion, where one person expresses his/her feelings and reasoning while the other person acknowledges, accepts it, and both parties work together to compromise and figure out a way to reduce that level of jealousy.

However, as we all know, relationships generally do not work that way. In most relationships, when one person expresses how he/she feels, the other person feels attacked and gets extremely defensive, making the level of jealousy even worse because now it seems like the partner has something to hide.

The expression of jealousy itself is not a sign of mistrust. When jealousy is not accepted well by the other party, it turns into mistrust on both sides. The person to whom the jealousy is being expressed, feels accused despite having a reason to or not, and becomes defensive. The person who is expressing the jealousy feels as if the other person has something to hide by becoming defensive rather than being open and becomes paranoid and neurotic that his/her feelings are being ignored and avoided.

When this occurs, trust cannot be resolved. Both parties can try, but there will always be this lingering feeling of whether the other person is still faithful or not, and hence, will eventually cause more and more accusations.

When jealousy is not properly accepted, it can also act as a trigger for impending acts of infidelity. When people are being accused of doing something that they are not doing, their minds instinctively go to the rebellion and the "I'll show you" mode. They begin to have the mindset that, if someone is already accusing them of doing something, and therefore, somewhat believes that it is already happening, they might as well just do the act they are being accused of because there is essentially nothing left to lose.

When jealousy is not well accepted, people become consumed with jealousy until they eventually tear relationships apart with neediness and mistrust or with anger and pain. Relationships can never work when jealousy meets aloof. Jealousy is inevitable in relationships, but relationships can be saved from it with understanding, and that is what everyone in any kind of relationship should strive for, whether romantic, familial, or social, because all "negative" emotions can be resolved when both parties understand the situations and are willing to work though the negativity.

Jealousy is also commonly known to occur ONLY when more than one party is involved. What if I told you that jealousy can happen within oneself, that we can essentially be jealous of ourselves? We can be jealous of the person we really are, the person we fear we are not allowed to be.

Our whole lives, we have been fed messages, either from our parents, the media, or our local communities, that we pretty much suck as ourselves and can only ever make it if we become someone else. And so, we listen, and we become someone else, only to the detriment of ourselves and the benefit of no one.

Not one single person benefits from us changing our demeanor and derailing from our true persons, but everybody loses as a result.

WE LOSE because we deprive ourselves from the chance of discovering the beautiful soul we were born to be, throwing out our uniqueness and becoming spawns of robots instead, and EVERYONE ELSE LOSES because they miss out on the chance to experience the amazing person we can be if given the freedom to do so.

Every person has a special heart that distinguishes them from the normality of the social world, and because of this, we develop the capacity to love ourselves and others. When we deprive ourselves from being the person we were born to be, we lose this ability and can no longer truly love outside of deception, so we lie because living in lies is all we know.

However, the longer we pretend to be someone we are not, the more we begin to realize that being someone else is FUCKING BORING! Who wants to go through their entire lives, following in the footsteps of someone else, and never having the chance to blossom outward or have their own say in any aspect of their own lives?

We all secretly want to be different and unique, but unfortunately, society still shuns on those who do deviate from the norm because WE LET IT. We become jealous of ourselves when we feel that itch inside of us wanting to break free, struggling to push its way out. We want our individualities to shine but fear they will be rejected.

We become jealous of the "us" we dream about at night, the only way we can visualize who we want to be without social criticisms. But jealousy of the self is a motivator! We want to be jealous of ourselves because it means we love ourselves enough to feel envy. We want that jealous feeling to shine stronger so it gives us the extra push we need to overcome our fears and bring out the inner soul that we have been hiding our whole lives.

Jealousy is a strong emotion that drives desires and actions into fruition. When we are jealous of someone else, almost nothing can keep us from acting on this emotion until we quell it. When we become jealous of ourselves, our human instincts, despite social influences, will stop at nothing to quell this jealousy.

CHAPTER 30
WE ARE SELFISH ASSHOLES

"Humans love to play victim. We thrive on being the innocent who gets crushed by those we blame. We thrive on pretending to be the weak being destroyed by the strong. We are not victims. We are manipulative. We know exactly what to say at the exact moments to get what we want." ℒ

HAVE you ever felt so connected to someone that it feels almost like a dream when you are with that person?

Have you ever felt so in love with someone that seeing

that person makes you breathless, and the thought of that person leaving makes it difficult to breathe?

Have you ever met someone who swept you off your feet in mere seconds and made you feel like royalty?

Have you ever spoken to someone who brightens up your day, puts endless smiles on your face, and makes you feel protected from all the problems in your world?

We have all experienced this feeling of breathtaking love, where we fall for someone so hard that we cannot fathom our lives without them. Although some people have remained with their "soulmates" from their teens to old age, the rest of us have not been so lucky. The rest of us deal with this cycle of back and forth, from hopeful and in love to devastation and rejection, only to transfer that over to the next person, and the next, and the next.

This is not because we are incapable of holding onto a person or a relationship; this is because these fantasies and hallucinations we have that "love conquers all" or "meant to be" are all fake. This is not what love did to us; this is what standards and expectations did to us.

Our minds have become so convoluted by what love should look like and how love should feel like that we trick ourselves into "falling in love at first sight" just so we can experience this "moment" that everyone else around us seems to be experiencing. We have become so good at lying to ourselves that we do not see it until months, or even years, later that the person we are with is not the person we thought we fell in love with. True, it could be due to one person changing over time, but the main reason is that we do not know who we get into relationships with, and we do not know who we fall in love with.

This is because we have become blinded with our subjective perspectives when we enter new relationships. The man we think is the man of our dreams could very well be a mediocre person that we have plucked out and subconsciously molded into the vessel of our desires.

The more time we spend with just one person, the more we begin to visualize that person as the ONLY PERSON we want for eternity. We begin to see this single soul as the "savior" of our romantic lives. We begin to mentally mold this person, this person whom we may not have even found attractive among a crowd of others but suddenly do because everyone else is out of mind, into the person we have been looking for all along, and the only one we would ever be with.

Our illusion of how we think we see the person we are with, not only ruins our opportunity for real potential love, but it manipulates and uses the other person, robbing their chance of being with someone who ACTUALLY WANTS to be with them.

How can we stop something that we do not even realize we are controlling in the first place?

Is it even possible to stop ourselves from falsely loving someone when we are so prone to leading with our hearts instead of our brains?

How do we know that we are in the depths of it BEFORE it is too late?

Can we learn to control our impulsive behaviors before they begin to control us?

We are not manipulative and terrible people.

We are people who have been told to behave in certain ways so many times that it has become instinctive. We have become so used to falling in "love" before falling in "like" that we have trained ourselves to rush into relationships before thinking. We not only begin to manipulate and brainwash others, but we also begin to brainwash ourselves.

The core of this problem is the need for validation.

When someone has feelings for us, but we do not necessarily feel the same way, we become addicted to the attention and the validation that this person gives us. We become obsessed with someone worshipping us that we do not even care who the person we are with is. We live in an age where we no longer fall in love with people themselves; we fall in love with what people are willing to give us and whether we believe that is enough.

When we fall in love with materialism and love selfishly, we set ourselves and others up for "infidelity without remorse." We lose our empathy for how someone feels, and we act based on what we want and ONLY WHAT WE WANT. We open doors to seek out other partners when the ones we have fail to give us everything we want.

When two people love each other, what they can and cannot offer each other is irrelevant. They love each other as the persons that they are despite the goods and services that they can provide. Love is not torn apart when one person refuses to become the "slave" of the other. It is only out of selfish love do we seek out other potential "slaves" that can continue the work of previous "slaves."

When people are in relationships where they report feeling unhappy and used, it is because they are.

We have become so independently focused that we seek out all aspects of life that can benefit, but not hurt, us. We run away from all, and any, sources of pain, ghosting and leaving behind others to deal with our betrayals and seek out other sources of pleasure. Because of this constant need for validation from others, the only way we can stop our patterns of manipulation and falling for people we do not actually want, is to simply TAKE A BREAK.

When we take a break from dating and relationships, we take a break from feeling the intense need to quickly get into one and do everything we can to control them into benefiting ourselves.

We can still form relationships with people, just not romantic ones that trigger our needs. We are half as likely to manipulate friends than we are to manipulate partners. Friends can come and go while partners are more intimate, so they are less likely to do all they can to please someone they like and trigger a dangerous path.

We need to stop feeding off the energy of others and start focusing on the energy we already have. When we spend so much time trying to control others and situations, we are expending more energy than our "victims," carefully crafting every word and every action, making sure we do not get caught. It is physically and mentally draining to control another human being, but we continue doing so because of the power that comes with it.

Why do we do this?

Insecurity.

Since the day we were born, we were told by everyone around us that we will never be good enough, that we will never amount to anything, and that we will always be alone if we decide to tackle life as the person we are right now. We have been told that we need to completely change our personas and become the opposite of who we are in order to be accepted by those around us. We are constantly being fed messages that the person we want to be is the person we should never be.

Girls are raised being told that they will never find husbands if they are independent and outspoken. Boys are raised being told that they must never be vulnerable and sensitive, or they will be socially rejected by their peers.

It used to be that, in order to remain in any sort of relationship, girls needed to be present but not heard, to be available despite what they were going through, to be serving and obedient despite how they were treated, and to always cater to and agree with their husbands to keep marriages alive. In modern days, this role has switched to men when it comes to keeping marriages alive, known as "happy wife, happy life."

Either way, every decade employs certain standards when

it comes to keeping a relationship or a marriage intact, and people are expected to blindly follow them or face lonely lives. This puts people in positions where they are forced to completely surrender for the sake of others, for the sake of "togetherness," and for the sake of "everlasting happiness," or remain "unhappy."

How happy can we really be as slaves to someone else?

How can our happiness stem solely from the happiness of someone else?

How can we possibly justify to ourselves that the way we feel and the way we behave can ever be thrown into the control of a stranger?

Can we untrain our brains?

Can we unlearn the habits that have been subconsciously worshipped for generations?

Can we teach ourselves to steer away from succumbing to the confines of those around us and finally learn to take back our own lives?

Humans are capable of so many feats when it comes to striving as independents. We know how to grasp onto the things we want when it does not involve others. We are resilient, and we face all sorts of adversities, from withstanding negative degree weather to scaling insanely high peaks to crossing ferociously dry heats of deserts.

We fight physical scars caused by wars and mental scars caused by PTSD. We fight death every time we face uncertainties and step outside our comfort zones. We have been through violence and discrimination, but time after time again, we recover and bounce back.

Then why is it so fucking difficult to tell the next asshole trying to control our lives to just back off?

Why do we live in a nation where people are so afraid of being alone that they will literally give up everything just to avoid feeling that way?

How is it that we can fight death but fear loneliness?

It is because we have been taught that defying death is awesome while remaining single is sad and pathetic. We are inherently social creatures who need to be around others so we feel needed and experience belonging. Dodging death is not in our inherent natures and, therefore, is seen as a great feat when avoided. When we fail to meet what is in our blood and expected of us, we become great failures to ourselves.

We have been told to grow up, marry well, and start a family; everything else we encounter along the way are just extras. But we can learn to detach ourselves from our emotions and avoid becoming slaves to strangers. By taking back our lives and avoiding serial dating, we train our brains to focus internally rather than externally.

We train ourselves to become more selfish toward ourselves and less vulnerable toward the selfishness of others. We can become selfish toward the self but remain compassionate toward others.

Loving someone does not mean completely surrendering.

Loving someone means finding equal balance between giving and taking without one side completely overpowering the other.

Loving someone means looking out for ourselves before looking out for others because we can only give to others when we have finished giving to ourselves.

Depriving ourselves of the goodness that we can give ourselves is the ultimate cause of pain to our physical and emotional health. We lose sight of who we can be for ourselves, the lovers we can be for ourselves, when we are immersed in trying to keep someone around by making him/her happy just because we fear being alone.

We fear ending up as the old woman with the twenty cats or the old man who resents everyone so we would rather settle for a stranger, an unfamiliar, than face the possibility of feeling lonely.

But the fear is all in our heads!

We only fear ending up alone when we have not lived it personally. Those who have braved through the anxiety of this fear end up completely loving their solo lives, never regretting not having settled. We turn to infidelity in our 50s because we regret having settled in our 20s. We run away and start over because we cannot admit to ourselves that we have failed ourselves by placing our entire lives in the palm of someone else.

For years, we have lied to ourselves that the stable and comfortable lives that we have been living are the lives that we want. We endure abuse and misery for decades until we finally snap, and we either rebel against all that we have fought for, or we die with extreme regret on our death beds.

If we learn to step out of our comfort zones and learn to live in the fear of uncertainty, even for just a little while, we prevent ourselves from both regretting and destroying our lives. If we cannot honestly say we are dedicated and happy with the person we are currently with, set him/her free so both are given the chance to find the person who we and them CAN be dedicated and happy with. Holding onto someone purely based on fear destroys the lives of many people: ourselves, our partners, and potential children involved.

We should not live in the mindset where we believe that it is okay to bring children into this world based on fear of being alone or based on societal pressure to belong and accommodate the standards others think we should live by. This only foresees neglect, lack of true love, regret, and worst of all, self-hate.

Short-term gratification can never exceed long-term sustained happiness, yet we let it take over, because at that time, it feels right. It becomes difficult for us to see beyond immediate pleasures, especially when we predict future pain.

We want to experience all the good before the bad gets a chance to reach us. So, we throw ourselves into destructive behaviors because, for a short while, they feel amazing with no IMMEDIATE CONSEQUENCES.

But what if we can foresee how our lives will turn out based on the decisions that we make?

How will we change our choices?

Will we even change how we decide on certain actions?

Is knowing the future and the consequences certain actions will bring enough to steer us away from choosing based on immediate pleasures?

Or will we still fall into the trap of instant gratification?

Take another hypothetical scenario, further into the future. What if we can experience, first-hand, both the BENEFITS and the CONSEQUENCES of actions, and then turn back in time to make our decisions, fully knowing how each one feels like and the pros and cons each one brings. Will we alter our decision-making to avoid long-term consequences, or will we STILL make decisions that lead to instant pleasure?

Despite how much we know and how much experience we have, we will always make choices that lead to instant pleasure, instant happiness, and instant gratification, whether real or false, whether for ourselves or someone else. This is because of the constant fears of "what ifs."

WHAT IF the long-term happiness never comes?

WHAT IF I die before I get to experience the benefits of my choices?

WHAT IF I do not take the instant happiness and completely regret it later?

WHAT IF I do not settle and end up in misery for the rest of my life?

WHAT IF the person I rejected is the person I am meant to be with?

WHAT IF this person was my true love, and now I will end up alone for the REST OF MY LIFE!?!?!?

WHAT IF!?

These "what ifs" are only results of insecurities. We only

question our futures and the unknown because we doubt that life always has a way of working itself out. We always want to be in control of our own situations. We make immediate choices and impulsive decisions because we would rather our lives fail in our own hands than in the hands of others. We rush to self-sabotage before life can destroy our lives for us. We rush to settle for the unfamiliar before others can call us "fuck ups."

We deceive ourselves into falling in love just so we can avoid feeling alone. We have so much, yet so little, control over our own lives to the point where we blame ourselves when others take advantage of us and abuse us. When we give our power over to those we have become vulnerable enough to trust, we blame ourselves for doing so when we are betrayed.

However, we do not fail when we decide to become vulnerable. When we give ourselves and our hearts to other people, we are building ourselves up to become stronger and more successful people despite whether we are accepted or rejected.

When we open our delicate hearts to love, we are demonstrating enough courage to be able to put our hearts into the hands of others rather than remain in our comfort zones and hold our love in because we fear getting hurt. Even if we are rejected, we can at least stop blaming ourselves for "failure" and start congratulating ourselves for being courageous enough to share our lives despite the risks of getting hurt and damaged.

Unfortunately, when we open our true selves up to the world around us, we also become flooded with waves of insecurity. We immediately start questioning whether we made the right decision by sharing ourselves. We immediately start regretting having said anything at all because we can never be 100% positive what others will think or how they will respond.

It takes a lot to speak up first, fully knowing that we have a 50% chance of being turned down but doing it anyway. But why are we much more willing to be vulnerable when it comes to falling in love than when it comes to admitting that we messed up?

Why is it so much easier for us to risk insecurity when it comes to admitting happiness, love, and joy, but so hard when it comes to admitting shame and regret?

We are always surrounded by insecurities, in our jobs, our relationships, our family, and even within ourselves. We have the tendency to always put ourselves down just when things are looking up. We tell ourselves that we will never be good enough so when things do go wrong, we will have already prepared ourselves for the worst, and when things go right, we feel that much more elated.

Reverse psychology is a complete hoax.

Similar to pills and self-help books, we use it as a placebo to make ourselves believe the self-detrimental lies that we tell ourselves, self-prophesizing our negative thoughts. We only experience our insecurities if we believe in them; otherwise, they just remain in hibernation inside our deepest subconscious and never flourish.

We bullshit ourselves with endless excuses of why it is okay to bash ourselves and our egos into the ground, and as a result, we willingly allow others to also bash us into the ground.

How can we stop our insecurities from ruining us when our entire lives have been filled with loved ones telling us that we should feel ashamed of ourselves, that we should doubt ourselves, and that the only way we can ever be accepted is to submit and obey?

Can we ever live a satisfied and fulfilled life without the constant worry of disappointing others and not living up to the social standards that society has created for us?

CHAPTER 31
ALL WORK, NO PLAY

"We share with others trauma that we would never wish on our worst enemies. What we fail to share is the strength that arises as a result of trauma. We have perished in the flames but have risen from the smoke. Surviving our deepest fears helps us fulfill our greatest dreams." ℒ

MOST OF US can live out our entire lives without significant physical or psychological trauma: we learn, we work, we love, we grow old, and we die. It makes life easy, but going through life with these simple and mundane routines makes us never feel the drive to CHANGE. We never experience what it feels like to hit rock-bottom, but we also never experience what love can be like for us outside of having to rely on person X or person Y to give us fulfilling experiences.

Not having hit rock-bottom (in terms of love), not having been ghosted, not having been abused, not having been left at the altar, not having been cheated on, not having been mentally disrespected and destroyed, and not having been beaten to the point of no return, leave us feeling empty, unfulfilled, and ignorant to the many possibilities of love that can exist because content prevents us from exploring.

Not having been through relationship trauma keeps us in a place of mundane satisfaction, where we are not quite sure where we belong, where we have sporadic doubts of staying or leaving the people we are with, and where we feel an itch to find something else but never pull the trigger to do so.

When we are not completely satisfied with the moments that we are experiencing but have not been destroyed by them either, we remain stagnant in our unsatisfactory love lives, sleeping next to people we may have settled for and having happy moments with our partners only when we engage in activities such as lavish vacations, other people, alcohol, and parties. We become distracted from who we are with and never fully realize whether we actually love (or still love) those we are with or if we only tolerate them enough where we do not hate them.

Couples who fight, argue, and cheat constantly interact with each other, allowing each other to face the anger and animosity that one person feels toward the other, and eventually forcing them to realize whether they love each other enough to work through their problems or whether it is time to call it quits and search for other potential mates.

Couples who become bored of their partners but never feel the drive to speak up or take drastic action toward someone or something else, remain in silence and continue to feel the breaths of "what ifs" until the day they die.

We can love people but not be IN LOVE with them. We believe that if we love, i.e., care, we should avoid hurting those we love in any way, including leaving when we feel unfulfilled. We find it extremely difficult to turn people down because we associate "not the right fit" with "rejection" and "we are not good enough." We find it easier to ghost those we care about because we believe that it hurts less than rejection.

When people tell us that they do not want to be with us, we take it personally and blame ourselves for it even though that may not be true. Even the strongest of us can be destroyed by feelings of not being wanted. It will never feel good to be rejected because we see it with a negative connotation. We associate rejection with being "ugly," "hated," "stupid," and "unlovable" rather than seeing the situation as being given the chance to avoid something that would have turn out terribly if we continued to let the interaction/relationship continue.

It is only after we have found others better suited for us that we begin to acknowledge that the people we have been so obsessed with are simply passersby, a taste but not a meal, a touch but not a hold. Only when we are truly happy, do we see how foolish we were, obsessing over those who were never meant to be with us in the first place.

I used to be obsessed with someone who specifically clarified that he could NEVER be with me, and that all he was looking for were people to mess around with (he even called himself "a piece of man-meat"). However, I did not want to believe him. I tried to make him change his mind. I became obsessed with telling myself how he was perfect for me, and I spent every night dreaming about how great we would be together. I tried giving him everything he wanted, giving up my own values, losing my self-respect, and hating people I did not even know just because they were associated with him.

This broke me, but I pushed on. I continued to tell myself that if I just kept being patient, just kept being supportive, and just kept staying positive, that he will come around, that he will eventually change his mind, and that he will want to be with me. Three months, six months, a year went by, and it only resulted in him pulling further and further away from me, eventually posting a picture on Instagram of him together with another girl in California.

This truth smacked me in the face like I had expected but failed to accept, forcing me to look within and realizing what the fuck I was doing. I forced myself to finally give up on this person that I was in love and obsessed with.

There is a certain point in an obsession where you feel so destroyed and so hurt that there is no coming back from it. There is only so much hope you can have for someone when, time after time, they continue to treat you like garbage.

I have had more than my fair share of experiences when it comes to the horrible actions of other people, letting one person after the next shit all over me while I just took it with a smile, metaphorically. But I was naïve. I wanted to be loved and cared for so much that I pushed my self-esteem and self-respect aside so others can take what they wanted and all that they wanted, leaving me in the dust when they were finished while I ignorantly told myself that they still wanted me.

I started dating when I was about 19. It took me over 9 years of abuse and neglect to realize that I deserve to be treated like a human being, something obvious and sad for those on the outside looking in but a serious reality hit for those also going through the same experiences.

It is still a struggle; I do not have it all together, and many days, especially on the low lows, I still let myself fall into the trap of being used and abused, remembering to pull out just before it becomes too late. When you have become so accustomed to giving into others and living your life for the sole purpose of making the person in front of you or next to you happy, you fall into this pattern where you no longer know what to do with yourself or how to live with yourself when you are no longer obligated to abide by those "rules."

To this day, even after pulling myself away from the toxic environments that I had created for myself and finding a relationship where I no longer chase, I still find myself full of insecurities. After having been with so many people who did not care about me and now finding someone who does, I continue to create a path of self-sabotage where I keep feeling like I do not deserve any of it. This never-ending feeling of insecurity ruins potentially amazing relationships, something I need to learn to break out of before ruining another.

However, before we can tackle and find healthy relationships, we need to work on ourselves and what it is we really want.

Is it a relationship we want, or do we just want to not be alone? Never get into any kind of relationship if it is the latter because it will only destroy you and the person you are with.

Hint: If you have recently come out of a relationship, whether healthy or toxic, you are not in a place where you are ready to tackle another one. You are in a place of limbo, where you have to figure out what it is that made the previous relationship end, how significant of a role you played in that, whether you will bring that same behavior or action to your next partner, whether you have flaws that you need to work on, and most importantly, whether you are actually ready to be with someone else or if you are only using new people as distractions from the old like the classic saying, "The best way to get over someone is to get under someone else."

So, when do we know if we are TRULY ready to move on, with a fresh perspective and a fresh start into a new relationship without constantly reminiscing the past? When we first get out of relationships, especially long-term relationships where we have so much history with our ex-partners, it is extremely difficult to separate anger from love.

When people leave us and break our hearts, or when we force ourselves to leave those we cared about, our minds become over-confluent with anger and confusion. All we can focus on is how much we hate our exes and how much we just want to get as far away from them as possible and move on.

So, we try, and we do, with finding a rebound as the most common way, latching onto said rebound, and deceiving ourselves into believing that we are actually in love with said rebound, when, more likely than not, we are only confusing love with the strong desire to forget. Some of us tell ourselves that we can completely separate anger from love. Some of us can even convince our rebounds that we are not confused.

When people leave serious long-term relationships, where they had so much love and care for their exes, and immediately try to jump back into the dating market without even waiting a week, they are looking for a distraction.

When people swear on their lives that they are completely over their exes and rush to start something new with strangers, they are looking for a way out.

When people say "I love you" within a month of dating, they are looking for a replacement.

How long can we live in denial before we realize that we forgot to slow down and work on our pain before jumping into new potential pain? How long before it takes us to realize that we no longer "love" the people we are with because we never loved them in the first place? How long before we stop distracting who we are and what we want from ourselves with what we want from others? How long before we can reach the stage where we no longer rely on others to make us happy?

Because they cannot.

No one can truly make us happy if we are dissatisfied with ourselves.

Only we possess the power to quell the pain that persists within us.

Pain does not go away; pain can only be dealt with head on.

Crush the heartache that courses through our veins by acknowledging it.

Forgive those who hurt us so we do not take the pain out on others.

Remember that, at the end of the day, the only person we have left is ourselves.

We can never rely on the presence of another person to fulfill a need if we cannot fulfill that need ourselves. We need to stop bouncing from person to person, constantly seeking new people to fill the holes that are missing within. One person can never satisfy all that we need for ourselves; only we can fill in the missing gaps.

Hence, why so many of us become unfaithful. We keep trying to find that ONE PERSON who can give us EVERY-THING we need, and when we do not, when we find out that the person we thought we have found can only satisfy a fraction of the needs we desire, we seek out others to fill in the rest of the gaps, therefore, leading to infidelity. We know all too well what it feels like to cheat on our partners or have our partners cheat on us.

It sucks.

I get it.

We feel an immense sense of betrayal and anger running down our spines as we experience the wrath that results from the disloyalty of those we loved and trusted. We put our hearts into the hands of those who were once strangers, letting go of our own control and allowing others to take part in the lives we have constructed for ourselves.

When we say "I love you" for the first time to someone we

still see as risky and untrustworthy, we are telling the other person that we see him/her as worthy enough to become vulnerable for.

When we completely open ourselves up, and when the other person takes that vulnerability that we have shared and destroys our trust, that person is telling us that we are not worthy enough to stay loyal or respectful to, that our willingness to be vulnerable meant nothing, and that the painstaking effort we took to force ourselves to relinquish control of the carefully constructed lives we have spent our entire lives building for ourselves meant absolutely nothing.

Learning to forgive after a partner cheats, physically or emotionally, is an extremely difficult task that almost no one can fully achieve.

Learning to forgive someone who betrayed and hurt us is a selfless skill that requires extreme amounts of patience, gratitude, empathy, and self-love.

CHAPTER 32
LEARNING TO LOVE

"Loving others is not the challenge. Loving ourselves is." ✍

To be patient is to truly understand that not everyone walks at the same pace.

Some of us are further ahead in our emotional discoveries and experiences when it comes to the kinds of love we seek. Some of us are slower to fall in love and should not be forced or feel obligated to rush into it. Some of us are slower to heal from past experiences and need more time than others before throwing ourselves into something new.

To be patient is to love selflessly when we are not getting what we need from the people we want it from.

To be grateful is to accept the things that we are given, whether big or small.

To be grateful is not to expect lavish grand gestures, but to expect nothing and relish in every small gesture or gift that we are given.

To be grateful is to love our partners for who they are rather than what they can offer us.

Too often, we choose our significant others based on what they have, what they can offer, how they can make us look better in front of our friends and family, and the potential life success that we can have with them. We forget that love comes from what we SHARE with our partners and the lives we can BUILD with them outside of materialism and success.

For just a moment, can we close our eyes and imagine how happy we can be when all we are surrounded by is stuff, stuff that we force our partners to buy for us, so much to the point where we are just collecting, with nothing having value?

Can we truly be happy living inside a mall?

Can we truly be happy when we willingly give people we are supposed to "love" ultimatums?

Can we force someone to buy our love?

Love stems from the willingness to do things for others; love cannot be bought nor can it be bullied into a corner.

Can we picture a life where the only things that exist are us and our partners, two people side by side who are not distracted by anyone or anything else?

Can we live with ourselves then?

Will we still stay with our partners?

Can we truly be happy and in love with the people we are with without any other distractions?

If we cannot, if we cannot picture our lives without our Tiffany jewelry or endless cruises and vacations, then we are in the wrong state of mind. Our minds are only ready for true love when we can honestly say to ourselves that we are completely willing to sacrifice everything for this other person, for this one person who used to be a stranger to us.

Only when we can truly give to ourselves, which can only be achieved through complete self-love and self-acceptance,

Only when we have 100% accepted the selves that we are,

Only when we have absolutely no regrets about our own lives and personal beings,

Only when we have experienced how to love life on our own,

Only when we can give to others without any expectations in return,

Can we truly be in love.

Love is all about giving. Love cannot exist when both parties take nor can love exist when one side gives while the other side takes. When both parties take, we are left with selfish and Machiavellian love, "loving" only to deceive others into giving us what we want. We only enter relationships to take, relationships that will never flourish and eventually drain all parties.

When both sides are constantly scheming against each other to see who can get the most out of the other, both sides lose. When we have relationships in which one side only gives while the other side only takes, we run into scenarios where one side becomes abused while the other becomes too controlling.

The giver is deceived into thinking that he/she is loved because of his/her selfless acts while the taker is constantly scheming to take as much from the giver as possible, getting away with it, and continuing until he/she has fully drained the giver of all life and savings before moving onto the next victim.

Relationships only work when both sides are givers, mutually giving without expectations, and unconventionally expressing love. We cannot rush others, just like we would not like others rushing us, but because we so often neglect the present moment and the other persons, we find ourselves bouncing from one person to the next, unsure of how to love because we are too focused on the future and on ourselves.

To be empathetic is to understand how our partners feel as a result of our actions.

Empathy means being true to the self as well as allowing others to be true to themselves. We are all our own individual persons, and every one of us has the right to love, hate, accept, reject, understand, stay ignorant, and strive for self-lessness or greed.

When we are empathetic, we tell those beside us that their lives are just as important as ours, that we are equals, that whatever pains them also pains us, that our troubles and our desires are no better than theirs, that we are not more impor-tant, and best of all, that we truly understand rather than just pretend to.

When we show empathy, we show that we care.

But can we be empathetic toward ourselves?

Think about it. We spend so much of our time either focused on taking for ourselves or giving to others that we rarely spend the time to really understand ourselves. Why do some of us only look out for ourselves while others expend more energy looking out for others? Is it necessarily bad that we choose our own wants and our own needs over those of our partners?

On the flip side, can it be bad if we become too involved in pleasing and giving to our partners while neglecting our own needs? Are we giving to our partners because we want to? Or are we only doing so out of insecurity and the fear that they will leave us? Too much time is wasted on whether people want to be with us or just fake it, whether people actually love us when they say it, whether we will get hurt if we continue/change the actions we are currently doing, and whether we should even waste time on unstable love.

Do I love him or do I just love the idea of being in love?

Do I want to be in a relationship or is it because this is all I know?

Is this how my life is supposed to turn out?

Am I so afraid of being alone or the idea of being alone, so afraid of being a social outcast if I am alone, that I force myself to love, blinded to the truth of I really want?

Can I just be alone?

Am I allowed to be alone?

These constant doubts continue to drive us into situations that we may not exactly want. We deceive ourselves into thinking and behaving in certain ways because we have been trained to do so. As children, we never got the chance to discover and understand ourselves before being taught to discover and understand life and humanity, while also being told that only materialism and social interactions can make us happy. We have been told that the ones who live alone are the ones who have been rejected and unloved, people we should not strive to turn into.

But what if these are the people who have discovered the secret to happiness?

The secret to rejecting social standards by understanding themselves fully?

Rather than striving to be with the best or striving to hold onto someone because we believe they "bring out the best in us," we need to strive to, once and for all, understand who we are rather than who we are meant to be. Humans are extremely complex beings where each one of our brains is wired differently, making us special and unique, yet we try too hard to be like everyone else.

We become ashamed of making mistakes because we believe that the more errors we make, the more we steer away from the norm. We run away from ourselves rather than learn to understand how we function, and we let our potential go to waste. We allow others to put us down because they feel threatened by our abilities to shine.

Notice that those who make it (i.e., influencers, motivational speakers, and those who seem to defy the laws of nature) have all rejected the notion that we must live by certain standards. They were the ones who have been hated and exiled for their unconventional beliefs, yet decades later, have managed to change the way we hope to find love and happiness. It is only after others have risked their dignities in attempts to change the world, do we find the strength in ourselves to do so.

It is time for us to stop being followers and start being leaders. We need to learn to take back what we were born to say and how we were meant to live. Humans were not meant to live in silence and fear. Humans were not meant to be overrun by those who are supposedly our equals. Influencers throughout history have made differences, proving that we are capable of speaking from our hearts and still remain supported.

We will always have to deal with haters who criticized how we live, what we say, what we do, how we respond, and even how we feel. But these people are just opinions, opinions that can either be followed or ignored. We can choose to walk away from toxic people whose only purpose is to bring us down. We can choose to walk away from harmful words of others, but we can never walk away from ourselves.

We can heal from others tearing us apart, but extreme guilt arises from self-hate and self-destruction. We are terrified of speaking out against popular opinions, not because it makes others hate us and cast us aside as unwanted and different, but because we are afraid to live with the shame that comes from within ourselves if we do so.

When we speak our minds and opinions in social settings and the majority of the group either rejects our ideas or completely disregards our voices, what do we instantly feel before anybody even gets a chance to criticize or mock us for our "unconventional" opinions (if they even do that)? We immediately feel embarrassed, ashamed, and like we should have never spoken out in the first place.

This is because we are our own worst enemies. We hold ourselves to such high standards that when we have not met them EXACTLY, we beat ourselves up. We tend to believe that the lower the self-esteem someone has and the lower the standards they hold themselves to, the more they hate themselves when things go awry. But it is actually the opposite. When people have low standards of themselves, nothing they do, normal or abnormal, will make them think less of themselves and feel more ashamed of themselves because their self-esteem are already so low.

But, when people have high self-esteem and think highly of themselves, any mistake will make them regret saying or doing ANYTHING at all because they "should have known better." In our minds, whenever we say something we believe is dumb, everyone around us just stops what they are doing and takes their own time and energy to judge us and laugh at us.

In reality, when we say something we believe is dumb, hardly anyone notices, and those who do notice DO NOT CARE. People are socially intelligent enough to know that everyone makes mistakes and everyone has flaws.

People DO NOT CARE if we say the wrong words, trips, slurs, or if we have toilet paper stuck on our shoes (well, they may speak up on the last one out of human decency because toilet paper stuck on our shoes is EMBARASSING!). People just want to go about their days and focus on their own issues and dumb mistakes. We think everyone around us lives in relation to us, that everyone is somehow part of our lives, but they are not. Only a select number of people come into and leave our lives for a reason; the majority of people only coexist with us, completely satisfied never having to interact with us.

But our minds refuse to let us think that way. We are wired to believe that everyone is tied to each other, and one person's mistake affects the thoughts of everyone within a two-mile radius. Our mistakes are our own, and we are the only ones who can truly tell ourselves whether we have made a mistake. When others judge us for making errors, they are simply ignorant to how life works.

We are all focused intrinsically on ourselves, yet we believe everyone is also focused on us, a paradigm that many of us find difficult to break out of.

CHAPTER 33
BE REAL

"Place your right hand over the left side of your chest. Do you feel that beating? That is you. That beating is unique to you and not anyone else. Do not let that uniqueness go to waste." ♈

HUMANS ARE the most complicated animals to walk this Earth.

We have the natural instincts of other animals, yet we also have the logic to drive ourselves insane.

We have what it takes to live a simple and happy life, yet we strive to reach toward the unthinkable, setting ourselves up for abysmal failure just so we can relish in high praises and success.

We have the ability to foresee future consequences based on patterns that we have already endured and stored into memory, yet we pursue the same paths over and over, hoping for different outcomes.

We have the resources we need to love and be happy with what we already have, yet we constantly search for reasons to be miserable and reasons to call ourselves "failure."

We do these things because we want to impress those who pay little to no attention to us, to boast what we have to those who do not care, and to hide what we do not have from everyone who breathes. We spend millions and millions of dollars dressing ourselves and our surroundings so we can show off just how insecure we really are when we believe THAT SAME ACT shows off how successful and secure we are. We spend hours and hours editing our lives on social media so we can pretend to have the life that everyone wants.

We go through great lengths to achieve what we believe everyone else wants, not limited to putting ourselves in debt just to chase the dreams that society has constructed for us to follow and/or completely faking how our lives really are through obsessive Photoshopping, to the point where we begin to live in our own lies and neglect who we are outside of others. We were born with minds that can be constructed into anything we want rather than just what we were told. We forget who we are because we try so hard to be those we are not just to impress our egos.

Day in and day out, we only take the steps in life necessary to show ourselves off rather than use that time to improve ourselves. We only do enough to get by rather than what we should to get through life. We want to be seen as "great," but we do not want to take the time and effort to achieve greatness because the illusion is all we need to deceive others. We do not see goals as worth achieving unless we have an audience.

For example, an artist creates a magnificent piece of art, posts it on social media, and receives three likes. Only a select few would continue painting while the rest would give up.

Why?

Because most of us only engage in activities so we can be accepted and well-liked by others rather than activities we actually enjoy. When we do something, such as paint a picture, and the crowd does not go crazy for it as we had expected, we give up because we no longer see a point in doing an activity that no one pays compliments to. That is why those who are able to continue painting after many times of painful rejection are those who paint solely for the love of the art, not for the love of the attention.

Those are the people who live and love for themselves even after failing.

Those are the people who do not need instant gratification and constant attention to continue engaging in activities that they relish in.

Those are the people who are truly living.

Those are the people we should follow.

Depression, self-hate, and low self-esteem all arise from trying to achieve goals we know we can never meet. This is partially due to the impossible standards that society has forced us to meet, resulting in "influencers" Photoshopping their lives in attempts to fool and keep up with the modern world.

We see these falsified images and resent our own lives for not being as "glamorous" as the ones we see online, even when we know that the images we see are not real. We fall into traps of telling ourselves that we are not worthy enough and not good enough because we do not match up to those who have millions of "followers." We hate ourselves and strive to do more, only to fail at attempts of instant gratification and give up, returning to self-loathing and illusions of failure.

What we do not see from influencers obtaining thousands and thousands of likes by the hour are,

Whether these activities are actually from REAL PEOPLE and,

Whether the smiles BEHIND THE SCREENS match the ones on the screens.

We fail to see that most of the world are in the same positions as us, achieving satisfaction and content rather than grandeur and success. We are forced to question whether we are truly happy when we are told that we can be happier if we have much more. We are forced to ignore and doubt the parts of our lives that we once found joy in and conform to parts of others' lives that we deceive ourselves into wanting.

What the hell!?

Why do we find it so easy to give up the things we once loved to chase after things we do not, while at the same time, falling into deep depression and self-hate as a result? Why do we find it so easy to be influenced by things we are smart enough to know are not true? We are intelligent creatures, with minds that can extend beyond unimaginable beliefs. We can GIVE endless advice on how we should not be falling for these schemes but struggle when it comes to taking our own advices.

We are intelligent at reasoning and working through problems but struggle tremendously when it comes to overcoming the mental blocks that prevent us from being able to stand our grounds and hold onto our desires and beliefs. Known as being one of the most difficult tasks that any human being will ever endure, self-love is a daunting one that many of us have attempted but few have achieved.

Complete self-love means giving ourselves undeniable and unconditional love despite all external factors that sway us otherwise.

Complete self-love means waking up every morning and going to bed every night without the need to compare ourselves to those we assume have it better.

Complete self-love is fully accepting ourselves for all the flaws we have even when others are telling us that we should not.

There are endless courses, lectures, self-help books, and "Psychology Today" articles that target our vulnerable sides when we do encounter brief moments of poor self-esteem, and we fall for their gimmicks. First, these sellers are only playing the game by knowing the EXACT moments we need "help" and when we will succumb to their false advertisements. Second, there is NOTHING wrong with us! We only fall for these marketing schemes and believe that this placebo effect works because we doubt our own mental strengths to survive without the help from "professionals." We were taught that we must strive to improve and be the "best," insinuating that there is something wrong with us.

How often do parents tell their children that they are perfect as they are rather than telling them they must change and improve in order to make it successfully and fit in with the rest of the world?

This is not necessarily the parents' fault, however. We live in a society where we are FORCED to change in order to SURVIVE. We blame parents too often for "not accepting their children," but really, most parents are only trying to build our strengths to make it in a world where they struggled to. That is why it is extremely difficult for us to snap ourselves out of feeling like we must reject who we should be and strive for who we are.

But, remember, the human mind can endure feats of greatness, including accomplishing even the most difficult of tasks.

Take a moment.

Close your eyes.

Imagine.

Bring yourself into the place where you are most happy.

What do you see?

Are you struggling to create an answer that you feel is acceptable and not completely stupid?

Well, stop it.

You do not need to come up with one.

The fact that you could even PICTURE a place means you can achieve self-fulfilling happiness and can change the mindset that you were taught to follow. Most of us still struggle with creativity because we associate it with rebellion, which in turn, becomes associated with going against the "correct" standards of life.

When we are stressed, angry, or frustrated, we often like to go on long drives or close our eyes and imagine that we are in a happier place, aka our safe zone. We have all the skills we will ever need to live the lives we want, but we still feel the need to rely on others because we were told to. Some people spend years in relationships and friendships that are toxic to them but feel obligated to stay for show.

We still believe that if we are not in a committed relationship by a certain age then there must be something wrong with us.

I once dated someone who seemed really confused that I was still single, immediately assumed that there was something "wrong" with me, and refused to take "nothing" as an answer. We look at people's outside appearances and automatically assume whether they are single or taken. We still associated "beautiful" people with being in relationships and "ugly" people with being single forever.

We still associate being single with being unwanted, so when we are chased, our egos become so enlarged that we believe we are entitled to it.

We are creatures of dichotomous thinking. When we have nothing, we believe we do not deserve anything. When we receive something, we believe we deserve it all. These, again, are lies that we have been fed. We are not selfish in nature, but the fables and fairytales we have been told since birth turn us into selfish beings.

I want to walk out my front door, without a man by my side, without a ring, without a short haircut, without a giant wart on my face, without my arm hanging off my body, and without acting like I am facing the apocalypse, and just walk down the street, undisturbed.

I do not need unwanted men coming up to me and thinking they are entitled to a date just because I am not married.

I do not need a man escorting me across the street because I learned how to cross the fucking street when I was two.

I do not need people asking me over and over why I am single just because I am.

I want to be able to travel alone to foreign cities without seeming like I want to sell myself.

I want to flirt on first dates without people assuming I am reaching for sex.

I want to JUST BE NICE to another human being without SOMEONE thinking that I am either flirting, home-wrecking, or prostituting.

I want to look in the mirror one day and tell myself that it is completely okay just being me.

Just me.

I want us to all join together, to make a pact to each other and to ourselves, that we will at least TRY (because I know that promises almost always fall through) to ACKNOWL-EDGE that these crazy relationships and dating problems we have are results of our transient and fleeting emotions, and that they DO NOT REFLECT who we are as people.

The next time we freak out over someone who breaks up with us out of nowhere and decide to aimlessly Facebook stalk him/her for weeks, REMEMBER that this does not make us stalkers. This makes us caring intellectuals who have shared our hearts and have had them broken. This makes us mature adults who had some wrong turns in life.

This makes us beautiful hearts who were not given the same love we had dealt. If caring too much and feeling hurt as a result of not receiving care back from people we had openly trusted makes us crazy, then fine, we are FUCKING CRAZY then.

Just because we become emotional from pain does not mean we should be locked up.

Just because we spew out crazy and insane statements about how much pain we are in does not make us at risk to ourselves.

Just because we handle betrayal by drinking, stalking, and hooking up with strangers rather than cry one tear, do yoga, and wake up automatically feeling better, which, by the way, NEVER HAPPENS because NO ONE walks away from a breakup, long or short, scar-free, does not mean we are "handling a breakup wrong."

Even those who cheat and crave to be with people other than their partners feel pain when it comes to a breakup.

Despite how difficult the relationship was, despite how much two people should not have been with each other, and despite how much two people find extreme happiness in others, there was a time and place where two separated individuals felt a connection to each other, felt joy, and felt the love that gravitated them toward each other in the first place, so much that, even if the breakup was justified or mutual, there will always be that sense of betrayal and the feeling of "what if."

From the outside perspective, or even when we have had some time to recover from our own traumatic experiences, the end of a relationship happens every day, and all the clichés that usually occur in relationship advice come into play. Even the best relationship therapists all narrow down their sessions to one take-home message: It will all be okay.

Will it, though?

Physically, yes.

As time moves on, humans see issues that were once amplified as no longer as serious as time helps to forget and distract, not necessarily heal. Even if we feel less congested mentally, and we are no longer in tears all the time, does that really mean we are "better"? Does that really mean we are "healed"? Even though we are no longer actively hyper-focused on a situation, it does not mean that we are not still affected by it.

In my personal experiences, this is the breakdown of my emotions over the course and end of a relationship:

Deeply in love and willing to do anything to keep this person happy.

Telling myself I am going to marry this person.

Hating this person and everything about him.

Hating myself for hating this person and unsure of whether to leave or stay, even after endless arguments and abuse.

Stalking and obsessively trying to contact this person after the relationship ends.

Stalking and obsessively trying to contact this person's family after the relationship ends.

Crying nonstop for months every time something reminds me of this person.

Trying to distract myself from this person by drinking heavily and dating every single person who expresses interest in me.

Completely ignoring my values and my sense of self by sleeping with strangers.

Ending at rock-bottom after waking up next to someone I do not recognize.

Coming to my senses by replacing men with activities that I could do alone.

Forgetting why I was so obsessed over this one person and no longer wanting to be with him or contact him.

Finding happiness in my life again and no longer wanting it to end.

Constant thoughts of the craziness and insanity that I am capable of…?

Number 14 is something that many of us either do not realize or ignore because we feel physically fine otherwise. We are no longer a mess, and we are no longer actively thinking about our exes. But that lingering feeling of what we are CAPABLE OF DOING, or that feeling of when a demon is taking over our bodies, never really goes away.

We may be healed physically, but after each experience of "craziness" that we go through, our self-esteem go down, our anxiety and trust levels go up, and we never really recover from the creeping memories of who we can become when we are in pain. This prevents us from wanting to start new relationships, we become extra clingy to try to prevent our new partners from ending it with us, or we go with the classic "I will break up with you before you can break up with me." We do not see it as serious problems now, and some of us do not even realize that these feelings are manifesting until we are already deep in them. No one, not even the best therapists, can unravel how our behaviors affect us subconsciously.

Our patterns continue because we never fully address the past. We focus on the present moments, trying to heal from the pain we feel CURRENTLY. We do not think about the future consequences of not dealing with these feelings before getting into new relationships until AFTER the patterns repeat.

We let ourselves become scarred by the people we are capable of becoming, and because we never address them, we are left with this lingering feeling that something is wrong with us.

I am not normal.

I will admit it.

I am addicted to love.

I fall in love too quickly.

I drive myself and others up the wall when I feel that love is fading away.

I experience losing a relationship the same way I experience being stabbed in the chest by a sharp knife.

I risk my life and dignity just so someone will stay with me.

I willingly allow others to walk over me and take advantage of me because I fear they will leave otherwise.

I tell myself and the person I am with that I am in love with him too soon into the dating phase, and I have trouble separating love from infatuation and loneliness.

I go back to exes and people I used to know when my dating life seems catastrophic, and I move too fast and then wonder why I am unlovable.

I give others what they need right off the bat, and I leave myself, and my heart, with nothing.

I stalk exes and obsessively contact their family in hopes for second chances when I have done nothing wrong and even when I am no longer in love.

I crave attachment and the idea of knowing I am with someone rather than wanting to be with someone.

I threaten to hurt myself and make up fake aliases to give exes reasons to not ignore me and keep them around for as long as possible.

I refuse to let people go even when I am with someone new, and I become overwhelmed with rage when they are no longer interested in me.

I disclose my entire life to complete strangers in hopes that the pity card wins me brownie points.

I am addicted to love.

And I am okay with that.

EPILOGUE
THE TURN AROUND

Three years later...

The phone rings

    Me (picks up): Hello?

    Him (enthusiastically): Hey! It's me!

    Me (fully knowing who is on the other line): Who's "me"?

    Him (confused): It's me! J! Remember?

    Me (still fully knowing): No...I really don't...

    Him (still confused and slightly disappointed): You

really don't remember me?! Are you serious? We dated for almost seven years!

Me (aloof and annoyed): Oh, right. Hi.

Him (excited): Hi! How are you!??! It's been awhile!

Me: Yeah.

Him: Hey! I was wondering if you want to grab a drink and catch up!

Me: I don't think so.

Him: Come on! One drink! As friends! It'll be fun!

Me: Yeah, I still don't think so.

Him (in a serious tone): Alright, the reason I called is because I've been thinking about us a lot, and I think I'm ready to get back together, you know, give this thing another shot and see how we do.

Me (thinking): Who the fuck does this kid think he is?! Three years to think!?? What, two years of partying, half a year of hooking up, another half of drinking, and a day of thinking? Cool. Cool. I feel so much better! THANK YOU SO MUCH FOR THINKING OF ME!

Me (irritated): This thing? Is that what our relationship meant to you? Just a thing?

Him (defensive): That's not what I meant. I'm just trying to tell you that I want to try again.

Me: Why?

Him: Because I think I still love you, and I know you still love me so, what do you say? Let's get back together! I forgive you, and I'm ready to try again!

Me: No.

Him: No? What do you mean? I do forgive you. Let's go out to dinner tomorrow!

Me: No.

Him (persisting): Come on! We can even split the bill! You don't even have to pay for me this time!

Me: No.

Him: No? What do you mean "no"?

Me: I mean no.

Him: But didn't you hear me? I still love you. I thought this was good news because you still love me.

Me: I don't love you anymore.

Him (confused): You don't love me?

Me: Oh my god. Get it through your thick narcissistic head. I DO NOT LOVE YOU ANYMORE! I DO NOT WANT TO GET BACK TOGETHER! I NEED YOU TO LEAVE ME ALONE!

Him: Wait, how do you not want to be with me? You're in love with me, and I'm giving you another chance. Are you seeing someone else? You're cheating on me?!

Me: Dude, regardless of whether I am seeing someone or not, which is none of your fucking business, I can't cheat on you because WE ARE NOT TOGETHER.

Him: But you're my girl. We promised to love each other no matter what.

Me: That promise was destroyed when you broke up with me three years ago.

Him: But I'm here now, and I want you back. You're mine forever. I love you.

Me: Dude, no! I don't belong to you! I don't love you. In fact, I still very much HATE YOU. NOW LEAVE ME ALONE!

Slams the phone down

Him (via text): Why'd you hang up on me!? I still love you, and I want to be with you.

Silence

Him (via text): Please talk to me. I know you're there!

Silence

Phone rings

Voicemail

Phone rings

Voicemail

Him (via text): Please pick up the phone! Stop ignoring me! I love you!

Silence
Phone rings
Voicemail
Phone rings
Voicemail
Phone rings
Blocked

Two days later, outside my apartment...

Him (cheerfully): Hey! What a coincidence running into you here! I was just in the neighborhood! I completely forgot that you live here! There was something wrong with my phone, and we must have lost connection the night I tried to call you. So, this is perfect! We can talk in person!

Me: Dude, are you fucking stalking me?

Him (dumbfounded): What? Of course not! I was just grocery shopping in the area, turned the corner, and there you were!

Me: You live in Jersey. You drove an hour and a half to come out here to grocery shop?

Him: I like the stores here better.

Me: The only store near here is Wholefoods, and you have one ten minutes from you. Plus, you're not even carrying grocery bags!

Him: I didn't see anything I like.

Me (scoffs): You're impossible.

Starts walking away

Him: Wait! Can we talk?

Me: There's nothing to talk about.

Him: I want to talk about us.

Me: There is no us.

Him: Lena! Please!

Me: We are done. For good. Bye.

Him: LENA! DON'T WALK AWAY FROM ME! DO YOU

KNOW WHO I AM?! I KNOW YOU STILL LOVE ME! WE CAN MAKE IT WORK! PLEASE! COME BACK!! I LOVE YOU!! I CAN'T LIVE WITHOUT YOU!

Continues walking away

Him: I DON'T WANT TO LOVE ANYONE ELSE BESIDES YOU!! I LOVE YOU SO MUCH! PLEASE TALK TO ME!!

Silence

Gone

Silence

The wind blows softly against the barren trees of autumn, whistling tunes of the forgotten, leaves fleeting across the roads.

Him (whispering): I love you….

AFTERWORD
WE ARE OVER. RIGHT?

"Sometimes we need to simply let go, let go of control, let go of promises, let go of hope, let go of the "what ifs." Then, maybe, we can begin to recover." ℒ

Part of me knew my ex was going to come running back. They always do. They only want us when we no longer want them, turning into the obsessive lovers that we once were. Do I regret walking away from him when all I wanted, for months, was him? Does part of me wish I had said yes to his request of getting back together? Probably, but at that moment, my brain was strong enough to overtake my heart.

That IMPULSIVE DECISION to turn him down saved me from a life of toxic love, otherwise, I would not be writing this book right now. Do I still think about him from time to time? We all do; we just hate to admit it. We all have some regrets when it comes to who we are with, who we have been with, where we are, and who we are. We will always have struggles with relationships, and we will always have memories of past struggles with relationships.

Maybe one day we will get back together.

Maybe not.

That decision is not up to me.

That decision is in the hands of life.

All I can say is, at the moment, I do not want him in my life.

But, then again, what do I know?

Will it ever get easier dealing with uncertainty and anxiety of potential heartbreak before, during, and after a relationship?

I wish I could stay positive and give you something to look forward to about love, but the short and cold answer is: no. Unlike many aspects in life, love is something that cannot be controlled, and the more we realize that there is nothing we can do about who love us and who do not, the more we want to try to control it. We want what we cannot have, and it drives us insane. With relationships always come uncertainties, and some of us would rather stay single than deal with the rollercoaster of emotions that comes with being with someone else.

After ten mind-fucked years of dealing with:

Flakey men

Broken promises

Suicide attempts

Criminal-like behaviors

Back and forth never-ending relationships

Lack of trust

Intense hatred for myself and others

Anger for the behaviors people are capable of, and

Complete self-destruction,

I still find myself in a mind-fucked situation.

It does not matter who I am with, how great the person I am with is, or how great I currently feel about my life and situation, the anxiety and constant paranoia will always be there. I am constantly overthinking every step I make in a new relationship, and how much I do not want to fuck up again because I know the events I am capable of spiraling down into if it does get fucked up.

I keep telling myself that if a new relationship ends, changes are going to be made on my end, I will get my shit together and act like an adult, and I will keep my emotions under control. But that does not ever happen, and that will not ever happen, because I cannot predict how my emotions will respond to certain situations. Who knows, I can very well wake up one day, lose the love of my life, and be completely content.

Sometimes I wonder why I let the loss of love affect me so much, even when I know I use it to replace something lacking in my own life. Sometimes I wonder how my love life would have been like if I had not let my emotions catalyze my self-destructive and catastrophic behaviors. Would I still be with one of my exes because my crazy behaviors would not have pushed them away? Or would I still be in the same position I am right now, realizing, with a clear head, that on-and-off relationships almost never work out?

Do I regret a lot of decisions I had made?

Of course.

Would I change how I react to breakups if I could go back in time and do so?

Probably not.

Because if I did, I would be acknowledging that who I am is flawed and needs to be "fixed." I would be acknowledging that feeling pain and having emotions are sins. I would be acknowledging that I need to become a completely different person in order to fit in with this world.

That is never going to happen.

Stay strong.

Let the crazy within you flourish.

I Love You

#OBSESSED

INSTAGRAM EXPOSES HUMANITY

A Crazy & Obsessed Series (Book 2)

CHAPTER 1
THE DARK WORLD OF INSTAGRAM

"Instagram is a social platform that has been tarnished by the ego of modern society. Instagram is where young hopefuls go to create and crush their dreams."

#love. #instagood. #photooftheday. #fashion. #beautiful. #happy. #cute. #tbt. #like4like. #followme. #picoftheday. #follow. #me. #selfie. #summer. #art. #instadaily. #friends. #repost. #nature. #girl. #fun. #style. #smile. #food.

ACCORDING TO THE LATEST INSTAGRAM "INFLUENCER" market, these are the top twenty-five most popular hashtags known to the social media world. However, it doesn't just end there. This list continues to multiply as we come up with new words daily that modern individuals can use to define themselves as "belonging," "prestigious," or better yet, "influencing."

For years, Instagram users have been living their lives, online and offline, solely based on trying to satisfy, not people, but hashtags, simple words that have suddenly skyrocketed to fame just because a handful of trolls on the Internet deemed them "cool," "popular," and "in."

We dedicate more time researching the best hashtags and key phrases to post than we do for research papers and class assignments. We schedule our days around the "best times" to post images on the popular app so we can "try to gain the most likes and followers." We deliberately take photos from different and unconventional angles so we have "something" to brag about, even if we don't stand by what we say, and even if we know our photos are doctored.

As human beings living in the contemporary civilization that is social media, we rely on any means we find possible to make ourselves seem more alluring and more well-rounded to the outside world. We deceive ourselves into believing that we are actually living our lives to the fullest, when in reality, we take stock photo-worthy images of a bowl of fruit sitting on our coffee tables with the caption, "Just moved into my new place by the beach in Miami!" #livingitup #beach-life4ever, when in truth, we have gone nowhere.

We experience mental breakdowns when our smartphones die before we get the chance to post selfies of ourselves with captions about how bored we are at work…instead of actually working. We purposefully dress ourselves up with makeup and new outfit purchases just so we have something new and different we can boast about. We spend hours learning how to use Lightroom and Photoshop just so we can alter our seemingly dull images into images that can potentially receive millions of likes and comments.

We try so hard to become someone, to become one of the many influencers on the Internet who may or may not be Internet bots, that we fail to realize how much we have become addicted to our Instagram lives, so dependent that we have even resorted to means beyond simple Photoshopping to get the followers we want; we have resorted to buying fake likes and fake followers.

"Local Woman Becomes Bankrupt for Temporary Fame."

"Instagram Fraud: Is Anything She Posts Real Anymore?"

"Travel Blogger Fools Public with Green Screen Backdrops."
"InstaFame or InstaFake?"

In today's society, the world of social media has become an addictive drug, a compulsion that does not discriminate by demographics. Originally cultivated as a simple mean of communication with friends and lost acquaintances, social media platforms such as Facebook and Instagram have opened gates for obsession and abuse. We hide behind our screens when we are too afraid to mock or torment others to their faces.

We block friends and lovers way too impulsively because we allow our personal feelings and strong desire for attention to overpower our connections. We give up friendships and relationships because we misinterpret Internet images and messages as personal attacks, or we become so focused on achieving a few seconds of fame that we expose our secrets and hurt those we love.

"Hangin' at the club with some hot new babes. Girlfriend ain't got no strings on me." #freedom #bachelorlife #infidelity

Since the rise of Instagram, other popular social sharing platforms, such as Facebook and Twitter, have declined significantly, with a 17% decrease in Facebook usage among American youth and young adults, from 79% to 62%, while the use of Instagram has increased from 64% to 66%.

The rise of social media, smartphones, and text messaging has driven families and soulful interactions apart, where young and once-naïve children can now be seen scrolling through Instagram feeds at the dinner table, where dating is left out in the cold when couples care more about the "perfect selfie" or "foodie shot" to post than the dates themselves, and where groups of friends sitting at the same table are seen texting each other.

We have become so alienated from one another that it almost becomes abnormal to make a phone call or to not use social media, becoming more attached to devices and virtual worlds than people we are with. We have become so disconnected from those right in front of us and the environment that surrounds us that we seek validation for connection elsewhere, aka, the Internet.

What happens when social media falls, coming to an inevitable end? What happens when our Internet lives are no longer recognized, or when we no longer have a sharing platform we can use to brag about our lives? What happens when that selfie we take is just an image that stays on our phones? What happens when we no longer have a horde of followers lusting over our travel and food images?

Will we still enjoy these hobbies we claim to enjoy? Will our lives still remain the same even when we no longer have an outlet to boast about our accomplishments? Will we still feel a purpose and drive to continue our lifestyles even when no one is around to see them? Or will we lose that motivation completely and admit that we only live the lives we claim to live for the attention of the those whom we do not even know?

CHAPTER 2
DETRIMENTAL CLOUT OF SOCIAL MEDIA

"You mean nothing!"

"Your life is trash. You should really accomplish more with your life."

"Your feed is nothing compared to hers. She has five times the followers and ten times the likes that you do. You're nothing. You shouldn't even be on social media."

"Everything you've done is pathetic. You don't know the first thing about traveling and, yet, you try to pride yourself on it."

"Get off the Internet. You're never going to amount to anything."

"If you don't visit 100 countries within the next year, you're done."

"You're a loser. Figure out a new hobby."

"Dude, you bought followers. Does your page even mean anything? How many of them are actually real?"

"Why are you catering to a bunch of bots? Do you realize how ridiculous that is? Wasting all that money just to showcase dumb pictures to a bunch of dumb robots? You're an idiot!"

"You better post a new country on your page every week. Otherwise, your page is useless!"

"Do you even like traveling? Are you only traveling so you can put it on Instagram?"

"Your pictures are terrible! You are never going to match up to the fame of others because your filters suck!"

"You need to learn Photoshop if you want to be #instafamous. Otherwise, you're a piece of shit."

"Are you even enjoying what you do, or is it all for show?"

"Are you even traveling for yourself, or so you can show others your life doesn't suck?"

"Are you even happy?"

TROLLING AND CYBERBULLYING affect over 90% of users on social networks, especially in college populations, and with over 50% of those populations resorting to successful suicides due to their social media obsessions, social media proves more deadly than alcohol and drug addictions combined.

The simple action of scrolling a finger up and down a phone can transform from a short five minutes of leisure activity into entire days wasted. People spend hours upon hours every day scrolling through posts from feeds of their fellow Instagram icons, aweing in vain over a life they wish they could possess while spending their remaining hours trying to concoct their own lavish posts, spending more time on their phones than on every other aspect of their lives.

Students neglect their studies and class assignments to take selfies in attempts to generate the most likes, as well as deprive themselves of sleep and nutrition as their focuses become consumed by the number of hearts they receive. Employees spend over half their time at work on their phones, taking multiple breaks throughout their days to scroll through feeds, neglecting their responsibilities both at work and in their homes.

"When people spend hours liking photos and creating the 'perfect post' but still do not see what they had hoped for in return, and they usually don't, depression and anxiety set in hard, and the addiction persists."

However, a lack of self-control is not to blame when it comes to Instagram addiction. These social sharing platforms are intentionally designed to become addictive so companies can channel optimal usage of their platforms for increased profit.

Addiction to social media can become just as intense as

addiction to heroine or alcohol. People can spend years hooked on something, whatever that something may be, that releases satisfaction into their brains, experiencing withdrawal symptoms such as extreme anxiety and feral anger when they try to step away, and throwing away their integrities and authentic lives for falsified ones in order to gain superficial approval.

"Cases of cyberbullying have risen drastically over the past decade with the increase in social media opportunities. The revolution of online correspondences has cultivated physical and mental damages to individuals all around the world, defined by online associations and advances that cause risks to secure and mental prosperities, and proven to employ life-long damages on those of all stages of life, especially young adults."

Victims of Internet cyberbullying have been known to experience critical antagonisms such as peer pressure, depression, substance abuse, eating disorders, and a reduced quality of ethics. It has become so dangerous that we find it difficult to distinguish between actual danger and perceived danger as we become disconnected from reality and begin to see the lives we have falsified as truths.

In 2019, a Canadian investigator conducted a research study with a sample size of 188 female college undergraduates and found that those who engaged in virtual comparisons of themselves with the broader population of females, real or Photoshop-constructed, dramatically decreased their self-esteems and self-perceived appearances when associated with those they felt were much more attractive. However, the negative consequences of these side-by-side comparisons don't just stop there.

A study published in 2018 in the Journal of Social and Clinical Psychology showed that quality of life and overall performance in daily activities significantly decreased with increased and unlimited use of social networks including, but not limited to, Facebook, Snapchat, and Instagram.

Online pressure and abuse increase nervousness and melancholy in individuals, youth especially, who constantly worry about trying to fit in and becoming well-liked and accepted by their peers, resorting to any means possible to achieve these goals regardless of whether they fall through the cracks and destroy themselves.

The more their likeability feels threatened, the more they feel the need to become attached to their phones and social media pages, without stopping until they feel secure enough to step away for even a few minutes, and never putting themselves in the position where they do not have 24/7 access to the Internet.

However, those individuals who scroll through their Instagram feeds late at night are the ones most vulnerable to the negative effects of the social media population, bringing out more trolls and deception as people become more sensitive to identity crises. This causes them to become more sleep-deprived with less motivation for other life responsibilities, channeling all their focus onto misinterpreting and envying that of which they see on their online networks. As a result, the feeling of helplessness and discouragement surge as they feel imprisoned by the words of those they don't even know or the images of those they want but cannot have, triggering their emotional reactions as opposed to their rational selves.

Research has also found that social media addiction provides a direct and positive correlation with stress and stress-related consequences, including dejection, negative body perception, and poor self-esteem, especially for young adults, late teens, and the female population, in which they respond by lashing out against their loved ones, seeking undeserved revenge in response to what they see on the Internet, and engaging in poor choices such as self-starvation and drug abuse in attempts to give their "followers" what they want or to become better "influencers" for certain crowds, creating an age where life choices are based upon the decisions made by the selfish desires of strangers.

Although social media was intentionally designed to help human beings stay connected to loved ones, colleagues, acquaintances, and missed connections, it has unintentionally also driven them apart, instigating constant competition and animosity against those who don't relish in their posts or against those who criticize images of others for their own attempted attention-seeking behaviors. Rates of kidnapping and murder have also been on the rise as individuals become so desperate to generate more followers that they fall for scams of "guaranteed likes" or fake photoshoots for "perfect Instagram pictures."

CHAPTER 3
DEADLY WRATH OF HASHTAGS

#gym. #summer. #workout. #autumn. #model. #instapic. #happiness. #motivation. #life. #cool. #hot. #music. #hair. #instamood. #beauty. #landscape. #repost. #ootd. #photography. #inspiration.

"Instagram is a drug, a digital drug, with an abuse of hashtags used to push our posts up the superficial ladder for all to pretend to admire. Hashtags are going to kill our generation."

LESS THAN TWO DECADES AGO, the word "hashtag" was not even in existence. The symbol "#" used to resemble the "pound key" on telephones but has now exploded into a symbol of representation and belonging. We cannot speak a simple phrase or write a simple post without the word "hashtag" spilling out of our mouths or through the tips of our fingers.

We feel the need to #hashtag every word we deem popular, and we sometimes even go as far as to make up words that don't even exist just so we can hashtag them. We waste hours scouring the Internet for the "most popular hashtags" or the "most commonly used hashtags" to enhance our profiles so we can portray ourselves as the best we can be.

We stalk "influencers" we admire and believe have millions of followers so we can steal their hashtags and gain the number of likes they receive. We fail to limit ourselves to just a few relevant hashtags because we possess the mentality that "more is better," and we end up falling into the trap of #overkill when we saturate our meaningful posts with hashtags we cannot even stand by because we use them more as competition than as personal labels.

Unfortunately, without hashtags, Instagram posts inevitably become lost in the midst, difficult to discover in a saturated environment where everyone strives to be someone. Our feeds and profile pages can only be known and potentially liked if we throw popular hashtags onto them; otherwise, we end up in a perpetual state of no likes nor followers. Even so, creating the "perfect" Instagram post has proven to be a difficult task for ordinary people who aren't celebrities.

Despite positioning at certain angles, polishing photos with the best filters, and coming up with creative and eye-catching captions, grabbing hold of the greatest hashtags can either make or break Instagram posts. It doesn't matter if we pour our emotional hearts out into our posts or if we take an image that represents a stock photo; if we don't slap on a

#metoo, our posts are considered #nothing. Someone who writes an essay on rescuing dolphins, with over ten humanitarian photos, can receive the same exact number of likes as someone who takes a selfie and throws on #selfie beneath it, an unfortunate truth that many Instagram users feel destroy the authenticity of social-sharing platforms.

CHAPTER 4
RISE OF INSTAGRAM TO NOTORIETY

LAUNCHED in 2010 as a photo-sharing application with a meagre 25,000 users, Instagram has taken over the social media world throughout the past several years. Unlike former social media hosts like Myspace and Facebook, Instagram requires minimal effort to show the world our "fantastic" lives, lives as popular as those seen on reality television shows. Instagram takes away the work and effort of having to construct long and interesting stories so people will stop their scrolling and pause for a moment on our pages.

Instagram allows us to spend less than a minute on an

image, where writing one simple sentence or hashtag can cause hundreds of likes to flock toward us. We are creatures who base what we like on what we encounter visually. We see Instagram as photo-pornography and find it way too easy to simply tap on a couple of images we find interesting and feed the egos of those who post them.

"As the demand for social media platforms increase, those who can accomplish ways to give users the most reward for the least amount of work have become the superpowers of the world, creating more addicting ways to get gullible zombies to create accounts so they can continue their rise to the top, fully aware that they are ruining traditional human-to-human interactions of our once-civilized society."

Nowadays, it's considered a "sin" to not have at least one social media account, whether it is Facebook, Twitter, Snapchat, YouTube, or Instagram, and if you have all five, then you are seen as someone who deserves to recognized and known, or so that's what we like to believe. The more social media accounts we have, the more we are seen as too desperate to fit in and trying too hard to portray a life that does not exist.

Having a million followers on the Internet, 99.9% of whom we don't even know, does not make us important and deserving of attention. Becoming an "Internet sensation" for mocking the elderly does not make our lives more worth living than the lives of others. Who cares how many likes we get per post?

Most of the people who like our posts are only randomly clicking on our images to get likes back, not because they actually believe our posts are magnificent.

Who cares if our follower count shoots up by twice as much in one day? What's the point of having thousands upon thousands of followers when we end up alone after putting down our phones?

Social sharing networks like Instagram have boosted our egos to unimaginable levels, and not in a positive way. We shame ourselves and others when theirs or our profiles don't look pristine, and we base our self-worth and importance by how many comments we receive on a daily basis.

We secretly (and sometimes, openly) judge others and demean them when they only receive two likes while we have received five, using these numbers as a measure of self-worth. We become so fame-hungry for virtual popularity that we forget how to be human, and we treat other human beings with disrespect and hatred just to climb that ladder of temptation to…nowhere.

Don't get me started on how we treat those who are NOT on social media. We see Instagram accounts as sacred rites of passage to life, and when we hear of people who don't have one, we either peer pressure them by making their current lives feel worthless otherwise, or we ignore them completely to avoid being associated with "unpopular" individuals, caring more about having a colony of followers online than a colony of followers in real life. When we are at the brink of death and ready to give up, who will be there to pull us off from the edge of the bridge? Our colony of Instagram followers commenting on our suicidal posts for us to step off rather than actually pulling us off?

"Your nose looks fake. I bet you had plastic surgery. You're a fake!"

"No wonder you're still single. Your face is too big, and you're too short!"

"How dare you wear a shirt supporting that company? You're a sell-out!"

"Ew! What the fuck are you wearing?! That's a fashion-don't!"

"I hate your face! I bet you don't have any friends. You're a loser. You suck!"

"Your voice makes me want to burn my ears. Get off the Internet!"

Instagram makes us ignore and reject those we used to call "friends" and "family," breaking up with our partners because the Internet does not approve or blocking our parents because we think they embarrass us. We isolate people we used to love in real life because the virtual world manipulates us into doing so rather than of our own choosing. We see close friends as scarred and flawed because we have tried so hard to fit in with the popular crowd that we would rather risk losing childhood friends than risk becoming isolated ourselves for having our own opinions and for standing our grounds.

We make decisions influenced by others that we later on regret…when it becomes too late. It no longer matters how long we have known people; one mistake or one misspoken word can cause us to banish and ghost those we care about, even when we don't understand why we are doing so. We no longer give people chances to redeem themselves because we have been trained to screen out those who don't meet specific criteria. We have been taught to only befriend those within the inner circle of popularity if we want to remain "popular," "well-liked," and "on top."

"Instagram is like a high school cafeteria. We sit with those who can boost our popularity, admiring the 'influencers' from a near distance, hoping to one day get the chance to sit with them. Sitting with those who are considered 'losers' will only

warrant harassment, and if we do not belong in any group,
we may as well eat in a toilet stall."

The problem with social media is that we find it that much
easier to unleash our criticism and negativity online because
we're not forced to come face-to-face with those we mock and
put down. Before the world of the Internet, we filter our
strong opinions, fearing shame or anger from those we taunt.

However, when we have that chance to hide behind a
screen like cowards, we become deadly and extreme, tossing
every insult and every criticism out in the open rather than
holding the hurtful ones in. We pick fights with everyone,
despite who they are, when we get to remain anonymous in
the process. We say things we would never have the nerves to
say otherwise, and we dispute back and forth even after we
have driven individuals to their own suicides, refusing to
stop until we meet our very own deaths.

If we take the time and stop to think about it, rather than
taking selfies in the middle of a highway, scrolling through
people's profiles and feeds is just a modern way of stalking
them. The word "following" means what it always meant,
despite whether it's over the Internet. We are literally
spending our days and nights stalking other people online
and trying too hard to be like them. It's insane! We are like the
crazy serial killers we see in movies, where the psychopaths
are obsessed with their prey. The only difference is, we don't
resort to killing those we stalk, not most of us anyway.

But, instead, we try to copy and be like those we admire,
generating account names, image profiles, captions, and
filters similar to those who generate the most likes in attempts
to also generate the same amounts of likes. It's not as diabolical as serially-killing people, but it's not something we
should be proud of either. We follow Instagram "influencers"
so much that we end up knowing more about their lives than
we do our own.

We follow their every move and force ourselves to behave like them, including eating the same food, dressing in the same clothes, and even speaking the same as them despite it being clearly fake. We become incrementally obsessed with complete strangers that our initial intentions of joining Instagram, whether socially, as a brand, or as a business, become lost because we give up our individualities to chase after "what's in" just because we believe changing ourselves will make us more well-liked. And if that's not bad enough, we sometimes even become envious of "Instagram pet influencers." How low have our lives sunk when we become less popular than a pig in a tutu?

"We judge others by their looks, their height, their skin color, their size, their age, their ethnicities, and their personal life choices when, secretly, we wish others would stop judging us based on our own."

"We criticize web-based profiles based on what we see rather than what we know, and we showcase our own profiles based on who we want to be rather than who we actually are."

"We put others down again and again over the Internet, pulling down their self-esteems, until they no longer have the motivation to continue and are forced to drop off the world of social media."

"We determine who we like and dislike based on how others on the Internet foolishly influence us, and we become miserable later in life when we regret having made decisions outside of our own choosing."

"We hate ourselves because the Internet tells us we are not worthy of life."

CHAPTER 5
INSTAGRAM AGAINST THE TEST OF TIME

INSTAGRAM. Facebook. YouTube. When it comes to social media platforms, what do we usually associate with happiness and success? Likes! We let our worth be determined by how many people approve of us on a daily basis, and when we receive a negative comment, we allow our lives to become destroyed by it.

However, what is it that makes Instagram stand out amongst these other social platforms, rising to the top at an exponential rate? The answer: feasibility and limited work. Even though we continue to base our lives on the approval of others on all social platforms, unlike Facebook and YouTube, both of which require more effort than just a simple picture, Instagram makes it easy to replace a single photo or a simple hashtag when they don't get approved. When we don't get enough hearts on an Instagram photo, we have no problem getting rid of it and slapping on a new one in its place. YouTube, on the other hand, is much more difficult to just delete and re-post because a lot of effort and time have gone into perfecting that video.

With Instagram photos, millions of people take 100 images of the same item or the same selfie at once, coating each one with a different filter with the intention of posting at least 40% of those images per day as each one fails to generate the expected number of likes. When that fails to go as planned, we enter a phase known as "Insta-pulse," where after scrolling through the endless photos we have on our phones and STILL failing to find one that works, we end up posting a mediocre image in its place because we believe that posting a shitty image is better than nothing at all because it shows that we are still actively present online and, therefore, alive.

For those of us desperate enough, we create five different accounts to increase our odds of becoming an influencer, one for our "fashion sense," one for our "foodie recipes," one for our "whimsical travels," one for our "desired musical talents," and one for our "selfie wall of shame." "One of them has got to be a winner," we tell ourselves as we lose motivation to continue posting onto any of them after two months of not getting the likes we expected.

"Immediate gratification is a bitch to our patience."
"Our captions can also make or break our posts, but let's face it, we all know originality means nothing as people tend to vote for overused motivational quotes and sappy song lyrics."

Instagram began as a social platform for connections and happiness through accomplishments and images others share. However, as the popularity increased, so did the competition as people began to sought after each other's profiles for the sake of getting tips or getting others to feature them on their profiles rather than seeking true connections.

We also tear down those we actually admire because, one, our comments on the photos of top influencers will definitely get us noticed and, two, we put our envy and jealousy on our plates and despise those who seem to be doing better than us with minimal to no effort.

Instagram allows for #like4like or #comment4comment because of its competitive nature. We falsely believe that if we spend 10 hours a day liking photos of others, then they will like our photos back, or we believe that following a bunch of people with the hashtag #follow4follow will get them to follow us back, and they do, for about a day or two, until they decide not to, exemplifying one of the most common scams in the book to generate followers without having to follow nonsense and irrelevant accounts.

More dangerously, Instagram's photo- and video-sharing features, plus their live feed opportunity, tempt users to take ridiculous selfies and narrate life stories of what they eat during every meal or describe their daily outfits WHILE they are driving to work or taking an exam. The live feed feature makes us feel the need to make EVERY PART of our lives live, whether people care about what we put out there or not.

Since the release of Instagram highlights, we have the people who post 1-2 highlights per week while the majority of us post 1-2 highlights per minute, telling entire stories about nothing on our highlights, whining about our days on our highlights, or filling our highlights with excessive photos we have left over from choosing our "best ones" to post.

Whenever we get a manicure, a new hairstyle, a new nose, or a new makeover, we can't help but overwhelm our profiles and boast about it, taking "flawless selfies" from every angle until we finally get one that knocks people off their feet. Similar to Internet stars and celebrities who are obsessed with posting new selfies of themselves daily, we try too hard to become noticed as we foolishly believe that selfies in vain and perfect external appearances are the only ways to achieve fame.

"Wealthier" IG users feel the need to showcase their lavish materialism despite whether they're living in debt, posting images of themselves in designer clothing, holding designer handbags such as Louis Vuitton or Prada with #fab or #lux while demeaning their followers as poor "peasants" when they can't also upload images of thousands of dollars in cash (which, by the way, is a stupid way to get targeted and burglarized). They find themselves living through social media, living via a constructed app that has inhibited their abilities to live in the present moment.

"We can travel to beautiful mountains in foreign countries and still only remain focused on our selfies and the perfect filters to post rather than the sceneries themselves."

"We can see beautiful sunsets but still choose to watch them through our screens rather than through our naked eyes. I once experienced a magnificent sunset over clear waters on a beach in Cape May, NJ, and over 90% of the people there whipped out their phones to videotape it instead of enjoying the moment."

"It's sickening how we cannot enjoy simple moments without feeling the need to share them with others as well."

"It's as if we think that unless we have proof of our travels or proof of the beauty we see, others will not believe that we have actually seen them. Who the fuck cares?"

"We do not need to prove ourselves to others. So, what if people don't believe that we have been to Antarctica? Those with proof are usually those seeking attention or those with Photoshopped images."

"Stop living for the approval of others."

When I had a semi-successful Instagram travel account of 20,000 followers, a micro-influencer account as people like to call it, I would always get messages and comments on places I SHOULD be visiting, allowing those comments to drive where I traveled to rather than visiting places I WANTED to go. I always felt the pressure to visit certain countries, wasting money on destinations I didn't really want to see just so I could hang onto my followers, and when I didn't have the time to visit these places, I saw my follower count drop off one by one when I failed to share new images. I saw my love for traveling slowly diminish as I struggled to keep up with the constant demand, and I began to question who I was traveling for.

Instagram users love consistency. Unless we're posting beautiful and flawless images every day of unique surroundings with savvy captions, we might as well see our IG lives fall through the cracks. People will begin to dislike us and find us as no longer worth following unless we can give them what they want all the time. It's no wonder being an Instagram influencer is a full-time job.

For those of us who are unfortunate enough to work 9-5 jobs without the freedom to spend six hours on a simple post, we struggle to keep our social lives intact. Not all of us can travel to a different country every week or dress in a new outfit every day. Unless our entire focus 24/7 is solely on Instagram, we're bound to lose followers, followers that take twice as much effort to gain back, followers we don't even know.

This competitive world makes us ignore memories and stories that make us unique. We lose confidence in ourselves and forget the past experiences that made us different and special. We see our ups and downs in life as flaws rather than as lessons. We see our personal preferences as damaging rather than as special to ourselves, constructing profile pictures based on feedback from critics than based on who we truly are.

CHAPTER 6
INSTAGRAM'S TRIUMPH OVER FACEBOOK

FACEBOOK ONCE RULED the social media world. The idea of allowing people to connect with those from same schools based on mutual friends and to find missed and lost connections (while also stalking exes and crushes left and right) provided the opportunity to truly judge a book by its cover and uphold the standards of society in order to be liked and in order to isolate others who just do not match up to the caliber.

Instagram, on the other hand, allows us to become Internet sensations by flashing our smiles and our asses without needing to be intelligent or speaking a single word. It has taken us decades back to a time where women should be seen and not heard, making humanity look shallow and superfluous.

However, for some odd reason and destroying what we have fought for all these years, Instagram's popularity continues to rise, with over 300 million users compared to the 228 million users on Facebook. Plus, we all know that when we're stalking others, all we care about are their photos and whether we look better than them.

Another reason why Instagram has taken over the reign that was Facebook is the false feeling of power by having "worshippers," aka "followers." Facebook's main connection is with friends, i.e., adding friends, blocking friends, poking friends, etc.

On the flip side, Instagram refers to these "friends" as "followers," where people follow each other like hungry dogs in heat, and so it's natural that the more "followers" people have, the more likely they are to believe they're royalty. The live feature and story highlights that Instagram offer also allow people to showcase their lives 24/7 with false beliefs that their "followers" are just sitting on their couches at home, pawning over the lives they wish they could have and envious of those they follow.

Instagram allows us to avoid the trouble of scrolling through feeds, where we can just click on several story highlights at once and see years' worth of life stories in a time span of 10 minutes.

"The use of social media has skyrocketed over the past decade."

"In 2005, only 5% of adults in the United States reported using a social media platform, whereas now, that number has increased to over 70%, higher among the younger population, with over 81% having some sort of social media life, paired with a continual decrease in intellectual knowledge and mental prosperity."

"Over 13% of adolescents reported being cyberbullied at least once in their online lives, and over 60% self-reported as being either supremacists, misogynists, or homophobes."

The Internet allows us to be anything and anybody we want that would otherwise be looked down on in real life. We have teenage boys presenting themselves as drag queens. We have middle-aged men presenting themselves as makeup artists. We have ordinary people presenting themselves as celebrities. We all hate the idea of catfishing but only because we hate being the victims of catfishing.

We live in a world where we feel forced to catfish in order to fit into this constantly moving civilization. We also date and flirt more often online than we ever have in real life. Exposing ourselves and becoming vulnerable to others online are much easier because that anxiety and that fear of rejection become relinquished. We handle rejection with more composure when we don't have to deal with those rejecting us face-to-face. We even have sex online, sending dick pics and nudes to more strangers than we do our own partners.

How did Instagram allow people to become so fake and so phony? As the app has developed, so has the weight of the world on people's shoulders to construct amazing profiles or risk becoming social outcasts. There are rules to posting on social media; it's no longer a relaxing activity to enjoy with loved ones.

These unwritten rules include how we can't post excessively, that the images we do share must be absolutely perfect regardless of what the photos are of, and we must post every single day even if we aren't in the mood or don't have the content. Authenticity has deteriorated as a result of this because most people online no longer represent who they are in real life.

"Who's to blame for this downward progression from authenticity to triviality?"

"Have societal standards become so high that we need to pretend to become what's socially acceptable in order to be socially accepted, or have the images of ourselves become so flawed that we can never be happy with who we are?"

"Why is it that we have become obsessed with creating accounts that represent those of privileged and famous people, continuing to fall into the trap of lavish lifestyles even when we know they're all fake?"

"We would rather be known as 'potential wannabes', 'social jokes', and 'sellouts' than not be known as anyone at all because negative attention is still attention. And you know how we play off and excuse negative attention? #haters!"

In the midst of fake photographs and accounts created by bots, the rise of "Finstagram" or "Finsta" has risen into popularity, otherwise known as phony Instagram. Finsta is especially popular among the younger generations as it has taken our desires to portray fake profiles and given us the opportunity and reason to create fake accounts.

We look at Finsta and think it's such a far-fetched and ridiculous idea to spend time constructing profiles that don't even represent the true persons, but at the same time, that's exactly what we do every day on Instagram when we filter and alter our images; we're just too oblivious and ignorant to realize and accept that our online profiles are all fake.

Although most people use Finstagram to troll others and post images of their "ugly" selves, which are most often truly unfiltered images, it's these same behaviors that make this version of Instagram that much more authentic than the actual version of Instagram. With Finsta, people don't need to hide behind a beauty shell nor hold back and refrain themselves from speaking their minds like we often do for Instagram to avoid being judged. With Finsta, it's okay letting our authentic selves be free.

CHAPTER 7

OBSESSION WITH THE INSTAGRAM PROFILE

Our Instagram profiles make or break our Instagram lives. In order to have any sort of social life or following, our profile names need to be on point, our images need to be pristine, and we need to post like we are people with captions worthy of being read. That means, we need to force ourselves to dedicate hours per image, per post, in order to receive any sort of attention, with the exact hashtags pasted at the end to really make our photos shine.

We start off with a certain message we want to portray or even just a few simple pictures we want to show so we can communicate with those close to us. However, somewhere between the midst of feeling like a loser and wanting to get noticed, we become the wannabes we mock in the first place, resorting to the same behaviors we swore to ourselves we never would.

How many Instagram profiles online are genuine compared to just masks? How many of the "influencers" we see are true influencers as opposed to bots or frauds? The problem is, we can't tell. We tear down those who are actually authentic, with real people trying their best to showcase their best selves, and we resonate on emotional levels with those who will never respond to or recognize us because they literally can't. We see what we want to see and ignore the signs telling us that those we seek to be are not even human beings.

However, it's not our faults for being so obsessed with seeking the perfect profiles. Subpar profiles are damaging and can present just as dangerous to our social lives. We're almost forced to manipulate our profiles in order to stay afloat. Otherwise, we might as well just give up Instagram forever. Bland-looking profiles are useless when it comes to the Instagram world because Instagram is all about pleasuring the eyes. Images that are dull and dark are less likely to grab the attention of potential likes while images that generate a theme with glamorous filters are more likely to attract followers.

If you Google "Instagram filters," you will see "influencers" and "wannabe influencers" selling filters left and right, and people jump over hoops to buy them because they believe "perfect filters" are key to millions of followers despite what is being advertised. In the Instagram world, a profile with 500 selfies adorned with perfect filters of luminescent rainbow colors becomes more popular than a profile with 500 unfiltered images of world travels.

But do we realize how desperate we all are to attract the attention of strangers, spending our hard-earned salaries on filters and outfits to please the eyes of people we don't even know? What people want is changing daily. The hilarious Internet cat that receives 10,000 likes in one day can barely achieve 5 likes a week later. Pink filters that were "all the rage" last month can become hated the next month. It's extremely difficult keeping up with the social media world because it's constantly shifting.

Those who are able to stand by their messages and their goals despite the changing world are the ones truly happy and proud of what they do. For the majority of us, we move with the changing world, jumping from fashion to food to travel to music to animals, unsure of which direction we want to turn our images toward and creating new profile after new profile to ensure that one of these profiles will showcase the themes we believe are "in."

We can't satisfy everyone on the Internet. There will always be critics despite how great our images look or how beautiful our filters are. We see fashion bloggers steering from couture and luxury outfits #ootd to food vloggers in front of iPhone cameras. We see foodies steering from #bestfoodever at hidden local treasures to selfies in front of Photoshopped screens of Paris. At the end of the day, who are we really trying to impress?

"Instagram influencers post images of themselves licking toilet seats and street lamps. How low do they have to stoop before we realize they're not worth following?"

CHAPTER 8
REALITY VERSUS DELUSION

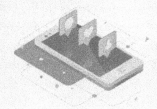

WHEN WE FIRST CREATED THAT coveted Instagram profile, many of us saw it as a fun opportunity to showcase our best selves and share our special moments with our friends and family.

However, somewhere down the line, we began getting addicted to it, thinking we are using this social media platform for ourselves, when in reality, we have turned into using it to make sure the world knows that we are better than others based on how many likes and followers we can collect, a way to boost our egos and show off to others that we have what they do not.

Needless to say, Instagram is a psychological mind-fuck that makes the majority of us hate ourselves. Despite being "loved" by millions of kids and adults around the world, this photograph-based platform is also a venue for elevated levels of anxiety, stress, depression, harassments, abuse, FOMO (fear of missing out), self-hatred for not measuring up, and dread for living lives seen as less significant than lives of others.

Of the major social media platforms we have all come to love, YouTube ranks the highest for promoting the well-being and prosperity of its users, with Twitter and Facebook trailing behind as second and third, respectively, followed by Snapchat and Instagram as dead last.

When we think about what we actually accomplish on Instagram, what are the first things that usually pop into our minds? We THINK we use Instagram in ways we are meant to on this platform, posting images, liking pictures of our friends and family members, commenting on posts and responding to posts on our own feeds, and sharing our major highlights with others so they can relish in our celebrations.

However, how we ACTUALLY use Instagram is a little different. After taking 1,000 images on one single trip or event, we spend days sorting through the best ones and choosing the best filters for them as natural lighting is just not good enough. We then post these images with witty captions that we either steal from others or off the Internet and pray that our one post will blow up with likes within the next hour. When that fails to happen, we remove that picture and repeat the process five more times before we finally either give up or run out of "good" pictures to showcase.

Next, we obsessively stalk other profiles and find the ones with the highest following counts, and like a lunatic, we like 30 images in a row of theirs so they will be forced to recognize us and check out our profiles in return. As we all know, one like or one comment from a top influencer automatically drives their followers to our accounts, and when that happens, our power begins to rise.

However, when that doesn't happen, we continue to obsessively stalk profiles of influencers and even non-influencers in attempts to generate some likes back. #like4like. And when that also fails, we pull out the vicious and manipulative tactics by criticizing images of influencers in attempts to start a controversial war that will indeed get us noticed.

After all, if an influencer posts an image with a perfect backdrop of Mount Everest while also wearing a sundress, we can't help but call them out as being fake; we're only saying what everyone else is afraid to say. We use Instagram as if it is our own personal game of cat and mouse, chasing after the one goal that everyone has of becoming a verified influencer and refusing to let anything get in our ways of achieving that goal. We allow our jealous and competitive natures to force us to tear down innocent people just because we hate that we are not them, and we destroy ourselves night after night for not being able to be them despite how much effort we put in.

Instagram's web-based photo option that's supposed to represent "real life" (but really doesn't) causes us to have unreasonable and unrealistic desires to reach for stars we cannot possibly grasp, creating low confidence and ineptness in ourselves. We see an image of an Instagram influencer prancing in front of an uncrowded Taj Mahal during peak season with #unfiltered, driving up our own anticipation for that same chance to also see the uncrowded iconic monument during peak season.

However, thousands of dollars and 20 hours on a plane later, we come to realize that this "unfiltered" image doesn't actually exist as we become surrounded by thousands of other eager tourists hoping to catch a solo selfie with the monument as they have also been fooled by Instagrammers, regretting their trips as they are now lost in a city with a language they cannot speak nor understand.

For about half of us, we're logical enough to realize that we have been tricked by photo manipulations or green screens. We're smart enough to not be fooled again by an image of the Great Wall of China or Times Square in New York City with barely any people, an image "influencers" just ripped off from Google. However, for the other half of us, we take this personally.

Despite the impossibilities, we still believe these photos are real and that the reason we cannot accomplish the same photos is because we have either arrived at the wrong time, that we are just unlucky, that we just suck at taking pictures, or that we just suck in general. Despite all the red flags pointing to fake Instagram pictures, such as the same cloud in every image, a pink hue over every photo that doesn't actually exist in reality, or the fact that there are no people at the most popular tourist sites, some people still choose to believe that their "influencer idols" are 100% authentic and still strive to become like them, as impossible as it is to do so, and as a result, we become demotivated to continue on as we realize we can never measure up to the photography skills of "the best."

"Instagram causes young men and women to hate the way their bodies look because they cannot Photoshop their mirrors."

"Instagram makes individuals feel like their lives are not worth living because they do not exude a glow of purple and blue hue."

"Instagram makes us feel pressured to do more and more even when we don't want to or else we're left feeling terrible about ourselves.

"Instagram makes us want to kill ourselves because our best always warrants negative comments from others, and trying to accommodate our critics will always warrant negative comments from ourselves."

And when that isn't enough, we resort to breaking the rules to drive our Instagram popularity up despite what it takes. We utilize banned hashtags, such as #adulting, #dating, and #fuck, at the risk of getting our accounts banned because we believe that using these hashtags will help us stand out and drive others toward our profiles. We will do anything to generate comments on our posts, whether positive or negative, because being the most controversial person on the Internet beats being a nobody.

#alone. #always. #armparty. #adulting. #assday. #ass. #assworship. #asiangirl. #beautyblogger. #brain. #boho. #besties. #bikinibody. #costumes. #curvygirls. #date. #dating. #desk. #dm. #direct. #elevator. #eggplant. #edm. #fuck. #girlsonly. #gloves. #graffitiigers. #happythanksgiving. #hawks. #hotweather. #humpday. #hustler. #ilovemyinstagram. #instababy. #instasport. #iphonegraphy. #italiano. #ice. #killingit. #kansas. #kissing. #kickoff. #leaves. #like. #lulu. #lean. #master. #milf. #mileycyrus. #models. #mustfollow. #nasty. #newyearsday. #nude. #nudism. #nudity. #overnight. #orderweedonline. #parties. #petite. #pornfood. #pushups. #prettygirl. #rate. #ravens. #samelove. #selfharm. #skateboarding. #skype. #snap. #snapchat. #single. #singlelife. #stranger. #saltwater. #shower. #shit. #sopretty. #sunbathing. #streetphoto. #swole. #snowstorm. #sun. #sexy. #tanlines. #todayimwearing. #teens. #teen. #thought. #tag4like. #tagsforlikes. #thighs. #undies. #valentinesday. #workflow. #wtf. #xanax. #youngmodel.

Many of us also turn to using robots in attempts to boost our profiles, from buying fake likes and followers (which will be touched upon more later) to deceitfully enhancing our popularity or utilizing software and apps that auto-like or auto-follow similar profiles to ours based on a few key hashtags. These bots are designed by companies to perform what humans generally do on Instagram, following/unfollowing and liking/unliking, but at an exponential rate, liking random images and randomly posting nonsense comments on users' profiles that don't add any value or sense.

Since one of the oldest tactics in the book for gaining more followers is to follow users, wait for them to follow back, and then unfollow them, bots are also designed to do this, but again, at an expedited rate, causing Instagram to catch onto this scheme and block accounts who are seen liking, commenting, and following at a rate more than the average human is able to do. However, despite accounts being blocked, we continue to do this anyway, waiting for our accounts to become unblocked and then repeating the process all over, until we are either banned completely, or we realize the truth that the results generated from these bots are only temporary, lasting for a month or two and then disappearing, causing us to lose both our money and our self-dignities.

#repost or #regram is another tactic that many IG users use to get their accounts noticed by others. Similar to #retweets, as seen on Twitter, where people see a tweet from someone else they find interesting or worthy of sharing and re-tweet it on their own accounts, allowing others to indirectly associate them with said brilliant tweet. Re-posting on Instagram is when we basically steal a beautiful image from someone else's account and post it on our own, with loose crediting to the original owner or no crediting at all. Some of us are decent enough to tag the picture to the original user while the rest of us either write #repost without a username or document the image as our own, all ways of which are stealing content from the original users.

We become so envious of the photography that others show that we feel the need to take from them rather than generate original photos ourselves. The more we scroll through Instagram, the more we come across accounts with the same exact images because we all lack originality. We find it easier to pretend to be influencers than to actually take the time to become influencers. For those more devious, instead of directly taking an image, we try to re-enact the images of influencers we find desirable, taking similar selfies or angles of materialistic items in attempts to generate the same number of followers they have. Because of this fraud, many genuine users have been forced to delete their accounts to prevent further identity theft, throwing away their hard work because we cannot find a way to create our own brands.

In my opinion, one of the most manipulative and controversial tactics ever featured on Instagram is the #giveaway. We all know what this is. A so-called "influencer," or even just anyone on Instagram, posts an image with sparkles, pretty colors, and the hashtag #giveaway in large and obnoxious letters. They then proceed to post below their obnoxious image a mega long post that entices other users with a "free gift," that may or may not actually exist, ONLY IF they like the post, comment about how much they like it, and tag at least 3-5 people on the post.

Not only does this allow the manipulative user to generate more likes and comments on their feed, but it also brings in new potential followers as everyone that is tagged now gets notifications from this post, exposing them to more and more posts from the original user. However, how many of these giveaways actually come to fruition?

Do those who promise free vacations or free puppies actually come through with their promises? My guess is, only about 30% of users who boast giveaways actually come through; the rest either make up excuses as to why the give-aways can no longer happen AFTER they have received their well-desired likes and followers, drag out the contest for so long that people eventually forget about the giveaway, or they announce "winners" so people will think the contests were real, when in reality, these "winners" aren't even real people.

Sadly, there's no way for Instagram to catch people who utilize these manipulative tactics unless enough people report them, and even then, Instagram MAYBE looks into it. This deadly competition among users has made the platform become unenjoyable as the ones who end up surviving are the ones who either don't care about trolls and thieves or those who become trolls and thieves.

CHAPTER 9
DESPERATE TO BELONG

THE GEORGE FLOYD incident of 2020 has spiraled protests all around America and the world, with chants of "Black Lives Matter" and demands of defunding the police force. For weeks since the incident, protests have risen in every major city with "Black Lives Matter" #BLM signs and graffiti, looting stores, blocking traffic, and creating chaos amongst an already chaotic world. At first glance, it seems as if these crowds of protesters actually care about the matter of respecting black lives. However, how many of them will actually take the time to support this matter when there isn't a protest going on? How many of them refrain from racist jokes when they believe no one's around to listen to their vulgar but honest opinions?

These so-called "activists" and "protesters" only seem to care when they know they have an audience. Scrolling through Instagram during these protests results in a 250% increase in "Black Lives Matter" posts and profile updates, claiming to be concerned and demanding justice for this cause. But, let's face it, unless you're dealing with this injustice directly, or even indirectly, you don't actually give a shit about black lives, just like you don't give a shit about animal rights or environmental health unless there's a protest going on or if the topic is "trendy" and "popular."

We see people with "Black Lives Matter" signs parading around town, but at the same time, they still see blacks as their stereotypes, calling them the N-word and fearing them. We see people with "Stop Animal Abuse" signs, but at the same time, they're killing mice and eating brutally-massacred cows. We see people with "Protect the Environment" signs, but at the same time, we see them littering and polluting the environment with overuse of hairspray products.

We only care about societal issues when we know we can take advantage of them. We want others to see us as "supportive" and "advocates" because we know those titles can boost our social status as people who care. Most "protesters" are only engaged so they can fit in, to have something they can post and brag about. Take away the popularity of the matter, and we see all those Instagram "support" come crashing down.

Most people on Instagram don't care about human rights; if we did, we wouldn't be bad-mouthing everyone and everything 364 days of the year and speaking up coincidentally only when everyone else seems to care. We try too hard to fit in, and it becomes obvious that we're only frauds.

Instagram protesters jump back and forth between issues

they care about because they want others to believe they're important and special, when behind the scenes, they're not even sure what they're supporting half the time. They believe that if they don't support the common cause, then their Instagram and social lives will be ruined because people would hate them for not "being supportive." When it comes time for one person to speak up about a serious cause, such as poverty, that isn't being celebrated and worshipped as royalty, how many Instagrammers will actually speak up?

CHAPTER 10
CONTROLLED BY STANDARDS & RULES

"Only post during certain hours of the day to generate the most likes."

"Make sure you have the most popular hashtags so others can find you."

"Use a filter that really shines, and keep these filters consistent so your feed stands out more."

"Respond to every DM and every comment that graces your account."

"Drown your posts in hashtags because those matter much more than your stupid captions."

"Photoshop out all the blemishes in your photos to match those of other users."

"Spend every waking moment liking posts on Instagram because that's the only way to get your profile noticed."

"Take images of everything you do because people want a story, not a few random posts."

"Dedicate your entire life to Instagram or delete your account."

THE MAJORITY of users spend their every waking moments dedicated to Instagram, waking up at odd hours in the morning, going to sleep at odd hours at night, and even skipping out on personal responsibilities, such as work and school, so they can post on Instagram at "optimal" hours of the day, since research upon research has been done to show that certain hours of days are the best times to generate the most likes per post.

We become so obsessed with these rules of posting at certain hours, liking 100 posts per hour, responding to every comment even when we're busy or don't want to respond, pretending to be always happy and fake even when we're miserable, and spending thousands of dollars on filters that don't represent our true images of life just so we can keep up with the crowds.

We become so obsessed with all of these standards that we neglect everything else for this one social app, literally letting machines take over our lives. When Instagram first came out, it was casual and fun, with friends posting images of their special moments whenever they wanted, and they were actually able to put their phones down for days before picking them back up to see how many likes their posts received, unbothered if the number remained low.

Nowadays, we become lunatics when we step away from our phones for even an hour, seeing our batteries dying as the end of the world, and literally locking our phones away or throwing them into the ocean just to prevent ourselves from checking Instagram every minute of every hour. We have transformed from letting Instagram portray the ways we want to live our lives into living our lives solely for Instagram.

CHAPTER 11
EXPOSING INSTAGRAM "INFLUENCERS"

"Every Instagram influencer believes his or her life is worth portraying in a documentary or worth writing about in a book. In reality, they're just people with narcissism and a lot to say."

WHO ARE these famous bloggers and influencers we so highly look up to? Celebrities? Motivational speakers? Athletes? Or just ordinary people with normal lives and normal problems like the rest of us? These "influencers" we see prancing around with fake paparazzi are our friends and our colleagues who started using Instagram with the same goals that we did: to connect with others and show off our best selves. However, what makes these ordinary people stand out as different from us? What do they have that makes them influencers compared to what we have? We're all just people, some with more masks and façades than others, with digitally-sculpted bodies, egotistical confidences, and pockets full of cash, but in the end, we're all the same.

Yet, it's these same factors that exclude people that make some of us more likely to become influencers than others. Becoming an influencer focuses less on how valuable, interesting, or important we are as people; becoming an influencer depends solely on how much we have, how much we can alter, and how much we can convince and manipulate. This computerized and web-based world of social networking has forced us to become superficial. It used to be that only celebrities, motivational speakers, and royalty were influencers. Now, the average Joe across the street or the average Jane next door can become our next role model, with a million followers through little to no effort.

Instagram influencers in the modern world have turned to digital alterations to maintain their influencing dreams, Photoshopping every image and buying every expensive outfit, dinner, or trip possible to keep their dream of becoming popular alive, without a care of whether they put themselves into debt.

Fashion gurus who claim to shop on a budget don't actually stick to a budget as they alter thousands of dollars of clothing to make them seem less expensive but still stand out. Travel influencers who claim to travel solo and on the cheap actually have an entire crew behind the scene, spending more than the average person normally would to rent out spaces they can use to take their undisturbed selfies. Foodies aren't actually down-to-earth home cooks as they hire famous chefs to cook for them so they can make their photos stand out by claiming credit for it afterward.

Not everything we see online is what people claim it to be. The people we look up to are either lying to us or burning through some serious cash to make their phony lives appear flawless. They carve out sections of their bodies, include images in photos that aren't meant to be there (such as trees in the Sahara Desert), and enhance even the smallest of images to seize Internet attention. How many of us have seen side-by-side comparisons of Instagram versus Reality, where Instagram shows a beautiful picture of a picnic by the ocean, but Reality shows a toy picnic set next to a puddle of water?

Instagrammers and other social media addicts deceive us into believing that their mundane lives are so much better than our mundane lives. They overextend their efforts to make simple things become worthy of adoring, proving their shallowness and insecurities. "Influencers" devote their entire lives into making sure that we believe their concocted lives are "natural," as if what they portray is how they live their everyday lives. Really? No one can afford to visit a new country every week for 8 years straight without having some sort of trust fund, and no one can afford a designer wardrobe in every photo when they claim to be "lower class."

Additionally, do influencers really expect us to believe that their picture-perfect face and styled hair portray the image of them "just waking up"? Despite the ridiculousness, we still eat it up, not because we actually believe these influencers are impeccable, but because we are envious of their confidence to put themselves out there while we hide ourselves in shame.

"Those who try their best to be something they're not are the ones who struggle with self-acceptance the most."

Just a few years ago, Instagram released the option for Instagrammers to open business, or creator, accounts, designed for businesses to showcase their products and work. However, shortly after it came out, Instagrammers discovered how to use this option to monetize from their posts by gaining a shit ton of followers and then getting paid for sponsored posts. While some have been authentically successful with this, others have found themselves scrambling to get noticed, buying thousands of fake followers just to meet the criteria of being an influencer so they can get paid for images they steal from someone else.

These "counterfeit influencers" have deceived people into thinking they're actually worth something when they simply resort to lying about their sponsors. No major company really checks up on the legitimacy of who tags them in their profiles. For most people, it isn't even about the money from being sponsored; it's about the exclusivity, the feeling of being able to "achieve" something no one else can. It's about feeling more important than others and the idea of being famous when they're actually not. Becoming an influencer sounds like a feat that takes time and talent to achieve, but really, it's just a popularity contest. These fake influencers buy their way into fame (like many celebrities do), raising colonies of fake followers that can never fully commit to them, and eventually flushing their money down the drain when everything comes crashing down.

Fake influencers appear to have everything that real influencers have, a web-based clientele, the appearance of fame and likeability, and top-notch pictures that seem too good to be true. But, the main difference between fake frauds and real influencers is their army of bots, machine-generated followers that often have no profile pictures, account names constructed from randomly typing on a keyboard, no postings themselves, no likes or followers themselves, and they comment on posts with phrases such as, "sexy," "cool," "okay," "fun," or "great," short, sparse phrases that don't really add anything or make sense.

For those who can afford higher quality bots, they usually end up with even more nonsensical phrases such as, "I like your video" when the post is a photo, "Very sexy queen" when the post is of a man, or "Hahaha, that is so funny" when the post is about someone's death.

Fake influencers sometimes even recruit their friends and family to create false profiles to enhance their accounts so it seems like they have more followers, or they create fifty different email addresses to create fifty different profiles and comment back and forth on the main one, making the original account seem like it has an army of followers, when in reality, it's still just one person. Fake influencers also use stock photos, claiming them as their own, or they simply pull images from anywhere on the Internet and re-post them on their profiles, choosing vague images where the person's back is facing the camera so they can play these stolen images off as self-portraits.

Fake influencers know they're fake, for the most part at least. Some have pretended to be influencers for so long that they have forgotten the difference between their real lives and their pretend lives. However, they still hold their heads up as if they are legit, and they present themselves as genuine despite not having an actual crowd, reputation, or sponsorship to back them up. They pretend to have sponsorship offers and post images and live videos on their feeds as if they have a following who will listen to them.

They use Instagram stories to narrate their entire lives, pretending like they are talking to a crowd because Instagram stories do not reveal how many people actually watched the highlights to outside viewers, allowing these fake influencers to cover up that zero people are paying attention to what they have to say. They spend their waking moments gathering tips and ideas from other influencers, real or fake, and pretend to act like them even though none of it matters. Some fake influencers can become so good at faking their social lives that it can become difficult for people to spot who's real and who's fake. For all we know, none of these influencers are really who they say they are.

Falling victim to the world of fake Instagram influencers can prove dangerous to any type of social media brand or presence we are trying to create. It distorts our image as a fraud, a fake, or a counterfeit rather than someone worth paying attention to, and fake influencers who become exposed will forever remain known as imposters on all social media platforms and in life, an unforgiving nature and a huge risk for potential influencers. Pretending to be an influencer with millions of followers will only continue to drain our pockets with no real gain in return and, eventually, we're forced to either give up our social media life or exposed ourselves as frauds as we realize we can no longer keep up with the demands of trying to cover the fact that we have purchased our fame.

An average brand or person trying to generate fame from an online presence without patience and hard work can blow over $200,000 a year on impressions and false hopes from "100% successful advertisements."

It takes years for a typical person to become a true influencer. Though, not everyone possesses this type of patience and continue to pile on thousands of "followers" within months. Their following counts are low and seem astronomical to the lack of content they have on their pages. There has been evidence of increasingly large numbers of Instagram followers overnight, with users swearing that it's their content that have brought in these followers, not their paychecks. Unless we're a celebrity or a phenomenal photographer of an extremely rare specimen (which I doubt we are), it is physically impossible to gain 10,000 followers in under two days. These spikes are usually from accounts with strange names and no followers or posts, dead giveaways that these are purchased bots. However, even for people who haven't bought followers, the occasional bot slips in every now and then because of the nature of showcasing ourselves on the Internet. Still, when 95% of our followers follow the same trend of a terrible name with no pictures, the excuse of "it just slipped in" is no longer valid.

Fake Instagram influencers are too often lured in by the use of hashtags. It is not common knowledge, but the more hashtags a post has, the more these users are targeted by an infestation of bots on their profiles. The standard number of hashtags used per post is usually two to three, five max. However, when we come across a post with over fifty hashtags, they are trying to lure in bots as bots frequently scan for posts with hashtags. Most people also believe that the more hashtags they drown their posts in, the more likely they are to get people to notice them. Unfortunately, hashtags only serve to make users look desperate.

"Love this!"
"Epic!"
"Delightful!"
"Awesome!"

CHAPTER 12

INSTAGRAM INFLUENCERS ARE FAKE

Purchasing Instagram followers and likes, or even Facebook and YouTube followers and likes, is a trend that has skyrocketed over the past few years, something so common that influencers and celebrities all over the world use to give their profiles a kick start as users are more likely to visit a profile that has 5,000 followers than one that only has 5. Despite being a tactic that can prove helpful at first, once people begin to buy followers, they become hooked, turning that 5,000 into 50,000, and eventually into 500,000 with a status claim as an "influencer." To make it more tempting, the cost of buying followers has gotten cheaper and cheaper over the years; the cost for 5,000 followers has become the price of a cup of coffee.

But, what's the point? What's the point of having half a million followers, or even 10 million followers, if none of them are real? The feeling of achieving something without any work always triumphs actual achievements because human beings are LAZY! We would much rather pay to have other people do our petty work for us while we take all the credit because the Internet has made it difficult to stay motivated to work toward achievements.

Even when people realize that they are only paying for bots that stick around for a week and then disappear in mass quantities, they still do it because it's so tempting. So many "influencers" have been caught buying a few hundred bots during their times on Instagram, paying for the impression of being successful until they can actually become successful, so much so to the point where we can no longer distinguish which of our followers are real and which are fake.

We buy so many followers that when these bots begin to drop off, we find ourselves compensating with more and more until we are elbow deep in debt. Bots will never interact with our profiles unless we buy comments and likes also, and even then, those are all still fake.

"Instagram started off as a social network to connect with others. The bots that have taken over have made us lonelier than ever before."

Many Instagram influencers have devoid themselves of true interactions. They don't care who's actually watching them or not as long as the few who are know that they are "the best" due to their large following. Buying likes and followers can never help an image or a brand grow. Of those 100,000 followers we have posted on our Instagram accounts, maybe only 10 of them are real, 10 real followers who quickly unfollow us when they see that out of 100,000 followers, we only have 5 likes. Bots provide no value, but then again, Instagram is all a number's game.

Even if these influencers aren't purchasing bots day and night, they still portray an image online that does not accurately represent human life. They give people false hope of being able to go anywhere and do anything they want with minimal effort and struggle, all while wearing designer dresses, when we all know that can never happen. Influencers pretend to support matters they don't actually care about just because they want to uphold a positive image, and they forget how to be real. They waltz around as if life is perfect and that everyone envies them, when they are probably miserable inside and struggling to keep up with the demand from their audiences.

"Are they really happy? Or are their smiles all forged?"

The images and faces we see on the Internet do not always mirror the images and faces that are hiding behind the cameras. No one wants to showcase a boring life at a 9 to 5 job, eating a simple sandwich because we are in a rush, or running into areas of foreign countries where we feel unsafe because those aren't the "glamorous lives" we want others to associate us with. We all want to put our best feet forward by showcasing the lives that we want, with others believing that we have amazing lives rather than the lives we actually live.

Because of this, these so called "influencers" expend all their money and energy on lives that they may not even believe in anymore but still struggle to keep up with just to fit in with the rest of the world. These influencers started off their careers because they truly loved what they were doing. Inevitably, the attention and fame that eventually caught up with them made them feel more powerful and under the pressure to keep up or crumble. This is especially true for those who rely solely on their Internet fame and appearances as their source of income.

"Imagine feeling under the weather but still pressured to have to carefully construct that perfect face and go climb that mountain we dread climbing."

"Imagine obtaining huge amounts of debt but still feeling the need to have to fly to that next 'promised dream country' or risk losing thousands of followers."

"Imagine hitting rock-bottom and becoming so desperate to keep up with the raging crowd that we're almost forced to Photoshop our entire lives or go places/do things that the crowd wants us to do rather than the things we love doing."

Hobbies have quickly turned from showcases of true interests to a constructed book of made-up fantasies that fool no one but the self. Despite becoming drained from how much trickery we impose on ourselves and others, we push on because we see our competitors continuing to post lavish images and beautiful selfies, gloating humbly about how special they are, that we feel the heaviness to also do the same.

Regardless of how perfect an image appears to be, it doesn't always reflect the happenings behind the scenes. Grinning selfies and loving couples don't always reflect reality. How many times have we seen dozens and dozens of images of people with blown-up shots of their engagement rings, with their fiancés in the far background and #special, #happilyeverafter, #engagedbitches, #bridetobe, #blessed, and #bflovesme? These images are designed to make us become envious of them because seeing those images makes our loneliness kick in, causing us to crave engagements and love lives of our own. We fool ourselves into wanting the lives that the newly-engaged have, taking wedding photos in the Maldives and having celebrities officiate their weddings, but do we actually want them?

What do you think is going on behind the scenes of big diamond rings and plastic surgeries? How much do you think people pressure their significant others into proposing to them and buying them the heaviest carat they can find JUST so they have something worthy of posting, or should I say, bragging about, on the 'gram. Let's face it, having a small wedding in a small church with a small group of people and a small ring is nowhere near as Instagram-worthy as lavish weddings that allow people to talk about them for months, filling their Instagram feeds with beautiful images of weddings cakes, flower bouquets, expensive venues, and pictures of wedding dress after wedding dress after wedding dress.

Over 70% of Instagram weddings don't last because people end up focusing more on their posts than their relationships, dragging around and controlling their partners so they can generate more followers by showing off things they foolishly believe others wished they themselves had. We only showcase our love lives to the public because we feel insecure about them. We think that by openly talking about them, we solidify that they actually exist, and we think that by taking selfies with our partners who stand next to us looking miserable, others can see how "in love" we actually are.

Those who share their "love" to the world aren't actually in love behind the cameras. Those who are truly in love would much rather share their love with each other in private than feel the need to drag the rest of the universe into it. Couples who appear happy in front of the camera are probably fighting and arguing nonstop once the cameras turn off. How many love lives will still exist when we take away social media? How many people will be exposed for "loving" just so they have something to post online?

The more time we spend on Instagram and comparing our lives to it, the more toxic it proves to ourselves. Instagram doesn't help us feel closer to our friends and loved ones like we all thought it would when we first joined back when it was released. Instead, Instagram makes us feel like shit about ourselves because we're always bombarded with the pressure to do more even when we're already doing our best, with constant harassments telling us that our best will never be good enough. We become so consumed by it, allowing it to become the first thing we look at when we wake up in the mornings and the last thing we look at before we fall asleep at nights. We become addicted with trying to get ahead of others that we begin to resent the lives we have outside of the Internet.

The "influencers" who we admire so much are not always as "perfect" and as "happy" as they appear. In most cases, they try too hard to show off how great their lives are compared to others. Those who are truly content with their lives don't feel the need to show them off. They're satisfied with who they are and continue living as is. Yet, many influencers feel the need to show others how happy they are doing the things they love because it's all a façade. We know this because we see travel influencers lugging 70lbs of camera equipment and crew around, taking selfies and videos of themselves talking about how much they're enjoying these foreign countries instead of actually enjoying them.

They don't showcase their lives because they're proud of them; they do it because they want to show others that they're so much better than them and can achieve successes that many others cannot. Instagram influencers who spend their sole focus on showing off their originality and happiness are the ones who are the most distraught, feeling the need to use distraction after distraction to forget how miserable they actually are. Influencers with over a million followers can become so disconnected from themselves, as they spend their entire time trying to connect with others, that they will become lost the day Instagram goes extinct, and like all social media platforms that come and go, it will. The more followers these influencers have online, the less they're likely to have in real life.

Faking happiness and joy are signs of psychological malnourishment and disturbance because we forget who we're pretending for. We forget that we're parading around in skimpy outfits and blowing our money on lavish vacations and makeovers just to impress people we don't even know. We forget that, despite how many people comment about how lovely our posts are, they don't actually care about us. Half of them are only commenting for hopes of receiving comments and likes back, and the other half are only commenting out of sheer boredom.

But we don't see that! We don't see that we're posting selfies of ourselves in lingerie to nobody except for creeps and perverts! On average, decent and normal human beings spend roughly 5 seconds per post they come across unless it's posts from people they are obsessed with. Most of the time, influencers are only faking their happiness for themselves.

"People who spend more time connecting with themselves are more satisfied than people who spend their time connecting with their phones."
"People who cherish the richness of life are happier than those who are desperate for love and attention."
"Minimalism has proven to generate more positivity in life than materialism."
"Competition does not hurt those who are truly proud of themselves and know themselves."
"Instagram can only destroy those who allow it or rely on it to control their lives."

"Can engineered happiness ever triumph true happiness?"

We live in a world where we have been taught the factors of life that's supposed to make us happy rather than allowing us to choose our own happiness. We associate happiness with a price tag and with quantity, vast quantities of followers, vast quantities of materialism, and vast quantities of money.

We have been brainwashed to believe that we cannot be truly happy unless we have everything and unless we have more than others around us do. We falsely believe that fancy parties and yachts dictate how likeable and important we are. We genuinely believe money can buy us happiness because we haven't put down our phones long enough to discover what really makes us happy.

"Influencers are the blemishes of the social media world."

"If an influencer stops eating, we also feel the need to stop eating."

"If an influencer sips champagne in France, we feel tempted to book a one-way ticket."

"If an influencer spends 8 hours a day at the gym, we automatically sign up for a membership we know we will never use."

"If an influencer wears an outfit that receives 60,000 likes, we run out to buy the same outfit."

"We live the lives of influencers because we're afraid of being left out."

"We live the lives of influencers because we do not love ourselves."

#fittingin

Instagram influencers are basically makeup artists with a fat brush of concocted lies and games to show the world. They spend so much time building up this online image that they never really take the time to focus on any other parts of their lives. Influencers live by their profiles, blowing all their money and time investing in mindless images that can all disappear one day.

"What happens when Instagram, or any other social media platform, finally comes to an end?"

"What happens when everyone decides to unplug?"

"What happens when social sharing networks become a thing of the past?"

"So, what if these influencers are pulling in $5,000 per sponsored post?"

"Will these so-called 'influencers' still have an income when Instagram perishes?"

"What talents will they have to share then?"

"Will they continue influencing?"

"Will they still be doing the things they claim to enjoy doing on Instagram?"

"Or will they immediately be forgotten as they realize that people don't actually care about influencers, seeing them as fakes and threats rather than as human beings?"

CHAPTER 13
THE ALGORITHM OF SUCCESS

IT'S NOT a secret that certain types of people are more well-liked than others in the Instagram world. If you've ever scrolled down the homepage, you can see that pictures of women in bikinis and shirtless men are almost always at the top of the page with the highest number of likes. That is because sex and the idea of sex sell. The so-called "pretty" people, women especially, are always more likely to grab attention than the average-looking people or those who post pictures of objects rather than selfies. The images of women who show off their asses and cleavage are bound to grab the attention of almost all men because they're either sleazy or find them attractive, as well as the attention of almost all women because they want to be them and need tips on how to become them.

But, this concept is nothing new. External beauty has, and will always, triumph when it comes to the Internet world because people are shallow. Dating apps focus solely on external appearances when users decide to swipe left or right, and Instagram is no different. Profiles who showcase six-pack abs, giant breasts, and model-like faces are more likely to grab attention than beer-bellies, flat chests, and zit-filled faces.

We don't like admitting it, but we all judge others based on how their faces and bodies look. The pretty girls and the muscular guys will always get the most views and the most likes because people feel like they need to like those who fit the standards of beauty. The more we continue to feel this way, the more we feed into the egos of these so-called "influencers," boosting up their profiles just because they're "hot."

We all think that we need to be attractive in order to be liked. We all try to hide who we really are, taking selfies at absurd angles just to show off our best selves, and only showcasing our faces when we have "good days." And because we all think this way, it becomes reality. Even people who aren't traditionally recognized as beautiful, such as overweight people, have blown up in the social media world.

However, the reason is not what we think. We all "love" images of plus-sized models and "big women" not because we think they're courageous and brave. We love them because they, too, are showcasing their fake selves, coating themselves in makeup and slim-fitting clothes, pretending to be people they are not, because even they believe that their authentic selves will not be liked. True, there are users who relish in the accounts of actual #nofilter images, but there is also always a crowd who will judge others despite what and who they post. We are judgmental by nature.

Admit it. The reason we refrain from being so openly judgmental on the Internet and refuse to be completely honest is because we don't want to stand out as being opinionated and risk societal hatred. Imagine opening up a post and seeing hundreds of positive comments about some random stranger sitting at the beach. We don't want to be the first ones to say something negative about the photo, even if we think it, because then we'll be seen as "haters" and warrant dislikes and unfollows. However, if we see hundreds of positive comments but also a small handful of negative ones, we have no problem expressing how we truly feel if we think the photo is hideous because then we'll know we're not alone and, therefore, will not be ostracized.

Mainstream media has promoted unrealistic beauty for years, more so since the rise of Photoshop, portraying stick-thin fashion models and chiseled celebrities in place of feasible bodies. This unrealistic portrayal of women and men has caused deadly consequences since, as models and gymnasts began starving themselves for their careers, and young boys and girls developed eating disorders trying to look like their icons. The world of social media has destroyed healthy self-esteem and body image, with Instagram playing right into the game. Altered body images now become common for gaining followers with curated Instagram feeds channeled toward making ourselves more likeable, yet, also more depressed.

Instagram forces us to parade around half-naked and post pictures of our external bodies on our profiles because it manipulates us into believing that those images get results. Because of how desperate we are, we go for it and expose our naked bodies online even when we don't want to. We willingly post nudes because we have been brainwashed to believe that people will like us more if we do so. This has gotten so bad that some people have taken advantage of this and utilize Instagram as their own personal porn stash.

The world of catfishing has also blown up as people started becoming less and less confident in themselves as being able to generate likes and followers as they are. They believe that if they don't pretend to be someone more approachable or more beautiful, then they'll never have the chance to become influencers, or even someone with more than 20 followers. Many influencers aren't fully themselves; some people pretend to be someone else completely. Others only post images of their backsides so people can never tell what they actually look like, and the rest of these Instagram influencers Photoshop so much on every picture that not even they can recognize what they really look like anymore. But how can they stay on top otherwise?

But, remember, likes toward posts that achieve desired attention are usually only directed toward one part of the image, the face, the ass, the boobs, the abs, the money, etc. These "devoted followers" who we all believe loyally follow and worship us are only attracted to parts of us, the shallow parts, rather than the entire picture. When someone likes our picture, it doesn't necessarily mean they like us; they just like the parts of us that they see. Over 80% of Instagram users who like posts don't even take the time to read what the posts say. They react with their eyes, and if they see something they like, they click "like," even if the posts mention murder or infidelity.

CHAPTER 14
INNOVATION TO SELF-REINVENTION

As INSTAGRAM GROWS, so do the people who claim to love the same things influencers do. Five years ago, there was only a small handful of influencers in each category, whether it's travel, fashion, fitness, or food. However, as the platform became more and more popular, we begin to see all these micro-influencers rise from nowhere, micro-influencers with small colonies of followers, racing for the higher positions.

These micro-influencers live life solely for Instagram and

try too hard to showcase every experience and every part of their lives. They strive to stand out by pulling followers from every direction despite what it takes, including buying followers and #follow4follow. They also spend hours researching and stalking verified influencers to see how they can reach up to their grandeur and status, regardless of whether these popular influencers are real people. They are usually the most insecure and often the ones more likely to fake their way through posts and copy verified influencers to stand out. This also makes them more likely to Photoshop their images and alter their videos.

Despite how hard we try, standing out amongst the influencer crowds just isn't enough. It has gotten to the point where we need to stand out from ALL THE CROWDS, including engaging in death-inducing and epic activities, where lives become at stake for who wins the biggest influencer crown. However, the problem lies in that the more these micro-influencers draw in the crowds that support them, the more pressured they feel to have to keep up with the demand, forcing them to change their original motives into something that pleases more than just one group of people. This causes influencers to go from showcasing what they love to what they feel they need to post in order to keep their positions as "the best."

"As an influencer, when I post something on Instagram, and it doesn't get 500 likes within the first hour, I delete it, pour my heart into more research on what sells, re-examine my angle, blame myself for not being as good as other influencers, and keep re-posting until my followers give me what I want. If my posts don't make me feel special and important, I beat myself up over them, become self-destructive, and either quit Instagram forever or open another (better) account."

Nevertheless, let's not solely point fingers at influencers who try too hard. What about their "faithful" supporters, the users, the trolls? The average person plays a much bigger role in the Instagram world than the influencers themselves because average people influence how influencers will create their next posts. Without average people to follow them, influencers would not exist.

People's desires change all the time. We may want travel pictures one minute from one influencer and then want that same influencer to become a bikini model, and in order to keep their followers, influencers give the crowds what they want, at their own demise. These new users are the ones who impact social media the most, manipulating influencers into posting what they want to see with false promises of following them. One strong voice can quickly turn an influencer's profile from 2 million followers to 200.

CHAPTER 15

INFLUENCER ATTRACTION AND REPUTATION

"We see these beautiful people in these beautiful places, and we automatically assume that their lives are as glamorous as their photoshoots."

"We see lavish cars and designer clothing and believe they come from wealth."

"We see a new photo of a new country every other day and believe they are living the dream life of traveling the world."

"We see their smiles every day and believe they have it all together."

"Glamorous images are often doctored or fake."

"Lavish cars and designer clothing can often be followed closely by debt."

"New country photos can mean luxury backdrops and green screens."

"Smiles can often have tears behind the screens."

I'M sure we can all agree that looking our best is the way to go when it comes to posting images. We even post our #freshoutofbed selfies with a face full of makeup and a perfect hairdo. We know that the minute we post a truly authentic no filter and no makeup image, we will receive 5x more dislikes than likes. We lie to ourselves that we need to be incredible and outstanding in order to feel good about ourselves even if our followers disagree.

Some people take this mindset way too far, mistaking "ridiculous and offensive" as "glamorous and beautiful." Instagram influencers often try too hard to grab the attention of the crowd that they forget how to be genuine. They allow their psychological rationality to become affected because the more they feel insecure about losing their followers, the more they become desperate to change their appearances. They develop an intense obsession with altering photos and acting exploitative and dishonest for the sake of advancing and being the best.

No amount of exercise or even plastic surgery will give us the images we proclaim are #100%real, and people know many of these are fake. The Internet may be gullible and weak, but it isn't stupid. People on the Internet all know (for the most part) that these falsified images are actually a hoax; they are just too scared to be the first ones to call out these powerful influencers on them and risk being branded as #unpopular and #troll.

On the other hand, let's take a moment to consider the influencers who actually have authentic photos. How do they achieve such amazing photos all the time without massive photo editing? I recently got the chance to catch up with a travel influencer I once knew while I was also part of the Instagram crowd. In order to capture these beautiful photos of famous tourist sites without all crowds, she has to wake up before the crack of dawn, multiple mornings in a row, due to uncertainties in weather conditions and other extraneous circumstances, and carry her entire camera set with her (all 50lbs of it) to her destinations, even if it means having to hike up mountains with heavy equipment and heels, all without getting herself dirty.

After spending over an hour setting up her equipment, she takes over 100 images of herself and then spend more hours sorting through them for the best ones, adding vivid filters over her images, and writing the perfect captions. If those weren't enough, most of her "amazing images" consist of layering, where she would take an image of her desired backdrop and an image of herself, separately, and stich the two together, making it seem as if her personal self is front of the beautiful backdrops. As an Instagram influencer, over 12 hours of her day, every day, is devoted to Instagram posts. With only 300,000 followers and the unknown potential of Instagram crashing any day, is all this hard work really worth it, or is it all for superficial attention?

While a lot of people on Instagram are fake, there are many who prove that being an influencer isn't as simple and easy as their images make it seem. A lot of effort goes into creating the perfect image, and there's bound to be stress along the way when we end up losing more than we gain, especially for fresh influencers who are trying to make a name for themselves. In the end, only the strong prevail, the ones who truly care about their worth as opposed to just their numbers, while those who are only in it to win it either become discouraged or bored.

CHAPTER 16
A PERPETUAL COMPETITION

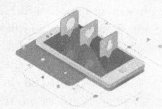

WHEN WE LOOK at social media accounts, such as on Facebook and Instagram, what's the purpose of even having one? The intention for such sites should be to connect with those we haven't seen in a long time or to connect with new friends. However, how often does that happen? Sure, there are people, especially those in their middle ages, who actually care about using the outlet for said reasons, but human beings are driven by competition. We fail to see our lives as worth living unless we have something to prove and show others.

We are social creatures who, unless we are able to compete

and show off our winnings and greatness over those of others, we struggle to find worth and meaning in life. For example, if no one is watching, if no one is around to see or hear us do the great things we claim to be doing, would we still do them? Would we still enjoy doing them? Are these hobbies still part of our beings and worth our time if we had no one to share them with?

"Social media is a place for us to brag about the things we're not actually doing so people will think we're not just sitting around all the time."

"Social media is a place for us to one up our friends and colleagues, showing them that we really did 'accomplish' all that we said we would ten years ago."

"Social media is a place for us to run one 5k race and show off our medal and athletic skills, excluding the time that it actually took for us to run it."

"Social media is a place for us to show off our new romantic partners, hashtagging how happy we are, when in reality, we're fighting 70% of the time, only stopping long enough to take a staged photo."

"Social media is a place for us to have accomplishments and do everything we can to rub them in the faces of others, whether it's winning an award or getting a job promotion."

"There's only so many angles of a piece of paper that we can take before it's time to move on."

We think that when we post on the Internet about how awesome we are, that people will immediately become super jealous and want to be us. And it's true. We see how great others are doing and feel left behind. We want to experience accomplishments also in order to beat our friends because no one likes being the "loser" of the party. We start doubting what we're doing with our lives, why we're not that famous musician that our friend is, why we're still stuck in an entry-level position when our co-worker is moving up, and why we're still Internet dating and bumming around when our sibling is happily married with two kids. And even if we didn't think we're losers before, we definitely start thinking we are after comparing ourselves to others and indirectly hearing that we have done nothing while others have done everything.

Not that I'm innocent of any of this, but I once knew someone who would just start recording everything she did in her day to day. I mean, everything, from the moment she woke up with elegant brunches to the moment she shopped at Saks Fifth Avenue in her gold Porsche with $5,000 daily clothing and accessory purchases to the moment she went out to expensive steakhouses with her boyfriend while flaunting her new engagement ring to the moment she fell asleep under the stars while lying on a beach in Hawaii. Great life, right?

It shouldn't be, because none of it was real. In reality, her breakfast consisted of a stale bagel in the car with spilled coffee, an office job where she slaved in a cubicle next to a man who sang off-key, drove an old 2004 Toyota Corolla, returned all the clothes that she bought, paid someone to be her new hot steady long-term fiancé, and basked on a beach along the Jersey shore, cropping out the backdrop. She played it off as truth for about three months, ran out of vacation days and stopped posting on the Internet completely. Her reasoning? She was "currently tired" from dealing with her busy social life and decided to take a break from social media.

This just goes to show, not everything we see online is a true representation of how someone is. All of or none of what we see can be real. We can be anyone or anything we want to be, or at least portray ourselves that way. Want to be a musician? Hit up Guitar Center and take a sick photo of yourself "strumming." Want to be a mountaineer? Take a selfie at the base of a mountain and chronicle about how you climbed and summited successfully. Want to be a competitive runner? Borrow a bib and have someone take a picture of you near the finish line.

No one needs to know or will know that we lie on our pictures unless they really look into them, which no one actually does. We go through more effort to look like we have accomplished something than it would've taken to actually do it. And, nowadays, people have gotten so skilled at Photoshop that it has become effortless to be anywhere in the world without having to spend a single dime. So many of the images on the highly-trafficked pages we see on Instagram are Photoshopped. How do I know? I don't! That's the problem!

However, this #fakeittillyoumakeit and #friendlycompetition are also gateways for the increasing rate of suicide caused by virtual stress and cyberbullying. According to the World Health Organization (WHO), 1.54 million people die from suicide every year, with a good fraction of that correlated to online-related drama. These suicide rates are known to have been influenced by not only personal factors, but social and environmental factors as well. As people become more pressured to fit in with the social media crowd, their emotional and mental health issues begin to take a toll for the worst.

Cyberbullying is no joke. This increasing problem has been linked to more suicide-related deaths than any other online matter, affecting mostly vulnerable, younger generations all trying to reach for that common goal of fame and fortune without having to do any of the work but post selfies. Sickeningly, it has become a trend for younger generations to harm themselves or commit suicide LIVE on their social media platforms, with their audiences cheering and booing rather than calling the cops, a shocking awakening for current and future generations.

The media loves to popularize and portray dangerous behaviors and toxic images that distort the minds of young individuals as they lose sight of what they should be following. Instagram provides higher risks for young adults as they promote pro-suicidal sites, message boards for planned homicides, and chat rooms and forums that allow groups of sick-minded individuals to come together and plot against others because the exclusivity makes them believe they can.

And if that isn't bad enough, users on Instagram all around the world are more likely to support these groups and ideas rather than prevent them because online presence allows people to say and support matters they wouldn't normally. We play these major roles in the deaths of innocent people, but at the same time, we pretend to feel sad and remorseful when these people actually do die, mourning with the rest of the Internet so we can feel a sense of belonging.

"Your Instagram presence is causing the death of another human being."

Unfortunately, online stupidity can be just as deadly as online bullying and cults. We find joy in seeing risky images on Instagram, such as taking selfies in front of a moving train and selfies while jumping off buildings with no experience, and without even thinking whether these images are real, we attempt to recreate them, landing ourselves in hospitals and death by attempting these same feats no sane human being would do. #YOLO

We also fall for gimmicks of challenges that would otherwise make no sense to us, including the Fire Challenge, the Ghost Pepper Challenge, and the Tide Pod Challenge. For those of you who are lucky enough to be unaware of these challenges, forgive me for exposing you to them now. The Fire Challenge is when we cover our bodies in flammable liquids and then set the liquids on fire, causing us to turn into a walking fireball, or a pile of ash, whichever one sounds more appealing. The Ghost Pepper Challenge is when we devour an entire ghost pepper, known as the hottest pepper in the world, without allowing ourselves to drink any milk to prevent our tongues from burning off. Finally, the Tide Pod Challenge, probably one of the more recent and memorable ones, is when we purchase toxic detergent Tide pods from the grocery store and eat them because the Internet tells us they are delicious while we end up in hospitals an hour later to have our stomachs pumped.

This is also not just exclusive to Instagram; people do these crazy and insane challenges all over the world on all forms of social media, not realizing how stupid they are even after they end up in critical care. Hospitalizations have skyrocketed since the last decade because more and more teenagers are landing themselves in emergency rooms for trying out acts they see on the Internet.

"In 2008, a Japanese forum shared that people can kill themselves using gaseous hydrogen sulfide. Because people have a habit of idolizing suicidal and homicidal behaviors, especially when they are portrayed online, shortly after, over 200 people attempted to kill themselves using gaseous hydrogen sulfide, with a 95% success rate." #suicide

CHAPTER 17
CRAVING A STRANGER'S ATTENTION

"FOMO = fear of missing out"

"Phubbing = ignoring the person you're talking to so you can look at your phone"

Is social media to blame for our downfall in mental health and drastic increases in depression and anxiety? In 2018, a research group at the University of Pennsylvania performed an experiment on a group of undergraduates, where they limited their use of social media, Facebook, Snapchat, and

Instagram included, to only 10-minutes a day while also measuring their resulting levels of depression. What they found was that spending less time on Instagram and other social media platforms a day can be part of the answer in how we can reduce our depression statistics.

"Our discoveries unequivocally recommend that restricting Internet-based life use to around 30 minutes a day may prompt critical improvement in prosperity."

Every day, we are distracted by the biosphere of social media. We allow notifications of someone liking our post or a new photo of someone we are following distract ourselves from reality. We check our phones the first thing in the morning and the last thing at night. We check our phones even as we are in critical conditions such as in car accidents and emergency rooms. We have let these pop-up notifications run our lives, and 95% of the time, these are notifications we don't even care about, yet, we drop everything we're doing to check them.

"Instagram can literally kill us."

We continue to check our feeds even when we're unsure of what we're checking; most of the time, we just feel the need to check for the sake of checking. We instinctively reach for our phones all hours of the day, when we're on a date, when we're in a meeting, when we're at the gym, and even at our own weddings. It's as if we feel possessed to reach for our phones every several minutes or, otherwise, we'd combust and explode. Millions of Instagram users actually become surprised when they find out how many hours a day they actually devote to this social media platform. Picking up our phones every minute will not help us win a million dollars nor will it help us succeed in life. The only results that endless hours of perusing on Instagram can achieve are anxiety and misery as we see low counts of likes and comments from trolls.

But, is social media to blame for our obsessions with Instagram and our risk-taking behaviors, or do we just suck as willpower and allow others to convince us into doing things we don't normally do, way too easily? Can we ever stop being under the influence of social media? Can we ever learn to just put our phones down for an entire day without sweating tears? Can we ever just unplug and live life without feeling the need to share every part of ourselves with others as if others even care?

CHAPTER 18
INSTAGRAM LANDMARKS

INSTAGRAM PHOTOS with perfect backdrops have become the new version of selfies with celebrities. Nowadays, people don't even take the time to look at our profiles unless we are in a room surrounded by marshmallows, absorbed by twinkling lights, or have the entire city skyline below us. And even then, we may still not get noticed. We always see these images of influencers with the same backdrops, such as hanging for their dear lives on *Brazil's* Pedra de Gavea, a cliff where people can hang off and pretend they are dangling a thousand feet in the air, when in reality, they are two inches from another rock below them.

But, because of this enticing photo opportunity, there are often long lines piled up with people hoping to snag this picture for the 'gram. But this is not even the worst of it. In more recent years, dangerous mountains, like Mount Everest, have become top of the list for photo ops, a dangerous endeavor. With hundreds of people dying every year, scaling Mount Everest is difficult enough in itself as oxygen supplies are slim the closer to the peak. If you've ever seen images of people climbing Mount Everest, you will notice that there's usually only one route up, forcing crowds to wait in line, diminishing their supplies. Now, imagine that but with dozens upon dozens of hopeful Instagrammers per day snapping selfies and posing for the perfect Instagram image as they near the summit. Not only do they put themselves at risk by losing oxygen, but other climbers below them are putting their lives at risk waiting for these ignorant climbers to finish taking pictures of something they may or may not even get to post.

But, fear not! Society has developed (and learned to monopolize) on how to offer opportunities for fantastic photo ops without the risks of death. Over the past several years, museums have popped up all over the world that feature rooms where people can go into one by one, where they are surrounded by beautiful and artificial scenery designed JUST for the sake of wowing the Instagram world and gaining those beloved followers.

Some of these museums include the Museum of Ice Cream in San Francisco, where rooms are coated in shades of pink and people can pretend to ride animal cookie carousels, the Color Factory located in both San Francisco and New York, which features an explosion of a rainbow, as if people really did eat a bag of Skittles, and includes a swimming pool of yellow balls, and Candytopia, the pop-up museum located in (you guessed it!) San Francisco and New York where Insta-grammers can become surrounded by all the sweets they can imagine as if it's Willy Wonka's Chocolate Factory, and where even people who are diabetic post images with #kidinacandy-factory or #sweettooth. The creators of these museums know what people want, engineering lights, fountains, indoor galaxies, and even rooms full of fake llamas to give people the opportunity to brag on their Instagram…and everybody falls for them.

Instagram's quick and effortless ability to easily showcase fake lives have put fear into the CEOs of other social media platforms such as Twitter. People fall in love with their eyes, and if they see a page of pretty colors and beautiful scenery, why wouldn't they choose that over a page of unfiltered shots featuring drug epidemics? Sometimes, people find it difficult to come up with the best captions to say, finding a great photo of themselves they want to post but struggle to find the words to go with it. With Instagram, this struggle disappears. Insta-gram accentuates imagery and symbolism so users are able to just take a picture, post it, and get thousands of likes without even having said a single world as we are often limited to a certain number of characters and given only one chance to wow the world in 20 words or less.

Have you ever walked into a famous historical site, such as the Westminster Abbey in London, the Sistine Chapel in Rome, or the Van Gogh Museum in Amsterdam, pulled out your phone, and have been disappointed when you're told that photography isn't allowed? Since the rise of Instagram, famous sites such as the New York's Metropolitan Museum of Art and the Boston Museum of Fine Arts have changed their rules on "no-photographs," now allowing photography into the buildings for those who have been dying to capture selfies in front of beautiful art.

We have been so persuaded by Instagram, feeling the need to take a picture of and post everything we see, that we become confused when we come across a place that confiscates our cameras as we try to use them. We have been so accustomed to taking lavish selfies that we no longer register that there are going to be other people around us as we take our pictures, and that we're not allowed to tell them to get the fuck out while we take our shots. We become so focused on our own little Instagram worlds that we forget that a real world exists beyond just ourselves. Landmarks and historic sites don't exist for the purpose of allowing us to have a bangin' Instagram.

During my travels through Asia, I visited famous landmarks such as the Angkor Wat in Cambodia, the Grand Palace in Thailand, and the Great Wall of China in, well, China. Rather than admiring these beautiful places, I was faced with more people than not either posing for selfies in front of them or experiencing these places through their phones, seeming more excited about allowing their followers to see how "happy" and lucky they are to be in these places than enjoying these rare moments themselves. Many Instagrammers never enjoy the places they travel to, the food they eat, or the clothes they wear because they do them all for Instagram.

I once knew someone who was always perfectly content wearing t-shirts and sweatpants until she joined Instagram as a fashion guru. Don't ask me why. But, six months into her journey of becoming an influencer, she had blown over $20,000 on clothes alone that she would only wear for her pictures. She dressed better for her Instagram pictures than she did for her brother's wedding! We dedicate our lives to Instagram, selling our souls and our bodies just to become #instafamous. Pretty soon, like all social media platforms, Instagram will be replaced. What will these influencers have accomplished then? How will they make their living when they can no longer exploit themselves for cash over the Internet?

CHAPTER 19
SELFIE ARMAGEDDON

TAKING THAT "PERFECT" photo can be just as easy as smiling or just as dangerous as dangling off a cliff, as long as users have the filters and Photoshop skills to polish it up afterward. It's actually shocking how scary some people's Photoshopping skills can be! We can see two famous adventurist influencers side-by-side, and while one is actually jumping off cliffs and dangling off helicopters, the other is jumping off beds and dangling off monkey bars.

Some influencers can spend their whole Instagram careers on Photoshop, never leaving their homes but still living the lives they claim to have because they can simply lie. We relish in people living lives that are not real, and we kill ourselves trying to be like them. We follow accounts that are heavily filtered more than we follow real accounts. We care more about living vicariously through other people's photos than we do trying to make something of ourselves, defending these influencers when they receive a bad comment like we know them like the back of our own hands.

Selfies have blossomed in the world of social media, boosting the term "egotistical" to a whole different level. We all know what selfies are, though some of us love them more than others. Selfies are when we take that camera or that phone and take pictures of ourselves instead of other things or other people. We position ourselves in our best angles, showing our best duck faces, and take over fifty images of the same face just to hate all of them except for one. You know who you are. Despite only being a few years old, selfies have become a normal part of everyone's lives.

Even though we think that selfies help us promote self-love and self-acceptance, what selfies actually do is further enhance our insecurities and emotional issues, aka, the more selfies we take, the more we do not love ourselves. Those who have true acceptance toward themselves do not need validation from strangers AFTER they have meticulously constructed the best images of themselves to show. It's self-destructive! This over-the-top behavior is simply a coping mechanism for people to feel good about themselves after lacking confidence, and seeking validation from others to fill the emptiness they feel for themselves.

"According to the American Psychiatric Association, there are three levels of selfie addiction: fringe (taking three selfies a day), intense (taking three consecutive selfies a day), and interminable (taking at least 6 selfies a day)." Hell, most of us consider even 6 a day as too little.

All around the world, people are snapping selfies, with women more likely than men, people in suburban areas more likely than in urban areas, and more likely on the western part of the world than the eastern part, with 61.6% of women obsessed with selfies in New York but only 55.2% in Bangkok, and an incredible 82% in Moscow. However, similar to checking Instagram eight times every hour, people feel compelled to take selfies, when they feel ugly, when they feel threatened, when they see places that look too enticing to not have a photo in, and especially when they feel bored. Look through an average person's phone. I guarantee you you'll see at least ten recent selfie images.

Like all other addictions, selfie addiction is a major problem. Yes, it's a thing. People can become so hooked on taking selfies that it becomes all they know and want to do. Take Danny Bowman, for example, a 19-year-old British high school student who became obsessed with taking selfies, fixating on it more than the rest of his life. He couldn't see past his actions other than wanting to take selfies, taking over 200 selfies every day, destroying his social life, and eventually dropping out of school. Who knew that being obsessed with selfies can destroy your life? In 2014, the story of Danny Bowman was portrayed as a young adolescent who became addicted to selfies, dropped out of school, and attempted to kill himself while going through withdrawal, a heartbreaking story many have failed to learn from.

Selfie addiction has become so bad that it has given rise to the psychological condition, "selfitis," characterized by a fanatic enthusiasm to crave taking photographs of the self and posting them on social media-based platforms for the world to see as a way of compensating for the lack of confidence. Taking selfies has become a movement. A movement! Contrary to common knowledge, taking a selfie is not just as simple as taking a picture of the self. Taking a selfie now comes with enhancements that are required to present the "perfect photo," a photo that differs completely from the image originally taken.

Nowadays, these selfies need to come with evolving filters and foundations that help alter and transform images on a different level before we allow our selfies to become posted on social media. Taking selfies is a way for us to feel good about ourselves when we can see a photo of us we originally think is ugly and then transform it into something amazing, despite whether this transformed image even looks like us anymore. Our selfies allow us to become the people we want to be but think we can never achieve. We become addicted because our self-esteems are so low that we need to create alter egos just to be able to share ourselves with the world.

"We take selfies because we can't stand the way we look in the mirror."

CHAPTER 20
RISKING LIVES FOR THE PERFECT POST

"One couple's Instagram profile has increased by 3,000 followers in one night because of a photo of them skydiving into a volcano."

"Instagram fashion guru gains an incredible 150,000 likes on one single post in one day for her shopping binge around the world, blowing $20,000 on makeup in Milan, $15,000 on shoes in Paris, and $50,000 on handbags in Monaco, all while claiming a humble allowance of $50,000 a month."

WHY DO we go through so much effort, risking our lives and our futures, just to gain a few hundred followers who may or may never interact with us? Is it just for the number, because we all know that maybe only about 1% of these loyal clones, if we're lucky, actually interact with us? Do we do it to boost our self-esteems? Can they really be boosted if we're suffering in other ways? Or do we do it out of envy, feeling doubtful about our own lives so we pretend to be others when we see images of them on lavish vacations or fancy dinners with their gorgeous partners and perfect outfits, and we feel like we're missing out on life by not living like them, giving ourselves mentalities that there's something wrong with our lives even when we didn't originally think so? #statusofmind

We have become so obsessed with trying to capture that perfect moment that beats out everyone else that we turn our lives into life-or-death moments. How many times have you seen posts on Instagram where someone is dangling off a plane, coming face-to-face with a bear, hanging with one arm off the top of one of the tallest buildings in the world, or taking selfies in front of moving trains and erupting volcanos? These senseless and dangerous acts would normally not be part of people's lifestyles, unless they are pure adventurists, but the world of social media have turned normal people with normal and mundane lives into people who risk everything they have just for that #perfectpost.

Influencers are the worst when it comes to uploading images no one really cares about, from their daily breakfast food they probably don't eat to every exercise they pretend to do to awkward yoga postures with pigs on their backs to expensive outfits they only wear once. Still want that charm that comes with being an influencer? Say goodbye to your life. The charm of being an Internet star comes with never truly being able to live the life you want without feeling the need to give others what they want to keep them #loyal. Influencers are at constant wars with their own minds, pulling back and forth between what they want to do and what they should do, compelled to put their lives at risk even when they don't want to, going to extreme measures just for temporary fame.

#socialmediabadass
#doitforthegram
#riskitall
"Do it for the 'gram." Really? We steal, we murder, we DIE, just so we can have something worthy of showing on Instagram?
"Is our life simply only worth one epic photo?"
"Will we die for Instagram?"

People desperate for Internet fame fall off high mountains and buildings regularly while trying to pose for the 'gram in attempts to catch an epic selfie and define themselves as #risktakers before plunging to their deaths. While attempting to take a selfie in Taranto, Italy in front of the beautiful waters, a woman plunged to her death instead as she toppled over and fell on top of sharp rocks. In Portugal, two children witnessed their parents fall to their deaths as they attempted to take a selfie on the edge of a cliff. We see these epic photos and automatically assume they are real, and we attempt to re-create them at our own expenses. Take the Magic Bus, for example, located on the Stampede Trail in Fairbanks, Alaska, where Chris McCandless was found dead during his Alaskan adventure. Since the movie about his life came out, many tourists have fluttered over to that same location for that iconic photo in front of the bus, only to find themselves trapped on the wrong side of the vicious Teklanika River that Alexander Supertramp also found himself, dying in attempts to cross the same dangerous river, never getting that chance to post.

Among the nations with the deadliest selfie occurrences,

Russia tops the list with the most fatalities per year. In 2016, a 12-year-old student died while trying to take a selfie of herself hanging off her 17th floor balcony, losing her balance, and tumbling down. A few months before that another student died while trying to climb an electrical tower in Moscow, when he was electrocuted during a selfie pose. If those weren't bad enough, Instagrammers are regularly lured into a toxic lake in Siberia, known for its turquoise waters, but also a dumping ground for chemical waste with a high case of bear sightings. Despite these concerns, when that opportunity comes up for epic Instagram-worthy photos, the thought of, "Shit, I'm going to get mauled by a bear" doesn't really cross our minds; instead, we can only focus on, "I need to get a close shot of myself with the bear."

"Selfies can cost us our lives."

CHAPTER 21
#OBSESSED

"The world is completely fixated on Instagram."

THE MEANING of a photograph has changed since the start of the Instagram nation. Remember the good times of disposable cameras, where we would have to wait weeks to have our pictures printed out at the store? Photographs used to represent a way to treasure real moments in our lives that we want to look back on years later and appreciate.

Nowadays, we use photographs as a base for how well we can enhance them to become something they're not, how well we can turn our photos into something that others cannot, caring more about what we portray to others in the present moment than what we can reflect back on later. We don't care about saving memories anymore; we only care about making others believe we have memories. We delete our memories when our photos are not well-liked or not good enough, and we create memories based on what others want to see, unable to look at ourselves in the mirror at the end of the day because we didn't take what we wanted for ourselves.

On average, Instagram sees over 4.2 billion likes per day. However, the majority of these likes aren't even genuine likes. The majority of these 4.2 billion likes either come from attempted users' tactics to gain more likes themselves by hoping the accounts they like will like them back or from bots that people pay for to auto-like thousands of images a day to fulfill that same #like4like tactic.

"When we see accounts with over 10,000 likes while we have 10, we become distraught, delete our photos that we have once been so proud of, and delete our lives."

"We put forward photos that we know will make others want to be us."

"We put forward photos that make our exes regret losing us and our crushes regret not being with us."

"We put forward photos that make others see how important and valuable we are compared to them, despite the fact that we're fake."

"We are willing to do whatever it takes to grab even one #like from one person, including bribing, sending nudes, and making obscene promises."

"We pay people to become our #followers because we fear not being able to get any on our own or not being able to get enough on our own."

"We sleep with sleazes who promise us false fame and influencer status, especially that well-desired #instagramverified status."

We pay strangers to pretend to be our partners because our real partners are not #Instagramhot, blowing thousands of dollars to portray a life that isn't ours. The more commonly known version of this is #Instagramboyfriends, men that women pretend to be with romantically who only exist in their worlds to help them take fantastic images of them holding a floating hand, sitting "casually" on large rocks, flashing their boobs beside a pool, and prancing in fields, all without allowing their "boyfriends" any screen time but with #beaulovesme.

Everyone has become so focused on themselves that people only exist to help Instagrammers boost their online presence. I can't even count how many times I have seen girls twirling in front of cameras with men bored behind the scenes, just to later see these same girls with #caughtoffguard. No, you're not fucking caught off guard, in your $5,000 dress and someone spitting water in your hair to mimic rainfall. This #Romaexperience allows "influencers" to have that #instabeau without any real commitment, a lie they hire to help them rise on the social media platform.

For those of you unfamiliar with the Carolyn Stritch incident, a #instastar and #blogger famous for her controversial shots of Disneyland, she successfully fooled Instagrammers for over 20,000 likes for her post of her walking through what looked like an abandoned Disneyland in California while wearing a polka dot dress.

However, what her loyal followers didn't know was that

rather than actually visiting this popular tourist destination, she plucked a photo from the Internet and simply Photoshopped herself into it. Photoshop and the Roma Experience are just two of the manipulative tactics people use to promote the weakening of psychological well-beings as desperate followers see images that have been falsely promoted as real.

"Those of us who accept ourselves and our failures wholeheartedly without trying to be someone else are the ones most successful in life."

"Instagram represents life. We become vulnerable and put ourselves out there even when we know there's a chance of getting hurt. However, when we do get hurt or when we find out people do not like us, we try a different method. We try being someone else, dressing up our bodies and faces to look like someone far different than who we are to begin with, looking like the people who gets the most attention and worship, all while feeling miserable and depressed on the inside. At the end of the day, we drink ourselves to sleep because we cannot stand who we have become. We pass out, wake up, and repeat this again."

We always see the same pattern, pretty girls and muscular boys, posting the same photos as everybody else but still remaining on top because of their external attractiveness. These unrealistic images of blemish-free faces, 0% body fat, and backgrounds without even a crack on the concrete have become the quintessential norm for posting. Nevertheless, at the end of the day, fakes will always continue being fakes and doing what they want with their time and lives; as long as we don't give into these concocted images, we can save ourselves from social media depression, and these so-called "influencers" will eventually fall.

Stop focusing so much of your time on Instagram. Unless

you're a sponsored influencer, these hashtags you throw out on every post aren't going to help you accomplish anything. A shit ton of followers who don't even talk to you and an increasing number of hearts aren't going to save your life one day.

We spend all our time on social media and Instagram. Great! Let's continue that when we're homeless. All social media influencers, as popular as they seem now, will eventually be forgotten, with nothing left to prove their existences with because they have done nothing else with their lives other than post pictures. Having one follower versus one million followers is not going to change a thing if there's no reward at the end of the line. Instagram is a constant competition with no winner and many losers.

CHAPTER 22
DECEPTION FOR ACCEPTANCE

PHOTOSHOPPING images used to be looked down upon. We saw magazine covers with parts of Beyonce's and Lady Gaga's bodies shaved off and riots broke out because of this injustice for altering images to fit the conventional standards of beauty. Just a few years down the line, Photoshopping has become the norm, an almost-expected if we want to stand out and keep up with the world. We are quick and eager to take lessons on the basics of Photoshop, but only just enough to make sure our followers do not disappear.

Unfortunately, sometimes even that isn't enough. Many of

us who purchase likes and followers for any social media platform are familiar with companies such as Buzzoid, Stormlikes, Famoid, and Sproutsocial, Internet companies that have become popular over the years for selling large bundles of likes and followers, for Instagram especially, at low costs. Those looking in from the outside would see this as deceitful and wrong, calling out those who use these sites as #frauds.

However, those in the midst of it become instantly addicted after their first purchase. The high from seeing a 1,000-follower count increase almost instantly makes us compelled to keep going so we can achieve that same high. These third-party sites compete with each other to see who can give users the most bang for their buck, increasing quantity, lowering quality, but still boasting "organic likes and followers."

Contrary to what these services boast, though their services are cheap, what really happens is that people spend that $20 or that $50 on these services, causing them to feel good about themselves when their follower counts spike by thousands overnight, just to watch them all drop two weeks later, with their real fans wondering how all their followers disappeared. This causes them to buy more and more in order to compensate for their loss and to hide the fact that they bought followers in the first place. This constant cycle of buying, losing, and buying more can quickly turn that inadequate $20 into $2,000 within only a few weeks.

Brands and celebrities are more likely to buy these likes, follows, views, comments, and re-grams than anyone else, tactics used in attempts to wipe out their competition and showcase their popularity. This is one of the most common tricks in the book. Buying your first hundred or first thousand followers will allow other users to see how popular you are and want to follow you as well, eventually (hopefully) turning those first 3,000 fake followers turn into 3,000 real followers. Not only does this rarely work, but this is deceitful for real users who follow these profiles in that they become enticed by products that may actually be terrible, and can also negatively impact businesses as they become exposed for being frauds and for purchasing popularity. Attempting to trick the system can hurt profiles more than they can help because once a user is caught as being a fraud, it goes public and becomes harder for them to recover.

Everyone says commitment is the key to Instagram success, loyal followers who will always invest time into liking and commenting on posts. Buying fake followers is not the same as having loyal followers. True that it may be, the numbers are still there. 5,000 is the same as 5,000, but 5,000 real followers are far different from 5,000 fake followers. 5,000 bot followers who never engage with profiles can easily expose that account as a fraud.

If an influencer account shows 5,000 followers but only gets 5 likes per post, what the hell is going on with the others? On average, real Instagram accounts get at least 5-10% likes per number of followers, giving an account of 5,000 followers an average of 500 likes per post, not 5. Simply typing "buy IG likes" into Google will result in hundreds of links connected to "genuine and verifiable likes" for as little as one cent per like, with bundles of 100 going for as little as $3! All these sites require is your credit card information and your Instagram name with permission for them to hack onto your feed and bombard your sad profile with a shit ton of likes and followers.

They then provide you with the option of either splitting up these bought likes among multiple posts or adding them all to one post, as well as the option of obtaining all your followers at once or spread out within a span of several hours. People often go for these sporadic options when they think they can avoid having others find out that they buy likes and followers. They think that by having their followers appear sporadically, they can make up an excuse that says their "post became a hit overnight."

However, despite how much we try to make these purchased followers look authentic, we forget that people can still find out the truth by clicking on our followers and seeing that all these "magnificent followers" overnight have no profile pictures, no posts, and account names we cannot even pronounce, giving us away anyway.

Instagram users are not the only ones to utilize fake likes and followers on their accounts, using counterfeit spawns to boost popularity. In 2019, Facebook discovered that over 2.2 billion users had utilized fake accounts, and in 2013, YouTube discovered that over half its traffic were from bots and paid laborers. As more people religiously purchase likes and followers, the amounts of genuine likes and commitments begin to decrease as people realize that their influencers are actually fakes. Regardless of how many likes or followers were actually purchased, paid commitment never brings the business loyalty as real followers do. How much business can business owners actually get when over half their followers are fake? If the goal is to sell more of their products, they are going the opposite direction as bots cannot buy anything and can never help with brand dependability. The best these bots can ever do is make profiles APPEAR better than they actually are, and what good does that accomplish anyway?

In 2019, the Institute of Contemporary Music Performance executed an extensive search and found that almost all their renowned students had purchased at least 50% of their Instagram followers. These purchased bots are often sought after to give big names a push ahead of their competitors, a way to pull in new followers if people think they're more famous than they actually are. We all know how difficult it is to achieve genuine followers. Even if we think people will never find out that we bought followers, it still stands out as suspicious when we gain a suspiciously high number of followers overnight for a subpar post. No one wants to take the time to wait for a trickle of followers to appear. We all want instant gratification, and we always want to take the easy routes to get the most rewards, making the idea of buying Instagram followers that much more tempting.

Gaining fake Instagram followers usually come within a matter of an hour or two, with notices that bring that desired feeling of being famous like celebrities. These notices become energizing for a day or two, with over 1,000 new followers in less than 24 hours, until we either feel the need to buy more and more to keep up with the demand, or we see our follower counts quickly drop off when we have tried to cheap out and buy lower quality bot followers, going from 20,000 followers to just 10,000 in a week (more expensive followers aren't that much better, dropping from 20,000 to 15,000 in less than a month at the cost of more than these followers are worth).

Cheating Instagram by selling fake followers, likes, and comments have become a major business for a lot of companies, so big that Instagram began cracking down on this illegal business and filed lawsuits against companies that sold these fraudulent accounts. Still, more and more of these businesses are popping up, and people are still buying them despite the risk of having their accounts banned.

Social Media Series Limited, a New Zealand organization, sold fake likes and followers through sites such as SocialEnvy.co, IGFamous.net, and Likesocial.co, where users paid between $10-$99 every week for these fraudulent activities. In only a year, this organization made over 9.4 million dollars, in which a claim was then filed against them for "drawing in and benefiting users with promises of phony preferences, perspectives, and devotees on Instagram," violating the US Computer Fraud and Abuse Act cybersecurity law.

"Inauthentic action has no spot on our foundation. That is the reason we give critical assets to recognizing and halting this conduct, including obstructing the creation and utilization of phony records, and utilizing AI innovation to proactively discover and expel inauthentic movement from Instagram."

~Facebook

What's the point of buying Instagram followers? Fake followers never actually interact with our profiles. Imagine traveling on a cruise to Antarctica, a dream come true, posting that experience on Instagram to share with your one million followers, and hoping to receive a surplus of likes and even new followers in return. However, the next morning, you wake up with only two likes and zero comments, wondering where all your loyal followers had gone before remembering that all your followers are fake. The more we buy followers, the more we deceive ourselves into believing our followers are real, and the more we engage in activities we don't even like to please followers who don't even have opinions of their own.

Additionally, for those potential influencers hoping to get sponsored, sponsors know when accounts are fake. They can tell when users have bought followers or not just by doing a quick scan of the types of people following them, whether they are trolls and bots, or actual users with lives and posts of their own. Once sponsors discover that certain posts have been a fraud, it immediately discredits these influencers from becoming sponsored by them or anyone else.

Instagram is a platform that holds a high personal stake in maintaining their foundation as a place where users need to invest time and energy into making it big, similar to all other social media platforms. Be that as it may, a multitude of fake accounts don't really accomplish this purpose nor make people feel human or invested. Because of this, Instagram has been making efforts toward decreasing unwanted conduct and fraudulent activity, working day and night to remove counterfeit records, creating mass decreases in Instagram followers magically overnight, whenever wherever, with famous Internet celebrities going from millions of followers to only a several hundred.

Instagram has become the most popular social media platform, and not necessarily in a good way as it has also brainwashed its users. Nowadays, we scarcely even look through Facebook posts or Twitter tweets, spending roughly seconds on each one before moving onto the next. With the recent crackdown on fake purchases, companies have become sneakier when it comes to providing services that won't get banned on the platform, promoting their services as "100% organic" and "GUARANTEED to not get blocked on Instagram," which all never really last, causing increased differences in prices when it comes to purchasing followers.

For example, buying 1,000 followers from StormLikes costs roughly $12.99 while buying that same number of followers from Mr. Insta costs $35.99. Despite the claims of "organic followers," fake followers are often exposed with names similar to a keyboard, random numbers and letters with zero posts as opposed to real users. These sites to purchase followers allow us to feed our needs of wanting more.

We start off with 100 authentic followers and feel the need to have more. So, we buy an additional 1,000, hoping that would satisfy our needs and desires. However, after we get that 1,000, we are still not satisfied, thinking we'll be even more satisfied when we hit 3,000. What happens when we hit 3,000? We see others with even more, so we aim for 4,000, 10,000, 20,000 to eventually 300,000 and counting because as long as the option to buy followers exist, we will never be satisfied with the numbers we have, constantly desiring more worship and more slaves as we crave the thought of actually being famous. As we see accounts bringing in 100 likes per hour, we question whether these accounts are real, even if, in the rarest of cases, they are. What photo can be so popular that it just pours in likes by the second? Are people actually reading posts or are they just randomly liking images as a tactic for their own profiles?

Human beings are social creatures, animals who pine for others to like them and worship them so they feel important. However, with the algorithm that is Instagram, only those who already have a shit ton of followers will receive likes on their posts while the rest of us become forgotten and unknown, making us feel the need to obtain those followers by any means possible in order for our posts to even mean anything. I mean, what's the point of spending so much time and effort on something just so no one can ever see it because we have zero followers, discouraging us from social media, or at least from honest social media?

Influencers looking to receive sponsors but only have four likes per post and 100,000 followers should think again. Without some sort of more authentic and loyal following, companies are less likely to sponsor someone with a bunch of followers but only one comment that says, "Great!." In addition, these bots will never share your posts with others on their stories, leaving you still unexposed to the broader IG crowd.

CHAPTER 23
#INSTADDICTION

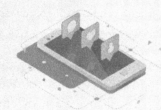

As we see the rise in Instagram influencers, we begin to envy them and strive to be just like them, pretending to show the world that we have something worth noticing also and a strong base of loyal fans who we strive to motivate and amuse. Consequently, as we hope, these loyal supporters show their appreciation for us by liking, sharing, and commenting on our photos and videos, all the while, we, as influencers, are paid handsomely for basically doing nothing.

This idea of being able to get paid for simple images empowers influencers and micro-influencers to fabricate a notoriety that makes them stand apart from their colleagues who aim for the same themes and outlets. Most Internet-based influencers always have certain themes they swear they abide by, only because they believe those are the most popular. One of UK's most influential influencers, Zoella, aka Huda Beauty, showcases her popular life as a beauty influencer, archiving every moment of her life through beauty products and tutorials.

Internet-based influencers are often seen as having the power to drive the mentalities and support of their followers, throwing content at them daily and believing they will see them or posting content solely based on what their supporters want to see, never really getting to post what they want to for themselves.

> "It wasn't until I joined Instagram in 2017 did I begin contrasting myself with others and wondering why I didn't look a certain way."

The psychological well-being of Instagram influencers is most often influenced by their followers. When influencers first open their accounts, there are already constant thoughts revolving what they need to accomplish and how they need to accomplish their goals in order to reach the status of "top dog." Their previous conceptions going into Instagram completely change when they realize they need to play to a different crowd in order to keep up with the increasing mainstream images.

> "When I first post something, and it doesn't get a fuck ton of likes, I become extremely disappointed and begin to doubt myself. I waste constant hours checking other influencers' pages and re-evaluate my scenario and how I can become more likeable and more entertaining."

"I let negative comments get to me, way too much, like I'm in a relationship with Instagram and constantly need its approval. One bad comment, and my day is ruined."

"Instagram has over 700 million active users and is developing each day."

"Instagram users 'like' roughly 4.2 billion posts per day!"

"Over 40 billion photographs shared, and 95 million every day!"

Having multiple Instagram accounts is common among celebrities and non-celebrities alike, with many having both genuine and fake accounts. VIPs and Instagram influencers often portray this to elevate their number of followers, meaning the more followers they can get per account, the more sponsors and cash they roll in. Significant influencers and celebrities have been known to make over $100,000 per Instagram post for doing nothing but parading around half-naked, showing young kids that this is what they need to be in order to also be famous. Some parents have also forced their kids to exploit their bodies as a means of gaining these desired followers and becoming Internet stars, forgetting what it means to be normal people with interests that don't need to be publicized to the world.

"In 2016, Instagram stories was released to showcase story highlights, Snapchat-style highlights where people can post pictures and recordings for easy access to their profiles, allowing users to pile random photos on top of each other and portraying them to the world over a period of 24 hours."

"It's a numbers game and super competitive; it's crazy how many followers and likes each person can get."

"I started by unfollowing influencers who have made me feel like my self-esteem is worthless. Honestly, I don't even know why I started following them in the first place."

"Realize that it's all fake, and stop comparing yourself to it."

"It's not real. Stop priding yourself on something that's not fucking real."

For the most part, although we are mindful of social media being fake with high standards that no one can ever meet, we still neglect to remember that when we compare ourselves to others on the Internet, we forget that the posts we portray are also not genuine while judging others for the same thing. Our insecurities continue to allow us to trick and deceive ourselves because it feels good to think, even for a second, that we are someone important, even if it isn't real.

However, the more we remain stuck in this mindset of believing we're someone we're not, the harder it becomes to break out of this pattern of loneliness. We end up believing that our fake Instagram lives are actually real, and we end up failing to be able to separate real life from this concocted life. We spend all our time and money on something that can and will never be real, and we become stuck in a mentality where we either give it all up and admit that we have been lying, or we continue holding onto this secret of being frauds.

We forget that, most of the time, the people we're trying to compare ourselves to online are fake themselves. So, what if they boast being true influencers with #nofilter? We don't actually know whether they're telling the truth. But, at the same time, we want to become like them so badly that we change our personalities and faces just to look like them, getting plastic surgery to make ourselves look better when these people we're trying to compare ourselves to have just Photoshopped their faces or are just fake accounts with stock photo faces.

"I need people who see me online to also see me face-to-face without asking themselves if a truck mauled down my face."

"On the off-chance that I have a flaw or blemish on my image, I delete it."

"If you see 3-4 pictures of me on my post, there's definitely a guarantee that I took over 100 before posting those few. I have to put my best face forward. I can't have the world seeing the ugly side of me."

"Before a photoshoot, I always take about an hour preparing myself, saturating my skin, putting extensions in my hair, perfecting my makeup, and so on. I also spend time rehearsing exactly how I want to position my body so I get my best sides captured."

"Although a few of us are attempting to keep it as genuine as possible, it doesn't change how online life is mostly curated and never shows the full picture."

"We trash-talk those we follow on Instagram, but at the same time, continue following them even as we hate them."

"We allow others to pull our self-esteems down, and we know it, but we still cannot get off the Internet. We find it difficult to cut the strings despite the deadly effects on us."

"Many of us hate Instagram with every being, and we constantly feel the need to leave, yet, we feel stuck, a feeling we cannot explain because of our addiction, especially if we're 'influencers'."

"Relying solely on Instagram as a source of income is deadly. Instagram is not a job; we can't expect it to sustain us in the long run. Once Instagram is done, so are we."

"Buying Instagram followers allows us to focus our time on others things rather than just Instagram. However, even as we try, it continues to suck us back in."

"The standard of what it takes to remain on top of the Instagram influencer board constantly changes; it doesn't matter how hard we try or how authentic we remain, what people want will always change, and pretty soon, we're yesterday's news."

"We focus too much on getting others to like us and getting by based on how we look. What else do we have to offer the world? What makes Instagram that much different from Tinder?"

"What will it take for us to feel good about ourselves? Destroy Instagram?"

We know we're addicted to Instagram and social media when the idea of posting stresses us out as it takes us hours just to post one image, but the idea of not posting at the required times stresses us out even more. When people, normal people at least, post images on Instagram, it's usually just as simple as choosing an image, throwing a random caption on it, a few dozen hashtags, and posting, putting the phone aside until the next morning. The rest of us, on the other hand, begin to twitch and seize when we feel like the option of posting online becomes inaccessible to us.

We spend so much energy invested in posting that the thought of not being able to post something at the scheduled times makes us feel paranoid that we'll immediately lose hundreds of followers if we don't. We become so dependent on Instagram that we lose sleep over not being able to post, always mentally preparing our next post, and calculating exactly what's needed in order to achieve the optimal amounts of likes.

We also let our addictions drive us insane and preoccupy our minds when we check our posts and only see 5 likes as opposed to our expected 500. We allow our self-worth and happiness to be driven by the validation of others on how amazing they think our lives are even when they're not. We drill it into our minds that if people do not like our posts, then they must not like us, and the number of followers we have dictate how well-liked we are.

But do you really think these influencers with millions of followers are really liked? Do you really think the lavish parties influencers claim to throw constantly actually exist, and that at the end of the day, they're not actually just alone in their pajamas? These "million-dollar accounts" may only appear so well-loved because other users either envy them or despise them. They see them as competition as opposed to idols. We stalk profiles of people we hate more than we stalk profiles of anyone else. However, we continue checking their feeds, wondering what they have that we don't and secretly hoping they post something about their own demise.

Additionally, as we all have done many times before, we become so obsessed with our profiles being 100% perfect that even after hours of perfecting our images and captions, we still end up deleting them when we don't receive enough likes per post or when we don't receive as much as our competitors. We face daily pressure with getting more likes, seeing the feeds we follow with thousands and thousands of likes per image and feeling like we can never compete. There's this constant bar we need to uphold in order to build any kind of image in the social media world. We hold ourselves to standards we cannot meet and allow our self-esteems to become crushed by the judgment of strangers.

Because of this constant wave of insecurity, we become even more attached to the app, refusing to take breaks even as we are engaging in important or life-risking activities. Do you know how many people skydive while taking a selfie and posting it, all while in the air? Do you know how many people speed down highways while taking selfies with their heads out the windows? Do you know how many people go backpacking in the woods and attempt to take selfies with bears as opposed to running away from them?

This idea of #FOMO makes it impossible for us to stop checking Instagram, whether it's checking our progress, liking other posts, responding to troll DMs that we receive, or simply watching live feeds. It has gotten to the point where we can't even eat dinner or watch TV without having our phones in our hands, or where we can't even sit through a meeting without itching to post about our breakfast because 11am has hit. We invest too much of ourselves into our Internet and web-based lives, wanting something we know we can never achieve or lack the motivation to achieve, disre-garding the events that happen in our actual lives to meet the needs of those in our online lives, and becoming agitated when people online do not like us or view us negatively.

Instagram posts are meant to make us feel shitty about ourselves, images posted by others geared toward making us feel inferior to them, from their extraordinary activities, expensive homes, and luxurious demeanor. Instagram users purposefully try to make us envy them and feel discouraged about our own lives and posts. Internet-based lives force a platform where people are forced to compare their sensible, yet, disconnected, real selves with their perfect, pristine alter egos, impeding their mental health and impressions of themselves. We are told to avoid showcasing our true selves and emotional sides because those are looked down upon, and we cannot tarnish our successful reputations online by portraying our true personalities.

CHAPTER 24
FABRICATING AUTHENTICITY

It's the age of 2020! Time to put forward our best Instagram games or drop off Instagram forever. This means, fantastic hues of filters, flawless live videos, pictures worth a million dollars, and the best concocted stories to portray our best selves. We attempt to deceive people about pretty much everything, from how we look to how we behave to how we speak to even what we do on a daily basis.

"I only wear cute and fashionable clothes. Like, ever!"
#OOTD #instafashion #daddysmoney #iwokeuplikethis
"I'm super, super vegan! I never eat meat products at all,
except egg whites, but those don't count." #veganlife
#kalenation #animallover

"I never wear makeup. I always have a perfect and flawless
face naturally. I think girls who wear makeup are trying too
hard." #allnaturale #freshface #naturalbeauty #bedface
#itrytoohard

"Oops, I didn't know they were taking a picture of me and
my perfect pose." #caughtoffguard #hotness #instastar
#nofilter

"I love animals. I am a huge advocate of anti-animal cruelty."
#animalrides #sittingoncamel #onceinalifetime

"I always keep random products by my side. I use them all
the time!" #sponsored #whatsitcalled #loved #awesome

"I cook at home like I'm in a 5-star restaurant. My friend's say
I'm the best chef around!" #masterchef #justwhippeditup
#noeffort

"I took this perfect picture on the first try! The other ones are
just backup in case I lose this one." #selfielife #perfectface

"I dug up this picture from YEARS ago with my childhood
friends! I can't believe I still have them!" #tbt #fbf #memories
#nostalgia

We willingly let ourselves become bankrupt by continuing to hide our false behaviors. Research has shown that the financial expenses of influencers who buy fake followers have risen to $1.3 billion. Influencers who feel the need to show off their wide number of supporters go through extortion to get an even bigger following, paying an average of $49 per 1,000 YouTube subscribers, $34 for Facebook, $16 for Instagram, and $15 for Twitter. In one investigation, it was found that influencers of the Ritz Carlton had over 78% fake followers, P&G with 32% fake followers, and L'Occitane with over 39% fake followers, an average percentage of 20% fake followers for influencer accounts with over 50,000 followers.

CHAPTER 25
EXTINCTION OF INDIVIDUALITY

THE INTERNET HAS BECOME a place of self-creation and self-invention, with more people using Instagram to promote and boost themselves. We live in a world where the Internet gives us the opportunity to become famous, Internet famous anyway. Look around, we see new stars popping up every day, from YouTube celebrity singers to Instagram models.

More and more people are dropping out of school to pursue their hopeful Internet careers due to how the Internet has taught us to believe that anyone can become famous and make millions of dollars on the Internet with zero to minimal effort.

We live in a time where we expect compensation for doing basically nothing but flashing our smiles or singing a poorly constructed song on YouTube and pretending to be a star. It has become so bad that even pet Instagram profiles have become so popular that they are beginning to make more money than those with normal 9-5 jobs. What pig needs to make $5,000 a month for wearing a tutu? We can't really expect to live completely off of our social media profiles, buying expensive houses and fast cars, before we realize that Internet fame only lasts a couple months before we become broke with no other prospects.

What happens when we no longer have access to Instagram? Will we still continue doing what we claim we love to do? Remember the "epic shock" portrayed by CNN, where the great social media platforms of Instagram and Facebook were shut down for 12 hours, causing a worldwide freak-out and people to become confused as to what they should do next with their lives?

People instantly feel disconnected due to the anxiety of losing all their followers, forcing them to attempt to send photos via other methods, even snail mail. We never think we rely on Instagram and social media this much until we no longer have access to them. We hear others say, "I'm not addicted to Instagram" all the time. Aren't they though? Most of us can only feel like we're part of something or are living when we are on social media, living only for others. We live and breathe Instagram, relying on it for every decision we make before acting on them.

Despite Instagram being down for only a measly 12 hours, a stretch of time that seems insignificant to most people as they'd rather be sleeping than freaking out over a stupid app, everyone else lost it. Businesses who spent hundreds on advertisements a day lost huge amounts of profit while many others saw this as the end of the world, having been so focused on this one aspect of life that they don't have a backup plan. We associate losing Instagram, WIFI connection, or even low battery on our phones with the same feeling as experiencing a breakup, heart-breaking moments that leave us wondering what we have accomplished with our lives and what we're actually capable of without the Internet. Nothing. But, this can happen. 12 hours without Instagram seems like nothing compared to 12 months without it, or even 12 years.

Don't quit your day job for your daydream of Internet fame. It's fun to chase something that probably won't ever happen for most people, but that glamorous hustle can very well one day disappear, leaving you with nothing but a crushed dream and a fuck ton of debt. Nothing is truly secure in this world, especially not our self-esteems.

CHAPTER 26
DISTORTION BETWEEN REALITY AND INSTAGRAM

For most of us, social media platforms such as Instagram, Facebook, and Twitter have become our second lives, lives we wish we could live but lack the motivation and time to achieve them other than online. What makes this different from catfishing? It's not. Although our personal information (well, most of it) remain truthful, we often alter our selfie images and descriptions about ourselves to portray lives we don't actually have.

Although we realize that many people share our same habits when it comes to posting the best and deleting the rest, some of us have taken this habit to the extreme, Photoshopping every bit of their reality so much that they themselves become disconnected from reality, unable to distinguish what's real and what's not, driving their psyches toward mental insanity and false self-perceptions. How much of an obsession do we need before we realize that we are not our Internet lives, no matter how much we try to portray our Internet lives as truths?

These influencers and big names that we're so obsessed with are far from living authentic lives. From their perfect complexions to their unusual optimism, how many people in reality dance around in ball gowns everywhere they go?

Unfortunately, only a few of us are able to distinguish between what's reality and what's not, attempting to reveal this fabrication of masks that exists behind the cameras of these unrealistic portrayals of everyday life. To debunk these false perceptions, more and more people have been exposing the truth behind these posts, including posting pictures showing before and after photos of "genuine" posts known as the #Instagramtreatment, and YouTubers posting videos revealing the appalling truth behind celebrated influencers.

"Avoid accepting what you see online as truth."

"Take Instagram posts with a grain of salt, and stop comparing yourself negatively to others."

"People you see on the Internet are not what they appear to be."

Do people really care whether photos have been Photoshopped, or has it become the norm? There's no longer a need for us to resemble ourselves as we are because we have now become forced to portray ourselves in comparison to how others portray themselves, despite having to color in our blue eyes green or filling in our teeth to make them appear whiter.

As presets have become more popular in bringing in mainstream users, more and more potential Instagram influencers have been going this route to keep up with the increasing demand, throwing away thousands of dollars on presets that give their images the sparkle, glimmer, and shine everyone craves. However, after blowing paycheck after paycheck on these presets, people begin to lose sight of their own image, their own vision of how they pictured their posts. They begin to feel uncomfortable posting a picture that no longer resembled them, feeling uncomfortable even after obtaining thousands of likes. We fail to realize that we put so much effort into activities we don't even care about, throwing aside our travel images for Photoshopped scenes and missing what we used to love.

"Modifying reality takes more effort than just living the lives we envisioned."

Still, for some people, altering photographs is the only way they can maintain their standard of living. Take an influencer, for example, who rose to fame through her beautiful blue hues that captured the attention of millions around the world. Because of this, there's that added pressure to continue showing blue hues on her photos in order to retain her followers and sponsors that allow her to make a living on the Internet. If she were to suddenly remove these hues to portray her authentic life, many of her followers would immediately drop off as they no longer want to follow someone with subpar photos.

The idea of presets and image altering is nothing new. People have been openly decorating and polishing their images for decades to conceal the truth, whether it's with Photoshop, plastic surgery, or makeup to depict themselves as people they are not. We continue to show false depictions of the real world, living in fantasy and neglecting the raw unfiltered world. Presets add to that contorted conviction of being able to dress ourselves without effort and have others envy us for a reality that can never exist.

CHAPTER 27
STRANGER APPROVAL FOR SELF-VALIDATION

"Our self-esteems and happiness are literally controlled by
Instagram and Internet validation."

"We struggle to feel good about ourselves if the Internet
hates us."

WHETHER IT'S an image of a man and his dog, an image of a
young woman in a club surrounded by her girlfriends, or an
image of a bride and groom on their wedding day, we all
want people to like our images because it means they are

telling us that they like us as human beings. We all portray ourselves as ALWAYS happy and positive, ALWAYS grateful for what we have in life, and HOW AMAZING our current lives are because we want others to give us that validation that we are well-liked regardless of how superficial our posts may be. Besides, who's going to like a post of a woman crying her eyes out from a recent breakup, a man angry and punching a hole through a wall, or a mom pissed off and yelling at her kids?

We all want to be reassured and told that what we're pursuing is actually something to be proud of as opposed to a waste of time; yet, we become angry and hostile when people do tell us what we're doing is a waste of time. We say we want the truth and honesty from others to #betterourselves, but when it comes down to it, we all only want to hear what we want to hear, seeing everything else as insults and offenses.

"Instagram and Snapchat are the most harming outlets to individuals between the ages of 14 and 25, affecting their self-perceptions as they believe the images of themselves they see online more than the images of themselves in the mirror."

Despite how much we try to tell ourselves that the images we see on Instagram are false perceptions, our brains continue to reveal what we see as truths, disguising what we know with what's in front of us. At some point in our Internet lives, we become so used to what we see online that we see them as truths and trust what we see over what we know.

Over the years, traveling has risen to the top in social media, with computerized settings being shown as significant and an identity for young adults, claiming themselves as travelers, wanderlusters, or travel experts after only having been to one international country. They are quick to show how fortunate they are, to be able to have these experiences, always portraying themselves in positive manners while also partnering with others who have the same ideals. Especially for millennials, millennials who can barely afford to live outside their parents' homes, travel has become much more than a simple 2-week vacation. Travel has become a lifestyle by which others strive to follow, bouncing from country to country and accumulating debt, never settling down until they are in their 60s, seeing career and family as second to seeing the world.

Despite what kind of traveler you are, embarking on an island hop along the Grecian waters, shopping your heart out at new and trendy stores in Milan, or meditating in the great unknown in India, these travel excursions have made it big on the Internet, causing people to travel more and more, even as they run out of money, in order to appease their followers.

In 2017, it was found that the "Instagrammability," or how well-liked a concept or theme is on Instagram, of posts rated travel inspiration as the top followed. We relish in images of notorious travelers far off in the distance of beautiful landscapes in France, images of women with their backs turned toward us and their hands reaching out to an unknown camera man, and images where you can swear these people have just stepped out of Cinderella's ball and wonder what they're doing on top of a mountain. Now, whenever you travel somewhere, you see other people attempting to re-create these same images, such as getting yelled at for having a photoshoot in the middle of a souk in Marrakesh or blockading entire roads just to reserve the Taj Mahal for themselves.

> "Seeing a beautiful picture of Istanbul doesn't mean we need to book a flight there."

It becomes sickening just how many people travel now just for that photo opportunity. No one really cares anymore about exploring a new town or seeing a different country; they all just want that picture-perfect image so they can brag about it online to people who don't care. People nowadays believe that if they can replicate amazing images, then they should be popular also. They just want that attention from others regardless of whether they are warranted.

We can follow someone's #travelgram all we want, admiring their beautiful pictures and pretend lifestyles, but when asked about the country and its specifics, very few know answers beyond the scope of "amazing" and "beautiful." It's disappointing how people no longer care about seeing the world; it's more about #doingitforthegram, something that can never replace actual memories. Years down the line, we will end up looking back at our pictures and not having those memories to match the images, regretting that we have lived for the Internet rather than for ourselves.

Web-based social networking has allowed us to portray the human experience as a meme, seeing and experiencing the world through one lens and one interpretation, causing more vulnerable individuals to neglect other parts of life or the idea that life moves in different directions and with different perceptions than that of which we see on the Internet. Individuals can become manipulated by what's truly reality when their scope of knowledge is only directed through one extremely limited channel.

Despite being the true ways human beings live their lives, satisfaction, positivity, and optimism have become the only acceptable character markers on the Internet world, superficial stances on life that almost no one experiences all the time. However, failing to uphold this standard of upbeat personalities and take on life, and rather, showing the "real," or aka "troubled," side of life, can lead to a precarious and unwarranted influx of trolls and critics. The only real way to avoid Internet hatred is by concealing external emotions, portraying ourselves to the world as the "person who is never flawed" or essentially, a robot.

Surprisingly, there are quite a few amounts of people, women especially, who report feeling ashamed and guilty when they share images on social media that do not coincide with the feelings they feel on the inside. Their constant blissful images with #blessed, #beautifullife, and #lovingit do not reflect the person staring back at them in the mirror at the end of the day. We try so hard to constantly show the best sides of us on Instagram that we forget what it feels like to feel anything.

We become so obsessed with seeing images of perfect people online and try so hard to be like them for those few minutes of fame that we end up feeling lost, confused, and hopeless about our own lives. We often forget that happiness is fleeting, just like all emotions, and that unless we're programmed to be happy all the time (don't say you are because you're not unless you're artificial intelligence), it is literally impossible to be #blessed all the fucking time. It doesn't matter how #beautiful we are, how #thicc we like to have others believe we are, or how #extra we like to pretend to be when we wave around a stash of Monopoly money, we will always have to deal with misfortunes and downfalls in our lives, some more than others, but not every day of our lives will ever be perfect.

There are some of us who fabricate entire Internet lives just for that shot at Internet fame, to become that "influencer" that most of us now associate as being celebrities who do more than just try to manipulate businesses for free stuff. We change our faces and backdrops so much and literally deceive others into thinking we're important because we're too lazy to actually put in the work, using face filters to make ourselves look like super-models when we're actually 20lbs overweight and posters as backdrops to make it seem like we're in front of the Eiffel Tower rather than in our bedrooms. The world of Instagram has become so fake that it makes it easier and easier to tease out who the frauds are. But what does it really accomplish when everything we have online are fake, fake posts, fake followers, fake likes, etc.? When nothing is real, it really doesn't matter what we post!

We can post an image of our bodies sliced in half or an image of us riding in a limousine surrounded by hundred-dollar bills and champagne, and our "followers" (more like fake followers) will comment with the same key phrases: "Yaaasss, queen!," "I love it!," or "Hahahaha," which doesn't even make any sense. Are those really enough to boost our self-validations? Knowing that a bunch of bots are liking our pictures? Does that follower or that like really matter that much when we know that we paid for them? We continue talking to our "followers" like they're real people with eyes and fingers to respond, but in actuality, we're only acting stupid for talking to, well, nobody. We think we're fooling others into believing we're so popular and so famous when our engagement rates are only 0.01%, a staggering low number for someone who claims to have 6 million followers.

So, what if we have that coveted verified stamp next to our usernames? Anyone can create a bunch of fake accounts and a bunch of fake sponsorships in order to get that. It doesn't mean they deserve it. We even go as far as to fake sponsored posts, taking selfies of ourselves with random products and throwing on the hashtag #sponsored, having others think we're special and getting paid for our posts when we're just fooling ourselves. It's all about the numbers, people! You have zero friends in real life, but five million online, and suddenly your ego goes up? We live in a world where we want so much but aren't willing to put in any of the effort, resorting to fraud and lies just to achieve what everyone strives to be. Can you believe being an Instagram celebrity is worth more nowadays than being an actual celebrity?

CHAPTER 28
EXPLOITATION OF LIGHTROOM FILTERS

ADOBE Lightroom (formally Adobe Photoshop Lightroom) has risen as one of the most popular software platforms to date as Instagram users have dependently relied on it to enhance their dull and monotonous photos. Lightroom allows us to upload our original photos and alter them depending on our likes and preferences, such as sharpening images, increasing contrasts, and even painting color hues over our faces. We can also adjust the white balance, modify exposure levels, adjust colors, fix spots, remove red-eyes, sharpen, and crop our images by using brushes to selectively adjust certain areas. Think, Photoshop, but for less skilled people.

Instagram has transformed our lives into a game of cat and mouse, in which we feel the need to be superior over others even when superiority is not warranted. We feel the need to show off our best selves to the world to the point where we also expect others to do the same. If we come across a subpar or unfiltered image of someone we know or don't know, we go out of our way to criticize them as being inferior to us, or we make huge efforts to showcase ourselves at the best places, with themed wedding destinations, unicorn parties, and pristine untouched beaches...whether they may or may not exist, just to one up them. After all, why be ordinary when you can take pictures of food at the best restaurants in town, spending hundreds of dollars on a meal just for Instagram, drink cocktails on tropical beaches just to say you were there, or abusing animals by riding on elephants, camels, and mules just to be able to brag to others about these "once in a lifetime" experiences?

Like how most of us are too lazy to generate real social media following without the use of alteration tools, most of us are also too lazy to generate our own filters, resorting to buying our presets from "Instagram influencers" who seem to have generated millions of likes because of their filters that can never represent the real world, spending thousands of dollars on filters alone in attempts to turn their minimal efforts at photography into money-worthy stock photos.

I once knew someone on Instagram who accumulated over $20,000 in debt from buying presets alone because the original ones she bought didn't bring in as many followers, so she continued buying and buying until, you guessed it, she's neck deep in crippling debt, all just for that chance to achieve perfect images that she can never truly claim as her own, resorting to begging, prostitution, and crime just to keep up with appearances, as like many other influencer hopefuls.

According to the BBC and the Huffington Post, over 30% of young adults between the ages of 20 and 30 spend their life-time salaries on promoting their online posts in attempts at those two seconds of fame, spending money they would not have otherwise for something that will probably become extinct in the next several years. We mindlessly blow all our paychecks trying to be like those we see online, trying to keep up with the ever-changing world, and trying to gain that coveted status and chance at becoming sponsored.

The irony is, we spend so much money and effort trying to be sponsored that we actually end up spending five times as much as what we would have made if we were sponsored. And when we find ourselves really struggling, with abso-lutely no way of continuing with our lifestyles, standing on chairs to take a restaurant quality photo of café food, buying and returning clothing we can't afford to boast our "lavish" lifestyles, and dropping our own images over someone else's face to pretend to be in places we have never visited, we delete our accounts.

"We believe life is not worth living until we can live it Instagram-style."

"We force our partners and families to pay for wedding destinations in extravagant places, like the Maldives or Santorini, just so we can have Instagram-worthy pictures on our accounts."

"We spend over $50,000 on a wedding dress, just to wear it in a couple of pictures and then never even look at the dress again."

"We manipulate our partners into proposing to us just because everyone else on Instagram is doing it, and we need to be part of the moving crowd."

We put our financial futures last because we're so busy accumulating debt by trying to achieve the impossible. That's why American and European millennials are having children when they're older and older. It's because they have spent all their time and money on Instagram that there's nothing left for them to raise a family with, putting their lifestyles of traveling the world and taking videos of themselves eating (yes, videos of people eating, called "mukbang," can generate up to millions of likes, believe it or not) over saving up for the future. Divorces happen so often because we have become so obsessed with the idea of relationships and getting a relationship rather than learning how to keep a relationship.

Those happy couples we see online are not actually as happy as they always appear. We only travel and eat in fancy restaurants because we want that chance to take that viral picture that will drive up our social media fame overnight, seeking out adventures solely for the purpose of social media rather than experiencing the interests for ourselves. This Instagram-based life is designed solely to make us feel as if wedding planning and relationships are easy, that traveling do not come with locals and tourists at popular sites, and that raising kids is the most relaxing activity in the world. We fall for these lifestyles and become motivated to try them out ourselves, just to find out that the Internet has lied to us.

"Because we keep buying fake followers and fake likes to enhance our Instagram accounts, and because we keep having to re-purchase these fake followers and likes to cover up that we bought them in the first place when these fake followers drop off, we end up becoming so addicted to covering up that we bought fake likes and followers that we don't notice how much we continue to spend on these fake likes and followers until thousands of dollars later, just to still see these fake followers and likes drop off. We take up second jobs, second mortgages, sell our belongings, steal, and other money we don't have just to keep covering up that we bought thousands of followers to begin with, until we either have to accept and admit we lied or quit Instagram."

So, we already know the vast amounts of people who spend their savings buying fake likes and followers, deceiving themselves into believing that these high numbers they have are actually real people. However, since the rise of these sites, sites created to sell people thousands of followers at low costs, Instagram has been cracking down on them and banning accounts for buying fake followers. As a result, people have turned to what we like to call "organic following," where instead of paying people for a shit ton of followers at once, we pay for services where real people help us boost our following by engaging in Instagram the "normal" way.

In other words, we pay for others to be us on Instagram while we sit on our couches and eat potato chips, waiting for magic to happen. But these services don't come cheap. These organic services can cost people up to thousands of dollars for a short one month of work. Another downside is, these services are never guaranteed, and even if they do get us 10 or 20 extra followers, they're not us, so our feeds and posts remain unoriginal and almost like we don't even own them, demolishing our chances of winning over a genuine crowd that we actually care about.

"As Low as $4 for 500 Followers!"
"100% Real Instagram Followers!"
"Purchase Instagram Followers!"
"Genuine Followers Fast!"

Adobe Lightroom contributes to the growing problem of impossible lives that people risk to achieve, including painting their own faces with paint because they don't realize that their influencers had slapped a filter on their photos. We see pictures that seem too good to be true because they are. Compare the Instagram pictures of influencers with one of their video highlights, and the person in the video seems almost like a completely different person than the one in the pictures.

Why do we spend so much effort turning our photos into a cartoon show? Everyone will know they're altered when we post them, but we continue to do it anyway and deny that they've been altered, even as we're called out for them. We become so accustomed to seeing altered and filtered images that we train our brains to believe that that's reality, and when we see real unfiltered images of people, we point those out as fake. What the fuck? No one has teeth as white as paper and waists that a baby can wrap its hand around. We see these altered images as so real that we expect people in reality to look like Instagram models, rejecting them if they don't. Imagine people altering and filtering their Tinder or dating app pictures. That is a very quick way to lure people in, yet, send them running the other direction when they see that you're not really who you portrayed yourself as online.

"Lightroom is a cutting-edge application that millions of Instagram influencers use in addition to fifty other apps to enhance their pictures."

CHAPTER 29
EVENTUAL COLLAPSE OF INSTAGRAM

Like all social media platforms, Instagram will eventually become outdated as more and more social sharing networks rise. The fall of Instagram, and even other popular social sharing platforms that currently exist like Facebook and YouTube, is inevitable, a sad truth for these so-called "Internet celebrities" and "influencers" who hope to make a permanent living from prancing around half-naked and asking for free stuff. I remember when I was a kid, people were obsessed with platforms like Xanga and Myspace, which have now become virtually unknown to younger generations.

"Trendy" platforms, as we like to call them, never last. We expend all our efforts and time rising to the top of Internet platforms that only bring us a few years of fame before the popular crowd jumps into the "next big thing." Facebook topped Myspace because of its ability to connect with others based on similar status, locations, and friends, pretty much an "acceptable" way to stalk people. Instagram topped Facebook for its ability to showcase maximum quality photos with minimal effort. But, this fame won't last. Pretty soon, another social platform will come along and dominate all existing ones, causing these influencers to become broke and homeless with no potential future prospects.

When Instagram falls, so do the interests that people portray on it. Will these food bloggers, fashion gurus, and travel adventurers continue doing the things they claim to love doing on Instagram, or will all those interests be tossed aside because they no longer have a platform to boast themselves on? Social media has become so popular because people can literally do nothing and gain everything, generating no useful skills of their own to survive in a social media-free world.

CHAPTER 30
RELEASE & UNPLUG

"Does Instagram make you genuinely feel good about yourself, or are you left feeling worse than you did before checking your social feed?"

"Have you ever tried to quit Instagram, just to find yourself re-activating your account days later?"

"Do you ever find yourself screaming and cursing about how much you hate the Internet and the fakes on it, just to find yourself taking and posting your own selfie soon after?"

"It's easy to start. It's harder to quit."

It's an extremely difficult task when we try to quit Instagram and social media because so much of our lives are validated by these platforms. Before I quit Instagram, I had over 20,000 followers and counting, feeling validated and important, almost like a star, when I posted an image on the platform and received thousands of likes (I know, conceited). Every like and every follow made me feel like I mattered and kept me motivated to continue traveling the world, even though at one point, I questioned whether I was actually traveling for myself or to please the anonymous social media environment. The hardest decision came when I decided that Instagram was sucking up all my time; my time was spent either taking the best pictures, coming up with the best captions, or scrolling through endless other feeds and liking random pictures just so they would like mine back. It became exhausting, but whenever I saw that slight increase in following, I literally felt like my life was complete. Pathetic, right?

Eventually, I made the decision to completely delete my account and never look back. It wasn't until stepping out of that world did I realize how fake Instagram actually is, with so many people bragging about themselves when over 80% of their followers are fake, and influencers with the nerves to ask for free stuff in exchange for publicity of them in a bikini with a hidden hashtag that promotes small businesses. It wasn't until I stopped obsessively trying to capture and film myself at extravagant places did I realize how ignorant people are for prancing in front of cameras in public, or running off to different places for that perfect shot.

Seriously, people take images of the dumbest things when they think they are influencing on Instagram, like lying on a sidewalk next to piles of trash or standing in front of a wall full of graffiti and calling it an "urban lifestyle." I went hiking at Zion National Park in Utah last year and, on my way back to catch the shuttle, my steps were blocked from crossing the street because two girls in sport bras and booty shorts were spread out on the road, yes, ON THE ROAD, taking pictures of each other with their butts sticking out, with the shuttle coming any minute (part of me had hoped the shuttle hit them just because of how obnoxious and selfish they were being. I mean, there were children there; they didn't need to be exposed to that culture).

When we step out of a world where we feel pressured to live life for other people or to live life only for the sake of showing others that we're better than them, we realize that we have so much more to offer the world than just our boobs and asses, and we realize how inconsiderate we have been while trying to keep up with the Internet, disregarding others and the world around us just so we can climb to the top of the influencer chain.

Nonetheless, Instagram is addicting, and it's addicting for a reason as the creators have spent time and research designing a platform people find it difficult to pull away from. From the minute we open Instagram on our phones, we are either bombarded by activity from others on our posts or by new posts from others that we can't seem to stop looking at because we're envious that we cannot come up with the same high-quality images. This continues to happen so often that, when the day comes where we decide we will not look at our phones, our anxiety will push us into wanting to because we know that there will be SOME kind of notification on it, making it difficult to step away for even a couple hours. We become so accustomed to updating our "followers" on our lives, commenting on other posts, or coming up with ideas for our next posts that we lose focus on what's important in life, spending up to 15 hours a day on a platform that, in reality, no one really gives a shit about.

We become engaged to a virtual relationship where we allow our moods and lifestyles to be dictated by social media, feeling discouraged and depressed if we are not well-liked, and only feeling optimistic and positive when someone likes our posts. We depend on Instagram to survive, proven by cases where people have threatened to kill themselves because they did not receive enough attention or to try to gain attention. Many people even fake their own suicides and mental illness just to get a few moments of fame from strangers.

When we step away from social media, we no longer have to live a life where we dedicate it to those around us. That's exhausting! We are free to do what we want to do for ourselves and at our own paces without the distraction of competition or others not liking the same things we like. We are able to spend more time with those we love and on things we actually care about instead of spending hours filming ourselves eating. We can enjoy what we eat and use the rest of that time on something else. We can now focus on generating content that we are proud of without the influence of haters telling us to stop, and we can wake up in the morning and NOT reach for that phone for once. Best of all, we can finally discover our true purpose in life even if others don't agree.

We learn to realize that remaining genuine to ourselves is more important than external validation because a life where we need to rely on others can never stay permanent as the interests of others also rapidly change. Although there is that constant fear of not staying connected with those close to us, social media is not the only way to communicate with people. When's the last time you picked up your phone to actually call someone? Although no longer a widely accepted form of communication due to chat, direct messages, and email, losing social media does not mean completely isolating your-self from the world.

"When I chose to give up social media, not only did I delete my Instagram, but I also deleted my online presence completely, Facebook, YouTube, even LinkedIn. I couldn't deal with the constant pressure and idea of having others judge me based on my online presence without getting the chance to know me. I wanted to be free from a world of cyberbullying and competition, and live more in a world where I can live life at my own pace."

CHAPTER 31
WILL SOCIAL MEDIA ANNIHILATE HUMAN CIVILIZATION?

"Instagram is a soul-sucking creation that will eventually destroy us if we do not crush it first."

THIS DEPENDENCE that we have on social media is SCARY! As much as we try to deny it, we live for Instagram. The phrase "do it for the 'gram" doesn't exist without reason. We have become so obsessed with trying to get that perfect shot that we fail to realize how stupid we look in public or how dangerous these acts are until it's too late. It has become an endless cycle of taking images of ourselves to show up others who aren't even looking!

I'm sure I'm not the only one who has ever tried to eat at a restaurant or relax on a beach, and suddenly, become bombarded by selfie-taking Instagrammers sticking their noses everywhere like they're the only ones who exist. Instagram has become a platform of nonsense, where people take images of pink walls and selfies while wearing fake mermaid tails and pretending to be mythical creatures. We go through extreme lengths for photos to share with complete strangers, risking our lives when we take selfies in the middle of a crowded road in New York City. Do it for the 'gram, guys. Do it for the 'gram.

Because we have become so reliant on this platform, we may end up perishing before Instagram does. An estimated 250 people die each year from taking selfies alone, all just for an Internet application. We follow movements we don't care about so we can get the attention of those who do, and for the chance to show others that we care about stuff also when all we care about is attention. The human population have become dumber and dumber as we no longer know how to think for ourselves or live for ourselves without the influence of others.

"The influencer hype will eventually come to an end, you know it, I know it. No one can sustain an entire lifestyle with no talent and a Photoshopped body. It doesn't happen in the real world! Pretty soon, these entitled influencers, who think they own the world, will face the harsh truth that they need to get real jobs."

"We have let our lives become controlled by external validations on Instagram that we now base our worth on how many likes we receive."

"We do not allow ourselves to feel good about our lives unless the Internet likes us."

"Instagram is the worst social media network for mental health and well-being. Despite the photo-based platform performing highly on means of self-expression and self-identity, it is also associated with high levels of anxiety, depression, bullying, and FOMO, or the "fear of missing out."

Instagram has gotten so out of control that any well-known online presence on the platform makes us believe that we are celebrities. We let this false fame get into our heads that, whenever we go out, we must end our days with millions of pictures that capture every moment of our awesome lives. We live in a culture where, unless we have proof through our pictures, no one will believe we did anything we claim to do. People have become so fixated with online expression over the years that the level of depression have skyrocketed as people no longer think they're good enough unless they have epic pictures.

Individuals become so obsessed with looking like the people they see on the Internet, whether real or fake, that they begin personal battles with themselves to achieve looks that are unachievable, including blowing millions of dollars on plastic surgery and suffering from eating disorders. This obsession detaches people from the real world, unaware when cars are headed their way as they pose for selfies, and neglecting their children as they have their kids take promiscuous photos of them.

"The world is turning into an inexorably innovation-adjusted society, and no one can live life fully without it."

This obsession with the perfect post on Instagram has gotten so real that it is now referred to as an art when people can post the perfect image, from taking a picture of the same fucking thing 20-30 times with over 15 styles of poses to sorting through decks to get the best ones to throwing on the most magnificent filters to really enhance the sky to spending hours coming up with the wittiest captions, just to do it all over again the next day because the current day is over from all that time trying to choose the perfect image. The mentality that most people have of needing to delete images that don't generate a ton of likes within the first couple minutes is detrimental. We lose sight of the genuineness and soul that comes with posting our first image, the image we actually liked, and instead, we present ourselves to the world the way the world wants to see us.

"You're not allowed to post more than one image a day on Instagram."

"If you get under ten likes on one post, you might as well quit Instagram forever because that's humiliating and pathetic."

"If your pictures don't look the best, you need to take them off the Internet because they're shit."

"If you don't have a selfie at the Giza Pyramids, then you can't call yourself a 'travel influencer'."

"When was the last time you didn't let Instagram control your life, where you actually went somewhere awesome without feeling the need to document it?"

Instagram-based life is taking control over humanity, as over 3 billion people around the globe and over 85% of Americans have an account on top of other social media accounts. The average American has roughly six different social media accounts, with Instagram, Facebook, Twitter, LinkedIn, and

YouTube being the most popular (more now given the rise of Snapchat and TikTok).

It has become so big that even pets and babies have their own social media accounts. What the hell does a dog or a baby need an Instagram account for? Not that they can use it. But, people continue to create these because they are unable to generate a following on their own, so they live vicariously through the fame of their infants and their pets, unless 4-month-old baby or a 2-year-old Labrador gets extremely upset when they only receive five likes on Instagram.

Instagrammers are always trying to brag about and show off their best selves to the world when they are actually just living in hopelessness, desperateness, and despair. We continue to live in futile ways, posting the best videos and staged images of ourselves, like having someone spit water on us to represent rain or having someone throw piles of sand on our asses to give us the "natural look," and we manipulate, in whatever ways possible, to get the most likes and comments on our feeds.

We experience the new reality as a life where we walk among others and continually compare ourselves to them, either seeing ourselves as inferior and need to change, or superior and letting our egos drive up our narcissistic tendencies. We become so obsessed, yet, then so embarrassed with the actions we engage in online, such as buying fake followers, that we either spend thousands buying fake interactions, or deleting our accounts completely if we cannot measure up or if Instagram purges are hard-bought bots. We post about our "hard lives" as an attempt to generate more drama and, therefore, more of a following when none of what we say is true. We pretend to have battles with ourselves and others just to appear controversial because people seem to follow accounts that defy the norms.

"Instagram has stirred such a war among strangers, calling

each other out for faking or stealing photos, that it has become part of daily life and a compulsion."

"We become slaves to our online worlds as we are fixated with what is portrayed online, driven by our animalistic desires to want attention by any means possible."
"We are addicted to Instagram."

CHAPTER 32
CONFESSION OF AN INSTAGRAM ADDICT

"I JOINED Instagram during the summer of 2018, well behind the game compared to everyone else. I never really cared about Instagram or social media; I just wanted to live for myself and do the things I love without the need to share them with the world. My hobby of choice was traveling. I haven't been to many places during my lifetime, and I really wanted to experience traveling to an international country alone. It seemed like such a dream come true, a moment I never thought I would be able to experience, that I wanted to document every moment for myself to remember a time I never thought would be possible.

I remember hopping on a plane to Sri Lanka for the first time, alone, naïve to the language and culture of the country, but ended up loving every moment, from the food to my interactions with the locals to the hostel stays to the elephant rides to hiking down to see the best waterfalls in the country. I experienced the most amazing three weeks of my life on this trip, spending more time on the physical experiences than on taking pictures and selfies, leaving the country with endless memories but only a few photos.

I didn't care. I didn't stand posing for hours, trying to capture my best moments and staging moments just to make my pictures stand out as stock photos. I was too focused on living in the moment and feeling free from the pressures of modern life that time flew by, and my limited pictures appeared crooked and blurry. I didn't care. I didn't need amazing photos to showcase my time in Sri Lanka; having experienced it first-hand was more than enough.

A few weeks after my trip, I started a new job. I told my new co-workers about my travel experience, and they encouraged me to put my pictures up on Instagram. Before then, I had never even heard of Instagram. I had a Facebook account, but I rarely used it so it became outdated. Deciding to give it a try, I signed up for Instagram, opened an account dedicated to my travels, and posted the three images I had from my trip to Sri Lanka. Over the course of the next several months, I continued traveling to more places, not for Instagram purposes, but because I had fallen in love with traveling from my trip to Sri Lanka.

I traveled alone to countries like Belize, Norway, Italy, Albania, and South Korea, and I loved every minute of my adventures. Taking only a few images again from each country, I posted those onto Instagram as well. I gradually posted images on the platform as I had them, never in a rush and never caring how many likes or followers I received. After eight months on the platform, I received over 200 followers with about 10 likes per post, which is far from a lot by Instagram's standards. But, I didn't care. I continued living life the way I normally would, never focusing too much attention on Instagram and only using it to post the few images I had each time, no filter, no altering, no Photoshopping, all 100% real with maybe one or two hashtags.

A few months after that, I started dating someone who had over 8,000 Instagram followers and counting. He was portrayed on Instagram as a 'fashion guru'. I didn't even know there's an online community dedicated solely to male fashion. He was so obsessed with his Instagram profile, taking images of himself in the same pieces of clothing, only mixed up, every day, and he refused to take a day off, calling Instagram his full-time job. Wait, I thought Instagram is just another social platform where people share posts with each other when they're bored or during their down time; never did I think people dedicated their time to Instagram like they would an actual job. Anyway, this guy broke up with me shortly after we began dating because he became offended when I called his obsessive fixation with Instagram 'stupid' and told him his captions seemed pretentious.

Come on, he was posting about the beauty of the world and how happy he was literally EVERY SINGLE DAY, and whenever we went out to eat, he refused to eat until he took the perfect photo and video of his meal. His food always got cold, and he never really ate his food because he would order the 'best sounding thing on the menu' despite being allergic or hating the ingredients. Despite me despising the pretentious and delusional attitude he showed, a part of me couldn't help but compare, compare my followers to his.

How was it that I was actually living a life, traveling the world and experiencing landmarks most people would die to see, while he took pictures at the same spots and dined at the same restaurants day after day, and still had thousands of followers over me? This began to tear apart my self-esteem. I became obsessed with my own Instagram account, constantly checking day after day to see if I had received more followers. To this day, I'm still not sure whether my strong desire for Instagram followers was due to the need to feel popular or the need to get revenge on this guy for dumping me by getting more followers than him.

My first attempt at trying to boost my following was to just travel to more and more places. I booked expensive tickets to popular travel destinations all over the world because I thought that would surely boost my following. $15,000 and memories of Greece, France, Japan, Iceland, Singapore, Australia, New Zealand, Peru, Egypt, and India later, my following only increased to a mere 500. Clearly, my plan to get more followers had backfired, and I couldn't afford to keep traveling the way I was. I needed a plan B. I spent days researching on how to increase Instagram popularity and began following all the rules, from posting at the 'best' times to liking and commenting on others' posts so they'll notice me and like mine in return to stirring up controversial conversations to offering random gifts to people if they liked, tagged, and re-posted my photos.

However, all that got me were lack of sleep, even less money, and my followers even began unfollowing me because they found me annoying and/or hated me for bashing on the profiles of well-loved influencers. I became desperate. Nothing I did was good enough to obtain those desired followers that I desperately wanted. I was beginning to lose hope.

Then, one day, I came across an article that featured an Instagram fitness influencer who was exposed for having over 50% fake followers that she bought online, followers that are Internet bots sold by companies in bulk to give Instagrammers all the numbers but none of the engagement. The influencer defended herself by saying that she only bought followers as a marketing scheme to obtain followers because people would rather follow accounts with higher numbers. I never finished the article. As soon as I found out that there's a quick and legal way to gain tons of Instagram followers, I went for it, never taking the time to think through the consequences my actions would cause.

I quickly Googled 'buy Instagram followers' and was surprised to find out how many results came up, with prices ranging from $0.01 per follower to $1,000 per month for 'organic' followers, whatever the hell that meant. I was surprised by how easy it was to buy an entire Instagram following account. Part of me knew this was wrong. I shouldn't be buying followers, right? What happens when I get exposed for also being a fraud? But, the temptation was too delicious. I wanted those numbers. I needed those numbers. Still plagued by my conscience, I found one of the cheaper services, a whole 5,000 followers for just a mere $30, typed in my credit card information, and with my eyes closed, I clicked 'submit' before my conscience took back control over me and made me change my decision. When I finally opened my eyes, I saw my payment confirmation and a note stating that I would receive my followers within the next several hours.

Barely two hours later, I checked my Instagram, and my following had gone from a mere 500 followers to a whopping 8,000, even more than what I had paid for. Of course, these services always give you more than you ask for to account for drop offs. Whatever the reason, I couldn't believe what I was looking at, a whole 8,000 followers. Granted, I know that number came from my credit card and that they were all fake, but just looking at that number gave me a sensational thrill I haven't experienced before: power. Any decently smart person would be able to click on my newly found 'followers' and quickly point out that these followers are all fake, all accounts with no profile pictures, long-ass names with strange characters in them, and 0-2 posts on each of their accounts.

However, I was banking on people not looking too much into who my followers were and more on how many followers I had. I know, from experience, that people tend to not really care who's following you; they only care that people are following you. They look at your number, your posts, and move on, never really taking the time to investigate your profile because, well, they have lives. Despite knowing my following was fake, I still pretended that I was hot shit. I pretended that I had a following of thousands of people who actually cared about my posts. This not only allowed me to brag to those I knew, but it also allowed me to take pictures of my daily life and travels as if I was actually someone worth noticing on the Internet.

I began to do the very things I hated, posing in public, taking selfies in public, pretty much everything we would normally do in the privacy of our own homes, I did in public. I had no shame. I even went as far as to buy more and more followers, never seeing my number as high enough, and even going as far as to strategically plan out how I bought my followers, only buying several hundred at a time and spacing the delivery times out so only a handful would show up on my account at once to make it seem more genuine. I thought I was outsmarting the system. I thought I had uncovered a secret that millions hadn't already tried before. However, my 'brilliant' plan was missing one crucial element: engagement.

Soon, people started getting suspicious, suspicious that the number of likes I was getting and the number of comments I was receiving did not match up, ratio-wise, to the high number of following I had. I had over 12,000 followers but only a mere 10 likes and 2 comments (if even) per post. A normal account with over 12,000 real followers would easily obtain hundreds, if not thousands, of likes and comments per post, or at least more than 10. My account was beginning to look fishy. It wasn't until one friend began digging into my account and trying to expose me did I really begin to take action. I soon learned that not only can you buy followers, but you can also buy engagement, i.e., likes and comments, both at different costs. Likes usually cost about $10 per 100, and comments about $30 per 50. I had already spent over $600 buying my followers and couldn't really afford to spend more on likes and comments.

However, I also couldn't risk having my account exposed and lose everything I had bought. So, with my eyes closed and credit card in hand once again, I bought 500 likes and 50 comments per post, every post, including the 220 past posts on my feed, just in case people decide to scroll down to see my pitiful history. I couldn't risk having them see that jump, from 2 likes per post to 500 only after a short amount of time. That would be too sketchy. Thousands of dollars later, I was finally able to fill all my posts with numbers that looked less suspicious, unless of course, people searched through those who actually followed me versus those who were fake.

Despite being in massive debt, I still saw this as not enough. I needed more. I wanted more. I ran out of vacation days to travel to more places so I began staging local areas around me as 'must-visit' destinations, where I would stage backdrops and drop endless filters on top of them to make my images seem more attractive. I also continued buying followers and likes whenever I heard that Instagram is purging fake accounts, a frequent purge they do once in a while to remove and expose phonies like myself. The more followers I lost, the more followers I bought back, a constant waste of money and trap I could not get out of.

This cycle, plus my continued addiction with buying Instagram popularity, eventually turned into my profile having over 100,000 followers, over 10,000 likes, and close to 500 comments per post, every post. I became so broke that I had to open up a whole new credit card just to cover these costs. Like all Internet stars, I pretended that I was a celebrity and deserved to be noticed wherever I went. I pretended I had sponsorships, taking pictures next to branded products with #sponsored.

No one ever called me out again. Some people believed that I actually had as many followers as I claimed to have. Others just didn't care enough to ask. Soon, my newfound lifestyle came to a halting end when I finally realized how much money I was feeding into this never-ending lie. It got to the point where I just couldn't continue this lifestyle anymore. By the end of all this, I was close to $100,000 in debt, spending close to $100 per post, just to keep people from finding out the truth. Shortly after, I deleted Instagram completely, never looking back, watching all that money I had wasted go down the drain as I went from being a nobody to being an Instagram fraud to being a nobody in debt. On the bright side, with all my fake followers, my number ended up exceeding that of the fashion guru's. I guess I won. Right?"

THE UGLY TRUTH

THE DARK SIDE OF BORDERLINE PERSONALITY DISORDER & THE EMOTIONAL MIND

A Crazy & Obsessed Series (Book 3)

PART ONE

CHAPTER 1
MY BORDERLINE STRUGGLE

My Story

SIX YEARS AGO, my psychiatrist preemptively diagnosed me with Borderline Personality Disorder on accounts of my "fluctuating moods," "manipulative lies," and "exaggerated stories." What the hell? Borderline Personality Disorder? What in the world does that even mean? A personality disorder? Me? Are you kidding?

What a joke! There's no way I could have a personality disorder. Is that even a real diagnosis? Personalities are supposed to fluctuate. No one can possibly have a stable personality all the time in all circumstances. That's ludicrous! This unqualified psychiatrist, with a master's degree in nonsensical lies, has no idea what she's talking about. I went to her for my depression, something I believe was also an overstatement, and now she's pointing out another mental illness in me? I bet it's just an injudicious scheme to try to render more money out of my insurance company.

I'm supposed to be distinctive; a personality disorder is the most preposterous disorder I have ever heard of. All I wanted were some simple pills, medication to paralyze and subdue the emotions that occluded my mind and made me hate my every being. I was not expecting to walk away with a brand-new label beneath my belt.

What the fuck is a borderline personality anyway? I refused to believe my verdict. Addicted to attention? False suicidal threats to prevent perceived abandonment? Constructed manipulations to deceive those around me into getting what I want? Destructive life behaviors due to impulsive decisions that I either fail to remember or deny later? None of those criteria sounded like me. Those all seemed concocted and used as justifications to diagnose me as "mentally insane" and throw me into the statistical pool of mental health diagnoses.

However, I was erroneous. Boy, was I mistaken! Have you ever heard of the saying, "You begin to behave like your label even when you weren't your label to begin with, just because someone in a white coat tells you that you are?" That's how I felt with my personality disorder diagnosis.

The more I was labeled and called my diagnosis, the more I slowly began to adopt it as truth. The more I started looking into my past actions based on the fabricated stories of several psychotherapists and psychiatrists, the more I began to forcefully connect the pieces together and believe a diagnosis I didn't even think was real.

Thinking back, my past relationships had all ended with me, on my knees, crying for attention, both during and after, even with people I never even dated. Breakups and unrequited love left me flailing and broken, a fish out of the water desperately searching for reasons to make others stay against their wills even if it meant I was seen as a sociopath while doing so.

I also somehow began to fear being alone and abandoned by those who didn't even matter to me, pawning for the slightest of attention just for the sake of having some. The end of relationships left me chaotic and frantic to replace the feeling of anguish and discomfort with literally anything I could grasp onto.

I developed strong attachments to anyone who acted like a parent and/or caretaker, exuding care or compassion, and I never gave relationships a fair chance to play through without feeling like I needed to control all parts of them.

I fled across the world on a whim to get away from myself after an excruciating breakup, somehow believing that was a therapeutic idea, only to end up calling my ex-partner from an airport halfway across the world, bawling my eyes out about how much I missed him even when I hated the relationship while I was in it.

I bounced back and forth between multiple short-term partners while craving for long-term companions I was never able to keep hold of, petrified to let any of them leave despite not being interested nor ready for the panic of ending up alone with no one. I always tried to have the loudest bark, engineering excuses, stories, and lies to get people to pay attention to and love me.

My impulsive actions never stood a chance when entering the realm of logical thinking; the strong instinctual and intuitive desire to take and demand overpowered any inch of common sense or rationality I had every single time. I purposely demolished positive aspects of my life in attempts to create unnecessary drama when I felt the current drama were not enough or when I felt attention steering away from my personal aura.

The constant need to feel more than I already was and want more than I actually deserved drove me into a hole I found difficult to crawl out of. The more my "tried and true" methods of manipulating others worked, the more inclined I became to use them despite who I shattered along the way. My struggle with a personality disorder I convinced myself to believe was existent left me with a constant personal battle of suicidal ideations and a disparaging lifestyle.

As a child, my parents never truly cared for me. Don't get me wrong, they were always there physically in terms of picking me up from school or feeding me when I was hungry, but they never truly understood me the way children believe their parents should. Even when they were around and physically nearby, I was still left feeling alone, neglected, and forgotten. I know, cliché, right?

My needs were never met mentally as I found myself constantly craving for love and affection, getting myself into accidents and injuring myself intentionally just to get my parents to notice me. Sometimes, my devious schemes worked. Other times, I found myself feeling even more disregarded and fragmented.

Most parents don't really understand the mental needs that children require in order to develop a mindset that does not become psychotic. The minds of young children are extremely malleable and easily influenced, so when they train themselves to believe a certain "truth" caused by their parents or someone close to them, they hold onto that belief as truth their entire lives, despite whether that belief is maniacal or malevolent.

Most parents believe that as long as their children have food on the table and clothing on their backs, then they are set for life. They fail to take the time to realize that children need to be nurtured and cared for mentally, to be understood and given the attention they seek rather than having their love bought with materialistic trinkets, or else they will seek it out elsewhere, including in damaging places. So, I did.

I sought out the care and attentiveness my parents failed to give me in the comfort of strange and random men, bouncing back and forth between men who paid the slightest of attention to me while taking advantage of and disregarding those I was already with. I began to see power in being able to grab the attention of people, casting them aside when I no longer needed them. This was the pattern in the endless mind-fucked cycle I called "dating."

However, at the same time, when I entered new relationships, more long-term and "stable" relationships than senseless hookups, I entered them hard, diving into them head first without fully getting to know who I was with and driving myself toward insanity when they attempted to leave, even after I had instigated the battles that caused them to want to walk away.

I saw each and every relationship like a puppet, a game which I could navigate freely when I wanted it to go my way despite my true animosity or affection toward them, and I had to have the relationships go my way or else I would feel like I could not breathe, hyperventilating with anxiety until I did something deadly to crush it.

I quickly turned from being extremely amorous and pleasurable to being withdrawn and antisocial to being neurotic and obsessed, chasing after those I neglected and never loved just because I dreaded ending up alone.

Loneliness was my biggest enemy. The fear of being left alone with my own mind drove me to a point where I would rather turn others against their own beliefs and intuitions than deal with the demons swarming inside my own mind. I guess my self-esteem was so low that sitting still with my own thoughts turned me into my own worst nemesis.

Imagine your worst moment as a child where other kids would constantly torment you, making you feel awful about yourself, and eventually causing you to take those taunts in as truths and accept every lie and every flaw they spewed to heart. That is what solitude felt like whenever I was by myself, a never-ending session of being bullied, enough to cause me to tear out my hair and scream into oblivion.

Every new relationship I entered made me feel as if my life was complete, with all my dreams coming true and everything I had ever wanted falling into place, ecstatic. However, because of this, on the flip side, every end of a relationship also made me feel suicidal as if my heart was going to explode if I did not do everything I possibly could to stop these massacres from happening. It wasn't until the end of relationship three and endless psychotherapy sessions did I realize that the problem weren't the relationships or any of the men; the problem was me.

I was my own source of the rage, disappointment, self-criticism, guilt, and depression that I constantly blamed my ex-partners for causing me, remaining in constant denial as I refused to take responsibility for any of my own self-destructive and Machiavellian behaviors.

Each potentially delusional end left me trapped in a black hole I desperately tried to crawl out of by engaging in toxic stalking and self-injurious behaviors, living a statistic. My deep sense of insecurity and trepidation of not being good enough for romance drove me to refuse to accept the truth in that others were capable of leaving me despite how hard I tried to prevent them from doing so.

The feeling of being left behind made me feel unwanted, used, and unloved. The thought of being forgotten made me revert to my child-like states, begging and pleading for attention from these ex-partners as if they were my caretakers and my life depended on them, propelling me into a further state of melancholy and apprehension.

CHAPTER 2
CASE STUDIES

Fear of Abandonment

As an easily influenced young child with a malleable and developing brain, Rachel was often ignored and neglected by her parents and left alone in the house. She had multiple babysitters at a time to whom she became attached, physically and mentally, just to watch them all leave, one by one, leaving her in tears and confusion.

Her mother never held her, and her father never told her he loved her. As she grew up, she became increasingly afraid of developing attachments toward anyone or anything for the fear that they will all leave her too, recreating the traumatic experiences and moments she suffered as a child.

However, when she entered college, she became obsessed with her philosophy professor. He was rugged and handsome, and she was certain that he was the person who would finally stick around and want to be in a relationship with her based on his beliefs on loyalty and trust. She wanted him. She enticed him, but he refused.

She became anxious and concerned that he would abandon her too, something she refused to let happen even though they were never together in the first place. So, she pursued him, doing everything she could to keep him from walking out of her life. When he transferred her out of his class, she followed him to his home.

When he refused to return her calls after she looked up his phone number on the school directory, she told his wife they were having an affair even when they weren't. She became extremely jealous when she saw him kissing his wife, and she slashed her tires early one morning. Rachel refused to stop her avenging behaviors, even when he filed a restraining order against her and moved out of state.

She became so focused on this one man and so terrified of the heartache that came with abandonment that she continued to follow him over the next seven years as he moved from country to country in attempts to escape. Her motivation became delusional for pursuing a man who never returned the same feelings, and she finally overdosed on mixed medications out of despair and desolation one evening in her car outside his home and died.

Rachel was so hyper-focused on her one goal that she was unable to calm herself down from her disturbed thoughts and behaviors. Her overwhelming emotions prevented her from thinking logically, and as a result, she reacted in inappropriate ways in attempts to stop the constant ringing and chattering inside her head.

She knew she needed to stop her infatuated patterns of behavior, but the piercing inside her mind pushed her to keep going. Her harrowing memories and past horrors of abandonment caused her to create a false attachment and perceived desertion toward a man who was never hers in the first place.

She idolized a hallucination with this man and lost contact with reality, engaging in behaviors that harmed both herself and those around her, threatening to harm herself if he didn't return her love, and eventually taking her own life.

Impulsive Behavior and Sensation Seeking

Madison was a straight-A student in high school, always obeying the rules and behaving as she was told, pleasing those around her. However, during her first job after graduation, she felt a sense of "feeling out of place" and "unfulfillment." She felt like she didn't belong in her mundane job as a nurse and itched to find something she loved, something she swore would complete her life once she figured out what that was.

She wanted the drive that made her feel more than the numbness she continued to experience. Decades of being mentally trapped under the rules of others made her feel out of touch with herself, and she no longer knew who she was or what she wanted. All she knew was she needed to experience some kind of thrill.

She impulsively quit her job, began shooting up on cocaine, drank heavily every night, and became a prostitute, all just to feel the "thrill" of being alive. She was intelligent but remained in constant denial of her actions, refusing to acknowledge the harm she was putting herself through. She knew her actions were out of control, but she refused to stop.

Soon, she became pregnant, not knowing who the father

was, and she had an abortion without even thinking through the consequences of those her action was affecting. She continued to steal from her parents over the next ten years without ever feeling guilt or shame.

Madison became emotionless as she quickly watched her life flush down the drain. Every night, she sat in her bath tub and cut her arm to relieve the numbing pain she felt inside. She hated her life, and she felt as if she could never go back to the life that used to be.

The human brain possesses a "braking system" that prevents individuals from steering wildly out of control when decisions seem out of the ordinary, and to prevent the mind from shattering into impulsive thoughts and the body from crumbling into reckless behaviors when emotions go awry.

People with Borderline Personality Disorder, however, possess braking systems that have become defective or malfunctioned in that they are no longer able to control the constant waves of emotions that devastate them, causing them to crash into a flood of consequences before their actions have been thought thoroughly through.

Madison was unable to control her powerful emotions and confused cravings of "what if" so she acted out with impulsive and self-destructive behaviors in attempts to curb her anxiety. She engaged in reckless behaviors with strangers and alienated herself from her body.

She jumped head first into promiscuous activities without thinking about sexual transmitted diseases or pregnancy until it was too late, and she experienced internal rage that eventually caused her to become suicidal.

Despite acknowledging that her behaviors were destructive, Madison refused to stop because her damaging behaviors also provided thrill and sensation, rushes of adrenaline and excitement when sexually acting out, binge eating, and abusing drugs that were strong enough to overcome all logic.

Unstable Relationships and Destructive Behaviors

Bridget started a seemingly healthy relationship with a man she "loved," spending day and night with her partner. However, six months in, Bridget began feeling bored in the romantic connection and started picking fights with her boyfriend out of nowhere. She told him white lies just to get him heated so his full focus would turn to her. She pretended she wanted to break up with him just to see him prove his love to her.

She started arguments from nothing and refused to back down until she won, even when she didn't stand by her own words. She only felt love toward her boyfriend when he was not around and when he was, she pretended like he didn't exist.

A year into their relationship, she noticed that her boyfriend was becoming detached. The feelings they had felt for each other the first day they met had disappeared, and she became excessively suspicious of his actions and intentions. She called him day and night to make sure he wasn't cheating on her. She showed up at his apartment in the middle of the night to tell him she loved him, and she became angry when he told her he preferred a few minutes where she wasn't smothering him nonstop.

His words made her become so afraid of him leaving that she became even more insecure. She grew livid toward and envious of every woman he spoke to even his mother and sister. She even threatened to kill herself whenever he chose to spend time alone instead of with her, continuing to suspect his adulterous behaviors even when he remained loyal to her.

Ultimately, he decided he could no longer handle her drama and overbearingness, and he broke up with her. As expected, this drove her insane. She needed to hold on even when he rejected her, buying him a ring and proposing to him at his place of work. She bombarded his phone with text messages, ranging from how much she missed and loved him to how much she wanted him dead. She stalked him endlessly, telling herself she was allowed to because he was "hers," and she could do what she wanted as a result.

One day, while he was walking to his car to go to work, she came out from behind the tree where she had been hiding for the past week and stabbed him in the chest, whispering, "I love you," as he fell, bleeding, to the ground.

Bridget had a black and white, dichotomous point of view. She went back and forth between believing her boyfriend was perfect and believing he was the devil. One minute, she was smothering him and the next, she wanted nothing to do with him.

Individuals with Borderline Personality Disorder, or BPD, have difficulty understanding the "grey" area, leaving them with the "go away / please don't go" state of mind, making it difficult for them to maintain stable relationships as they continue to instigate fights and create unnecessary drama to feel a sense of arousal, only resorting to "love" when the other person wants to leave.

BPD is typically mirrored through erratic moods, turbulent personal relationships, the inability to control anger, and self-destructive behaviors. People who suffer from Borderline Personality Disorder are frequently irate and quick to take offense at every word or action related or unrelated to them.

For causes not apparent to others, BPD victims unexpectedly become sad, irritable, nervous, or angered. They find trouble in accepting life as is without the constant need to stir up anger or drama. They fear abandonment, but at the same time, provoke it repeatedly by plaguing others with unreasonable complaints and demands. They either vilify or extol others and themselves, a condition known as "Splitting."

These sudden rejections are often followed by intense attachments or increased attention-seeking behaviors. In the mind of a BPD victim, one single person can be both a saint and the devil, roles that switch back and forth when this one person fails to meet impossible standards and expectations of the BPD victims.

Long-term ambitions and dependability often contradict a "borderliner's" personality where they lack a clear sense of self to remain a stable mindset without constantly seeking more, often talking about frustration and inner loneliness without grounds to hold their statements up on.

Borderliners engage in risky behaviors such as reckless driving, excessive spending, irresponsible drinking, and promiscuous sexual activity, as well as express threats of false suicidal ideations and desires, engage in attempted suicide without the desire for actual death, and execute self-mutilation as a means to grab the attention of others but only when others are around to witness their cries for help because they often tend to see the slightest of problems as catastrophic and unsolvable.

People with BPD experience emotional and unpredictable shifts of sensations, and they often find it difficult to maintain a steady ground after unleashing these emotions. The rapidly shifting emotional environment of people with BPD forces those around them to walk on eggshells, cautious of speaking or acting in ways that could further trigger the BPD victims.

People with BPD can also experience serenity, anger, depression, and euphoria all within a span of a few minutes, often causing people to mistaken them with victims of Bipolar Disorder, leaving Borderline Personality Disorder a misunderstood mental illness and phenomenon, often left unnoticed, untreated, and forgotten.

CHAPTER 3
THE BORDERLINE PERSONALITY

What is Borderline Personality Disorder?

BORDERLINE PERSONALITY DISORDER is a psychological condition marked by persistent inconsistency or recurrent instability in emotions, mood, perceptions of the self and others, personal relationships, and self-esteem.

Approximately 10-14% of the general population and 15-20% of patients in psychiatric hospitals suffer from BPD, more often than not, as a comorbid disorder with another chronic mental illness. The prevalence of this disease for women is 2-3 times higher than for men, similar to how women often suffer more from depression than men.

This increased occurrence has often been linked to premenstrual anxiety, incestuous relationships, or harassments from close family members during childhood, conditions more widespread in women than in men.

This persistent or intermittent victimization and brutalization eventually leads to weakened relationships, foreseeable failure and pain, increased distrust in men, and an overconcern with sexuality, sexual promiscuity, lack of inhibitions, deep-seated depression, and a seriously damaged sense of self.

According to the American Psychiatric Association's Diagnostic and Statistical Manual of Mental Disorders (DSM-5), personality disorders are characterized as persistent, omnipresent, and inflexible patterns of vision, thought, and/or actions that cause severe disorder or deficiency in the minds of human beings. These behaviors include struggles in personal relationships, incoherent and irrational cognitive habits, and poor management of urges and emotions.

Individuals with personality disorders are often difficult to live and work with because they struggle with proper and appropriate reactions to stressors of anxiety and constructive criticisms.

Borderline Personality Disorder (BPD) is a mental ailment that results in a twisted self-image, impulsive behaviors, unpredictable and intense relationships, and extreme emotional responses toward normal circumstances. People with BPD find it challenging to normalize their thoughts and mindsets, leading them to self-harming and self-demoting activities.

BPD is more commonly seen in western cultures and societies, where the concepts of "individualism" and "independence" are more widespread. Western societies measure and promote the value of success based on how much individuals achieve in both their professional and social lives in COMPARISON to those around them, pressuring individuals to live a constant life of competition or risk "falling out" and "losing."

This idealism makes people strive to create drastic differences between them and their peers, stepping away from the commonalities and norms of traditional society to achieve greater goals beyond the scope of ordinary life. Because of this lifestyle, most westerners develop a phenomenon known as "Self-Absorption," which have been highly correlated with BPD.

Self-absorption drives individuals to focus on a single aspect of life, aka themselves, and as a result, they develop this increased desire to improve the self through any means possible, including risking the emotional health of both themselves and others by constantly seeking attention through radical measures even when that self-absorbed attention is not validated.

Eastern societies, on the other hand, function more as social groups rather than as individuals. They prioritize giving and sharing rather than taking, adopting a more selfless belief in attempts to promote the greater good of society and others rather than themselves.

Because of this, easterners are less likely to fall into the temptation of developing the "Me Syndrome," where the focus of everyone else needs to be on them. There is less of a drive to engage in intense and impulsive behaviors to thwart attention toward the self.

CHAPTER 4
PSYCHOLOGICAL ENTITLEMENT

What is Psychological Entitlement?

THE TERM "PSYCHOLOGICAL ENTITLEMENT" refers to the belief that specific individuals or groups of individuals are entitled to earn more or deserve more than others without reason. They focus on the ideas of "right," "deservingness," and believe that when people contribute to a cause or to a situation, they are obligated to receive something in return for their contributions, a term known as "Psychological Privilege."

However, as we all know, this is usually not the case when it comes to the game of life, and so when people do not receive what they believe they are entitled to, they become extremely upset, viewing the situation(s) as "unjust" or "unfair," seeking out compensation for their work even if they do not deserve it and refusing to contribute further to causes even when their contributions were minor.

Psychological privilege creates individual differences between those with extremely high psychological entitlement levels and those with moderate to low psychological entitlement levels.

Those with high levels of psychological privilege are more inclined to believe they are more deserving than others are even when they are not, while those with low levels of psychological privilege fail to believe they are deserving even when they actually are and constantly pull their levels of self-esteem down.

Individuals with high levels psychological entitlement are more likely to agree with statements involving "wanting more," "being liked," and "deserving better" on the self-report Psychological Entitlement Scale because their minds have been construed into them believing they deserve more, a phenomenon where they truly believe they are worthy rather than just pretending they are worthy due to self-absorbed opinions of themselves or egotistical thoughts.

When psychological entitlement is represented in romantic relationships, there is an increased havoc of negative consequences on relational behavior, thoughts, and emotions. Individuals in relationships who report having high levels of psychological entitlement often respond negatively to relational conflicts and are often less empathetic, less respectful, and less willing to understand the perspectives of their romantic partners.

These individuals are also the ones who are more prone to aggressive behaviors, feelings of rage, and are more likely to act violent toward their partners, especially those who criti-cize them or challenge their opinions, a positive correlation with domestic abuse and assault.

BPD victims who struggle to accept the negative conse-quences of life and relationships are more likely to become increasingly susceptible to overwhelming emotional distress and distraught. Individuals with high levels of psychological superiority often expect experiencing positive feelings and outcomes as fundamental human rights, becoming agitated and disappointed when the universe fails to align with their needs. As a result, they resort to brute force and manipulation to re-rotate the universe until it does meet their desires and expectations.

Hallmarks of healthy personalities and mindsets include the ability to tolerate frustration and delayed gratification, and a resilience to intense adversities in life even when they seem unfair rather than falling through the cracks of the obstacles that come with the complexities of life.

Interpersonal symptoms that often co-occur with border-line personality individuals include physical, sexual, and mental abuse, both in childhood and adulthood. These patterns of abuse trigger a chain-reaction of increased inap-propriate efforts to avoid abandonment, impulsive suicidal and self-harm behaviors, and chaotic personal relationships due to a desperation to avoid abandonment distress.

Childhood abuse makes it difficult for adults later on in life to feel secure about their relationships with other people as children are often vulnerable to initial impressions. They develop the negative impressions they have experienced into core beliefs, such as, "I'll never be good enough for love," "I will always be alone forever," "No one cares about me because my life is useless and insignificant," and "If they won't stay, I'll have to make them stay," causing them to lack faith in those they are supposed to trust, such as parents and caregivers, and force trust from others instead.

Psychological trauma manifests in emotional damage as a result of distressing incidents, where those individuals affected lose their abilities to cope with the overwhelming stress that encompasses them. These distressing incidents can either be perceived as hallucinated threats or actual threats of physical and/or psychological harm.

BPD victims commonly experience psychological distress from past or existing traumatic memories, or they subconsciously create pre-constructed thoughts of past or existing traumatic memories that never existed.

Traumatic events or incidents that result in borderline personality behaviors and judgments are extremely subjective. What is perceived as disturbing versus what is not solely depends on the person experiencing the defining moment.

The definition of "traumatic" depends on how the affected individual defines it, assigns value to it, and is physically and psychologically disturbed by the situation. A situation that is seen as "traumatic" is most often an occurrence that correlates with a sense of embarrassment or disappointment, causing the individual to become silenced, rather than an incident that causes physical or mental pain.

In many cases, embarrassment and shame are the largest factors associated with trauma. It is much easier to become psychologically scarred by moments that demean the self-esteem and pride than by moments that cause physical or mental pain such as sexual abuse or harassment.

Other factors that contribute to how a particular individual defines trauma include cultural and societal beliefs, the availability of surrounding social support, and the developmental stage of the individual's mental state.

Borderline Personality Disorder drastically takes a toll on its victims' self-perceptions of themselves and their surrounding situations, causing them to react in ways that are generally not part of the norm nor accepted by society. Their intense fears of losing attention or those they claim to love drive them toward a mental state where they partake in extreme measures to prevent this actual or imagined perception of abandonment, leading to dysfunctional relationships.

The paranoia caused by their assumptions and premonitions causes their personalities to switch within the blink of an eye as they transition from seemingly loving in relationships to revengeful and loathing without reason or trigger. They experience extreme mood swings that are both unexpected to themselves and others, lasting from a few hours to a few days.

This phenomenon is known as "Emptiness Feelings," where individuals lose contact with reality and engage in risky behaviors that are detrimental to their well-beings, constantly seeking something that does not exist and throwing aside their stable careers, relational connections, and values to chase after uncertainty.

CHAPTER 5
THE CONSEQUENCES

Physiological and Psychological Consequences

Victims of Borderline Personality Disorder can experience extreme and intermittent panic attacks, especially when their means of seeking attention and preventing abandonment have failed, causing them to feel near death unless they achieve their goals of manipulation.

Panic attacks are manifested by waves of fear driven by an abrupt and immobilizing force, causing the victims to feel as if their lifespans are shortening. Sufferers report feeling increased tension and anxiety paired with shortness of breath and the feeling of their hearts uncontrollably beating out of their chests.

However, panic attacks are usually triggered in those with BPD, coming and going as different situations arise, such as the reoccurrence of romantic relationship separations with the same or different people or other panic-inducing situations where individuals feel threatened and unable to escape their own apprehensive mentalities.

Shame often goes hand-in-hand with attention-seeking behaviors in victims of BPD, frantically trying to prevent themselves from experiencing humiliation and mortification so much so to the point where they do whatever they can to manipulation situations to avoid the shame.

Shame is a conscious emotion that constantly reminds us of self-inadequacy, indignity, dishonor, remorse, and disconnection, a sign that specific situations or people have disturbed our positive feelings and optimistic mindsets. Constant and repetitive shocks of shame cause individuals to perceive themselves as flawed, damaged, and deranged, unable to fit in with the rest of the world so they seek out drastic measures to save themselves from being seen as "imperfect."

Desperate motives to avoid experiencing shameful feelings can often lead to addiction as BPD victims anxiously strive for admiration and responsiveness from those who threaten them by engaging in radical actions that prevent what is deservingly theirs from being taken away. They tend to correlate success with attention and believe that unless they are likeable and favored by all, then their lives and reputations are meaningless and worth nothing.

The terms "anger" and "rage" are often misunderstood by many as interchangeable. Although anger and rage are both considered results of emotional outbursts, they are correlated rather than mutually exclusive, as anger is simply a fleeting and temporary feeling that a person experiences when he or she feels offended or betrayed, while rage is an action of revenge and retaliation, a consequence that arises from the feeling of anger.

Rage is an intense expression of wrath and hatred that results when an individual is unable to properly control his or her anger. Anger, on the other hand, is often perceived as a healthy and normal means of expressing the self, an emotion that can usually be controlled or quelled if tackled from the right direction.

Rage is often perceived as a toxin that plagues and destroys the human mind, driving it toward a state of self-destruction when the lives of others and situations around them do not align with their own, making them unable to cease until the mind has been demolished to the point of no return.

Rage can sometimes manifest as a complete blackout of consciousness, where individuals cannot recall their actions when they were in the state of rage, their bodies behaving in ways that were disconnected from their minds.

Borderliners often experience rage when they behave in unpredictable ways; their anger motivating them to seek and do all they can to achieve their irrational and illogical goals, turning into weapons of self-destruction when they realize life continues to move on regardless of whether they achieve what they desire.

The dichotomous mindset of borderliners also makes it difficult for them to recognize feelings as transient emotions that can be disregarded rather than as strong forces that over-power their entire bodies and cause them to pursue and attain despite their deadly methods.

Many victims of BPD often express feeling "hollow" or "empty" on the inside, like there is a hole deep inside them aching to be filled but unsure of what is needed to fill it. Because of this, they constantly crave for something, something more that they are not able to identify or obtain, leaving them feeling lonely and unfulfilled, mindlessly trying to fill that void with shallow activities such as sex, drugs, and/or food.

However, because of this inability to identify their true source of emptiness, these shallow replacements are often never enough to truly satisfy their cravings, simply feeding into a dark, black hole instead. The more they attempt to fill this never-ending hole of emptiness, the more they fuel their impulsivity as they resort to jumping into decisions and actions without thinking through the dangerous penalties of their risky judgments.

Famous philosopher, Baruch Spinoza, once described sadness as "transferring a person from great perfection to smaller perfection." Sadness or sorrow is a mood that resembles an increased sense of disadvantage, failure, loss, and dejection.

When this emotion persists for extended periods of time, chronic depression and suicidal thoughts often result, leaving the ones affected feeling silenced, crestfallen, and withdrawn into the self, lacking the desire to engage in interests that were once appealing.

When these lingering feelings of melancholy are paired with severe and transient mood swings, they begin to resemble symptoms of Borderline Personality Disorder, an illness often confused with Bipolar Disorder.

However, the key difference between those with Bipolar Disorder and those who suffer from Borderline Personality Disorder is that victims of BPD more often than not act out because they have motives of seeking attention and believe their conducts of abnormal actions will help them achieve their sensational goals.

Paranoid and dichotomous ways of thinking that are seen as abnormal to the average human being become standard ways of behavior for those with BPD, including disturbing and demotivating thoughts on how they are terrible people for existing or how their lives do not matter as much as others.

These thoughts lead to uncertainties about their sense of selves as they experience extreme lows and paralysis for terse, but repetitive, periods of time. This paranoia results in constant anxiety over thoughts of loved ones leaving or abandoning them, the fears of separation causing them to act out in attached, dependent, and envious manners, often accusing their romantic partners of actions not being committed just to develop that sense of security.

When accusations and confrontations fail to resolve their worries, borderliners resort to obsessive stalking behaviors, accusing those around them of infidelity and tracking the steps of those who stay and leave. This paranoia can become so intense that BPD victims often find it difficult to separate reality from their constructed false accusations, believing and experiencing past "memories" of events that never existed in the first place.

This leads to patterns of dysfunctional relationships where those suffering find themselves extremely attached one minute with intense loathing toward the same partners the next minute, or becoming bored of those they are with only after a couple months and seeking out attention from others due to the initial thrill of being wanted and loved, constantly placing threats on their current relationships.

BPD victims often experience two types of behavioral impulses: a self-harming impulse and a self-destructive impulse. Self-harming impulses often include physical injuries to the selves, such as individuals cutting their arms with razor blades or purposely burning themselves on hot surfaces to feel any sensation. These impulses are usually driven by feelings of numbness or sadness, causing them to harm themselves in order to feel or as cries for help for unwarranted attention.

Self-destructive impulses, on the other hand, are portrayed in the form of reckless and irresponsible behaviors such as binge drinking, toxic drug abuse, excessive promiscuity, overeating, aggressive driving, shoplifting, destruction of property (self or others), and spending or gambling even when they are in extreme debt.

These sorts of impulses drive people to jump into risks before thinking through the consequences of those risks, such as the dangers involved in unprotected sexual behaviors, the deaths that could result from excessive drug use, and potential criminal records that could result from acts of kleptomania.

Self-destructive impulses are also often paired with fits of severe rage when these compulsions are halted or stalled from fruition, such as getting caught when trying to steal a magazine that was potentially seen as "the thing" to fill the emptiness inside or becoming bankrupt because playing that round of cards was the "satisfaction" needed for fulfillment, driving borderliners to seek out other, sometimes deadlier, ways to justify their needs.

Borderliners often claim to desire stable and healthy relationships, but time after time, they unintentionally hinder and destroy their chances of maintaining positive relationships. They have constant worries about failing to meet relationship expectations and maintaining positive relationships that they subconsciously seek out flaws in their partners and relationships even when there are none.

These insecurities tend to amplify when relationships become more developed and stable as borderliners repeatedly tell themselves they do not deserve love or happiness, that something must be wrong for their partners to stay, and they continue to question whether they are making mistakes until the stable relationships eventually do come to an end.

When these relationships end, borderliners are driven into the arms of those offering unstable relationships, those who confirm their self-destructive thoughts and anxieties, leaving them even more broken and prone to increase their borderline thoughts of wanting more and more attention from more and more toxic people.

The intense desires of those with BPD for relationships and "love" are often driven by overwhelming needs to fill the endless void inside their hearts.

However, borderliners struggle to maintain these relationships as they wrestle back and forth between making both their disease and their partners happy, a constant push and pull as both sides battle it out in the borderliner's mind, eventually coming to a crash and spiraling into a cycle of disappointment, delusion, and anger when the borderliner is unable to satisfy the needs of either side.

Partners of borderliners often find it challenging to maintain steady relationships with them as they find it difficult to satisfy their constant desires for attention and their unconventional lives of impulsivity.

But, beware, borderliners are difficult to spot, and those who enter romantic relationships with them do not realize what they are capable of until it becomes too late. Borderliners tend to begin relationships with high hopes and enthusiasm, seeming like the "perfect partner."

They provide comfort, compassion, and excitement, making their partners feel loved and wanted like most partners in normal, stable relationships. However, these acts of love, respect, and passion are all short-lived as the positive optimism of borderliners can quickly turn into negative responses and aloofness.

It does not take long into entering a new relationship before borderliners are triggered into suspiciousness and life-threatening anxiety, leading them to revert to dependent and clingy child-like states where they feel physically and mentally unable to let their partners go for the fear of being left alone again like they once were by their caretakers.

As a result of this foreseeable potential neglect, they engage in overly insecure behaviors such as excessively calling their partners (even in the middle of the night), physically sticking to the sides of their partners at all hours of the day (even when their partners are at their places of work), and becoming angry and skeptical when their partners ask for even a few minutes of space.

Victims of BPD commonly associate "asking for space" with infidelity and rejection, unable to see that people are naturally independent and have minds and lives of their own; entering into relationships do not mean the partners need to stick by each other's sides at all times, a truth unbeknownst to most borderliners.

Rather than acknowledging reality and the norms of life, borderliners become irrationally angry when their partners request time away from them, threatening to harm themselves if their partners do not physically stay with them at all times, and becoming jealous and seeking revenge when partners do decide to walk out, whether temporarily or permanently, sometimes even threatening to harm the partners' family members and friends, whom borderliners view as the nemeses who try to take their partners away from them.

Borderliners in relationships also teeter back and forth between feeling breathless and taken away by love, loving their partners until death, and feeling distant and emotionally withdrawn toward their partners, loathing them and not wanting anything to do with them, constantly lashing out with verbal abuse and denial toward their partners until they reach their breaking points and hint toward separation. That is when the gears inside the borderliners' minds switch.

Similar to their views toward themselves and life in general, individuals with BPD also possess a dichotomous perception when it comes to romance, portraying a "love-hate" relationship with themselves and with their partners.

Unlike "normal" individuals who enter relationships,

borderliners either see their relationships as "perfect" or "destined for disaster." One small argument or one slight disagreement is enough to automatically trigger borderliners to assume their relationships are coming to an end, unable to compromise or live in the "grey areas" of how seemingly "normal" relationships are supposed to function.

An individual with Borderline Personality Disorder often experiences a demoralized or uncertain sense of self, feeling inadequate or fundamentally flawed with no apparent reason, along with constant switches in how they feel about themselves and how this feeling affects their relations with those around them.

Their seemingly inexplicable anger, impulsiveness, and mood swings often push others away despite the intense desires of the borderliners to experience loving relationships. This rapid switch in personalities and the manners in which they understand themselves is known as "Identity Diffusion," where the individuals actively change their perceptions about themselves, feeling "on top of the world" one minute to "nonexistent" the next.

This unstable image of the self leads to eventual existential crisis and frequent changes in jobs, friendships, relationship partners, aspirations, and beliefs. The crisis of the unknown is one of the most common causes of self-injuring and risk-taking behaviors.

The constant shift in personality and goals of an individual suffering from BPD can cause their partners to become confused as to who they fell in love with, leading to relationship turmoil when the BPD victim cycles between love and hate.

One key characteristic of a borderliner is interpersonal hypersensitivity, meaning they find difficulty in maintaining stable and mutual beneficial relationships with others, always taking offense from what others say and never being able to truly trust the words of someone else. Romantic BPD relationships are often painful and conflict-laden, starting fights when nothing is wrong and become apprehensive that the partners will leave even when there are no signs that point to it.

On the other hand, they can also quickly shift to feeling smothered and afraid of intimacy with no apparent triggers, withdrawing from their partners just as quickly as they attach to them. The resulting consequence of these shifts is an inexorable back and forth pull between affection and attention to abrupt detachment and loneliness.

Borderliners also experience a phenomenon known as "Vulnerability to Abandonment," a condition where they constantly watch for signs of people who will leave them or people who will consider leaving them, even if these signs are minor such as a night out with their friends without the borderliners or a small family trip without external parties, and borderliners perceive these minor events as premonitions of separation and abandonment.

These "signs" drive borderliners to engage in extreme measures to prevent their premonitions from becoming reality, including public scenes of begging, stalking behaviors of their partners' every move, physically withholding their partners from walking out of their sights, and expressing dark lies, manipulating their partners by misrepresenting the truth and construing stories that provide leverage to prevent their partners from leaving such as feigning deadly illnesses like cancer or imminent responsibilities like pregnancy.

Although quarrels are often common and normal in healthy relationships, even the most minor of arguments, such as a partner mentioning to a borderline victim their dissatisfaction with how they failed to wash the dishes, can trigger an emotional downward spiral, causing the partners to feel like they are walking on eggshells.

Partners in BPD relationships are left feeling stuck and silenced, unable to discuss important issues or their own emotional feelings in the relationships without triggering a major conflict or having the borderliners threaten to harm themselves.

Borderliners often take the opinions and feelings of others personally, correlating the dissatisfactions of others toward an external situation with dissatisfactions toward the borderliners. They become defensive as they feel they are being attacked, and their minds instantly turn toward impending breakups and divorces when their partners are simply expressing their opinions and feelings.

When borderliners first enter relationships, they experience a phase known as "Idealization," where they place their partners on pedestals and feel like they are living in the "honeymoon phase." They falsely believe they have found their "perfect match," their soul mate who will save them eternal emotional pain and damnation...in every single new relationship they enter.

However, as the relationships progress, this idealization begins to diminish, reality sets in, and problems start to emerge, even if from nothing. When borderliners realize that their new partners are not faultless (this reality often sets in shortly after the relationships begin but can also occur years down the line), their idealized perfect images of their thought-to-be "soul mates" crash.

Because borderliners often suffer from dichotomous thinking, they have extreme difficulties accepting flaws as part of human life and that everyone, even them, makes mistakes. As a consequence of this, their idealizations quickly turn to devaluations, and they begin perceiving their partners as horrible people, leading their partners to feel unloved and depreciated, and the cycle resumes.

CHAPTER 6
COMORBIDITY

Borderline Personality Disorder Comorbidities

PSYCHIATRIC COMORBIDITY IS COMMONLY FOUND in most mental disorders, characterized as having the presence of two or more disorders in the same person at the same time, with symptoms of two separate diagnoses often overlapping and creating false diagnoses and a challenge in clinical treatment.

One of the most common comorbid symptoms that often coincides with Borderline Personality Disorder is an excessive need to harm the self, the physical body and mind included. Self-injurious behaviors are actions in which people engage in deliberate damage, such as self-harm or self-mutilation, toward their own bodies.

Self-harm behaviors usually occur when individuals want to inflict pain onto themselves as cries for help or as suicidal ideations, often leaving scars on their bodies as signs of psychological turmoil and causing damage to their tissues and veins to the point of no return. These are the individuals who usually want to die.

Self-mutilation, on the other hand, entails purposeful destruction or alteration of the body, such as extreme scarification, without the desire to actually harm the self to the point of death. However, this is not to say that people who self-mutilate do not also have suicidal thoughts, as many who self-mutilate also engage in suicide attempts that result in death from their injuries.

There is a common misconception that those who engage in self-harm or self-mutilation behaviors do so for attention as many also engage in these behaviors in the privacy of their own homes and make attempts to conceal their scars and wounds. The inflicted individuals can often become ashamed of these actions and hold them secret, especially if they are vulnerable and sensitive to rejection from others.

Self-injurious behaviors are common among individuals with Borderline Personality Disorder. Statistics show that over 40% of university students had engaged in self-harm or self-mutilation behaviors at least once while at least 10% had engaged in these behaviors at least ten times, with those who had experienced childhood abuse and neglect at higher risks.

Triggered by deep senses of desperation, uncontrolled depression, and a longing for death, suicidal behaviors tend to be more episodic and intermittent for borderliners as they often fluctuate between feeling fine and feeling despair, one of the most problematic aspects of BPD.

According to the World Health Organization (WHO), depression is the number one cause of illness worldwide, with over 300 million people suffering from this condition, with occurrences ranging from Major Depressive Disorder to Dysthymia to Postpartum Depression to Seasonal Affective Disorder.

Research has shown that almost 83% of individuals who suffer from Borderline Personality Disorder also suffer from a comorbid depressive condition. Because of this, many borderliners go unnoticed and are mistakenly diagnosed with a depressive disorder rather than a personality disorder.

Borderliners who experience comorbidity with depression often report feeling hostile and detached from other human beings, reporting passive-aggressive violence paired with active suicidal threats and co-occurring, non-lethal, self-injury behaviors.

They become dysfunctional, with extreme episodic dysphoria, recurrent temperament outbursts and agitation, depressive and anxious irritabilities, and feelings of loneliness and stress-related angst with serious dissociations.

However, these depressive symptoms only arise in those suffering from BPD when they are triggered by an external force such as perceived rejection or abandonment, and they usually subside when these forces are eliminated as depressive symptoms are often forms of communication for how the individuals mentally feel.

But depressive symptoms in those with BPD are not always reported as simple sadness; BPD depressive symptoms have also been associated with feelings of anger, shame, loneliness, and emptiness, where borderliners report feeling jaded and agitated with desperate solitude when they are despondent, their depressive episodes often caused by interpersonal losses such as the loss of a relationship.

Depressive symptoms also include recurrent depressed and empty emotions, as well as feelings of guilt, worthlessness, and helplessness with a loss of interest in previously-enjoyed hobbies. Those suffering from depression also experience decreased strength, difficulty in focus, memory, and decision-making, and increased risks of drug, sex, and alcohol addictions, further complicating proper diagnosis of the personality disorder.

When addictions are paired with Borderline Personality Disorder, the BPD symptoms only amplify, increasing the antisocial and manipulative nature of these individuals. Addicts are just as likely, if not more likely, than borderliners to react impulsively and destructively, with mood swings ranging from severe depression to intense psychosis, and engage in acts of deceit and risky behaviors, further paralyzing and destabilizing their relationships, finances, and employment.

Post-traumatic stress disorder, or PTSD, is a mental illness often caused by severely stressful situations, with major symptoms including hallucinations, nightmares, anxiety, and uncontrollable traumatic flashbacks, usually categorized into four classifications: disturbed thoughts, avoidance, negative thoughts, and mood changes. Many individuals who suffer from PTSD struggle with re-adapting to normal life and experience frequent reoccurrences of these symptoms periodically.

The comorbidity of BPD victims who also suffer from PTSD is between 25-60%, with sufferers of both types reporting early childhood trauma as opposed to those who only suffer from PTSD alone.

Individuals diagnosed with both BPD and PTSD generally experience more psychological and physical difficulties getting through life compared to those suffering from either BPD or PTSD, with increased complications in controlling their emotions and augmented mood swings and anger as a result of abandonment. This comorbidity also further increases the original symptoms of BPD, including emotional dysregulation, dissociation, attempted suicide, and self-mutilation.

Attention-deficit / hyperactivity disorder, or ADHD, is a chronic disorder that affects millions of young children and often persists into adulthood, affecting males at a higher prevalence than females as symptoms are more passive in females, with males becoming more hyperactive while females becoming less attentive.

Symptoms of ADHD include chronic difficulties in sustaining attention, hyperactivity, and persistent patterns of impulsive behavior that affect home, school, and work life. Symptoms often begin before the age of 12, with initial symptoms of low self-esteem and instability in interpersonal relationships for children.

Adults who struggle with ADHD, although not as common, find difficulty managing time, planning and setting goals, holding down a job, and often struggle with relationship issues, self-esteem, and increased addiction.

Literature consistently reports a high prevalence of co-occurring ADHD and BPD. Approximately 27% of an outpatient cohort of 372 individuals suffering from ADHD report also meeting BPD criteria based on the structured clinical interview for DSM-IV (SCID-II).

In another study of 181 adults, approximately 38% of individuals diagnosed with ADHD also met the criteria for Borderline Personality Disorder. A high co-occurrence rate was reported in a study of 118 adult females from outpatient clinics seeking treatment for BPD, where over 41% of these individuals met the criteria for ADHD during childhood and over 16% reported ADHD symptoms.

In a population survey by the National Epidemiological Survey on Alcohol and Related Conditions of more than 34,000 adults, they found that the lifetime comorbidity of BPD and ADHD is 33% while the prevalence of BPD alone in the general public is only 5.2%.

Impulsivity is a common overlap between those struggling from BPD and ADHD other than the two being considered "developmental" disorders with initial occurrences in childhood and adolescence.

However, despite the overlap in symptom, impulsivity in the sense of ADHD and impulsivity in the sense of BPD are drastically different. Impulsivity in ADHD includes constant interruptions and intrusions, often sticking their noses into the conversations of others even when unwarranted, and finding difficulty in remaining patient.

These behaviors in childhood can give rise to impairment of social functioning and self-damaging behaviors in adulthood, resulting in reckless driving, promiscuity, and aggression in interpersonal relationships, indirect results of childhood impulsivity.

Impulsivity in BPD victims, on the other hand, is characterized by direct self-damaging habits of reckless driving, promiscuity, and aggression in interpersonal relationships rather than acting as second-hand symptoms of another cause.

Eating disorders are another common comorbidity that is often found in individuals with BPD. Eating disorders are a series of psychological conditions that lead to unhealthy eating and exercise habits which can cause deadly health complications if left untreated.

Approximately 20 million women and 10 million men in the United States alone have or have had an eating disorder at some point in their lives, and by the age of 20, nearly 13% of Americans experience at least one type of eating disorder, with symptoms ranging from food restriction to food binging to purging behaviors such as vomiting and/or overexercising.

Among all eating disorders, three of the most common types include Anorexia Nervosa, characterized by an obsessive fear of weight gain and an unrealistic perception of body image where sufferers see themselves as overweight even when they're not, Bulimia Nervosa, characterized by excessive use of purging behaviors such as vomiting, over-exercising, and/or laxatives and diuretics use in attempts to keep weight down and is often paired with impulsive behaviors, secrecy, and intense feelings of shame, guilt, and a lack of control, and Binge Eating Disorder, characterized by an uncontrollable need to eat, but unlike Bulimia Nervosa, is not paired with the compensatory need to dispel the food intake.

However, of all the major eating disorders, Bulimia Nervosa is the most prevalent as a comorbid disorder with BPD, with common overlapping symptoms including impulsive and out-of-control decision-making and a dichotomous thinking where bulimics feel a strong need to dispose of the food they consume or all hell breaks loose.

The purging desires of bulimics can become so strong that the individual deep within the wraths of the eating disorder are often strongly influenced by complicated feelings that overpower logic and reason, and the affected use their behaviors as methods of communication instead of words.

Although the exact relation between Bulimia Nervosa and Borderline Personality Disorder is not well known, eating disorder symptoms, such as purging, often begin as a coping mechanism for individuals, providing temporary relief and numbness for the intense feelings of depression and anxiety being experienced, leading the individuals to continuously return to these symptoms for further relief.

Furthermore, sufferers may also engage in self-harm behaviors as a means of punishing themselves for the guilt and shame they feel from their purging behaviors. According to a study by Dr. Mary Zanarini and her colleagues at McLean Hospital, individuals suffering from Borderline Personality Disorder have a higher chance of also developing eating disorders than the general population without this condition.

She revealed that over 53% of patients with BPD also met

the criteria for at least one other eating disorder, 21.7% for Anorexia Nervosa and 24.1% for Bulimia Nervosa, compared to the 24.6% prevalence rate for all other personality disorders. Bulimia Nervosa individuals are predicted to have a higher comorbidity rate with BPD because victims of both illnesses have connections with physical, emotional, and sexual trauma during their childhoods, placing them at higher risks.

Roughly 80% of individuals with Borderline Personality Disorder experience some sort of suicidal behavior, including self-cutting, self-burning, and literal suicidal attempts. This is because they often experience this impulsivity of "having to" commit suicide when they don't get their ways, living mindsets of live-or-die situations.

Because of this impulsivity, individuals with BPD are more likely to commit suicide than any other psychiatric disorder, with 4-9% of individuals with BPD who will die by suicide, 50 times higher than the suicide rate of the general population.

This increased rate is likely due to painful negative emotions that sufferers often try to quell with further actions, with the most common ways being through self-injury and substance abuse. These suicidal ideations can have lasting effects on individuals with BPD, leading them to reject potentially beneficial treatment methods.

According to brain imaging scans, individuals with BPD have increased abnormalities in the metabolism and structure of their brains when compared to healthy individuals, which explains why they tend to have increased impulsiveness and aggression.

Research has shown that there is less grey matter in individuals who are more prone to high suicide lethality while those with low suicidal lethality have increased grey matter in their brains.

Of the BPD victims who had attempted suicide, roughly

89% of individuals were shown to have less grey matter than their counterparts, and out of the BPD victims who had not attempted suicide, only 56% of these individuals had decreased grey matter, showing that decreased grey matter in the brain has a positive correlation with successful suicide behaviors and BPD symptoms.

CHAPTER 7
DARKNESS BEYOND

Darkness Beyond BPD

INTERNAL CONTROL and the dysregulation of self-esteem are closely related to the false perception of grandeur that results from feelings of inferiority, fear, and worthlessness in which individuals feel the need to compensate for their low self-esteem with an increased sense of superiority, exceptionally high self-centeredness, delusions of unfulfilled desires, and limitless achievement, creativity, and elegance.

However, grandiosity is malleable. It can frequently

change when individuals become susceptible to vulnerability that causes them to become less shameful and guilty of failure. However, for these individuals, signs of weakness are almost never shown, and instead, they act out their shame and guilt in ultimatums, manipulations, reprisals, and/or suicidal threats.

Narcissism is often characterized by an excessive grandiose ideation of the self, a king who sits at the center of the universe, and all people and things around this "king" shall worship his every need.

Individuals with Narcissistic Personality Disorder (NPD) have extremely fragile self-esteem, and as a way to compensate, they overly enhance their egos and praise toward themselves, refusing to show empathy or weakness to anyone for fear of others discovering their "flaws."

Instead, their delusions drive them to exude a sense of undeserved entitlement, expressing illogical control and emotional manipulation toward those around them.

Individuals suffering from Narcissistic Personality Disorder exhibit similar symptoms to those suffering from Borderline Personality Disorder.

Both personality disorders experience intense fears of abandonment and become unable and unwilling to face the consequences, and instead, twist and downplay the words of their counterparts, constantly feign being the victims, and blame others for all the misfortunes occurring in the narcissists' lives, never accepting defeat or responsibility for their actions.

However, unlike borderliners, narcissists are less likely to engage in self-injurious behaviors as a means of seeking attention. Narcissists are more likely to seek out attention and avoid abandonment by denying and avoiding as opposed to begging and pleading, always putting themselves and their best interests first while disregarding the feelings of others.

Symptoms of those with Narcissistic Personality Disorder

include an exaggerated sense of self-importance, with a high delusional obsession for achievement, greatness, praise, and entitlement while taking advantage of others who could potentially benefit them.

They often remain self-absorbed, believing they are destined to be something greater than what life has given them, and they constantly seek out opportunities to enhance their "greatness" even if it means leaving the lives they have behind with no concrete goals to chase after, running after justified self-worth with privilege only they believe they have.

While the exact correlation between individuals with NPD and individuals with BPD has not been widely studied, few studies have found a positive co-occurrence between the two, with 16-39% of individuals suffering from BPD also meeting the diagnostic criteria for NPD.

Research has also shown that narcissistic individuals are more treatment-resistant and less likely to improve when their symptoms also overlap with symptoms of borderliners. Individuals who suffer from this comorbidity are less like to eradicate the symptoms of either disorder (19%) than individuals who only suffer from either NPD or BPD (6%).

The comorbidity of NPD and BPD can prove to be deadly in relationships. Both types of individuals tend to exploit their romantic partners in order to achieve what they want, plus, both groups are often paranoid and extremely fearful of loss and abandonment, creating a stressful emotional apocalypse for the partners in these relationships.

There is substantial evidence that shows how the Dark Triad traits of Machiavellianism, Narcissism, and Psychopathy correspond with the Cluster B personality traits of Antisocial Personality Disorder (APD), Narcissistic Personality Disorder (NPD), Borderline Personality Disorder (BPD), and Histrionic Personality Disorder (HPD), in how individuals who score high on the Dark Triad traits equally score high on the Cluster B personality traits, with psychopathy having the strongest correlation due to its high impulsivity characteristic.

Niccolò di Bernardo dei Machiavelli termed the trait "Machiavellianism" as "dispositional patterns to promote self-related goal achievements regardless of boundaries, rationalizations, or fairness." Individuals with this trait often are aware of the patterns and behaviors they are capable of and engage in but disregard the need to spare the feelings of others when reaching toward their goals.

Similar to narcissists, Machiavellians seek to take what they believe they are entitled to regardless of who they destroy along the way. These malevolent individuals score high on tests of callousness, impulsivity, coercion, aggression, and grandiosity, seeking thrills and successes regardless of who they inflict pain on or annihilate.

A study by Frodi and colleagues in 2001 identified the Dismissive-Avoidant Attachment Style as the most common descriptor of psychopathic criminals. Similarly, a study by Salteris in 2002 concluded how individuals who commit acts of violence are more likely to experience unstable and disturbed attachment styles.

In adults who experience traits of psychopathy, those with factor one traits are more likely to be linked to a hostile attachment style, with low avoidance and low anxiety, while those with factor two traits are more likely to be linked to a fearful attachment style, with strong avoidance and high anxiety, and are often in coexistence with drug abuse and aggression, consistent with individuals experiencing borderline personality traits and insecure narcissism.

Borderline Personality Disorder has been seen in some of the world's deadliest criminals, more so in female criminals than in males. Among them include Aileen Wuornos, an American serial killer and prostitute who confessed to shooting 7 men in Florida within a time span of 12 months, Jeffrey Dahmer, an American serial killer and sex offender who murdered, dismembered, and cannibalized 17 boys and men in Wisconsin and Ohio, and Kristen Gilbert, an American serial killer and former nurse who murdered 4 men in Massachusetts by injecting them with large doses of epinephrine to induce cardiac arrest.

Wuornos dealt with a rough and traumatizing childhood that left irrevocable damage on her psyche. In addition to enduring sexual assault from her grandfather, her mother also abandoned her when she was just a young girl, not realizing this truth until she was 11 years old.

Because of this early abuse, Wuornos developed behavioral problems and explosive temper in her early teens, making it difficult for her to maintain stable relationships as her childhood trauma forced her mind to enter primitive and dissociated mindsets, later being diagnosed with Borderline Personality Disorder at the age of 46.

As a child, Jeffrey Dahmer was severely deprived of attention as his mother suffered from constant depression and suicide attempts. He also discovered his homosexuality, but because of his fear in telling his parents and coming out with his sexuality, he, instead, fantasized about dominating men he could not have by any means possible, including murder.

Despite being diagnosed with BPD, Schizotypal Personality Disorder, and Psychosis during his trial, he was still convicted as legally sane and sentenced to 15 terms of life imprisonment in 1992.

On the outside, Kristen Gilbert seemed like any ordinary young woman, intelligent and with a lively personality. However, her borderline personality overtook her very early as she became addicted to attention, constantly wanting more and more for the thrill and security and manipulating her romantic partners into giving her what she wanted.

She had a volatile relationship with her husband while continuing to have affairs even after she had kids. During her 15-month sentence for a possible bomb threat, Gilbert attempted suicide, more for the excitement of drawing attention to herself than for death itself, causing medical authorities to diagnose her as borderline.

Victims of Borderline Personality Disorder almost feel as if they are not themselves, constantly moving in between relationships and hobbies, spontaneously jumping from one person or thing to another.

They experience high highs at the beginning of each new experience they encounter, such as new relationships or a new change, but these excitements never last long as BPD individuals often become bored of their stagnant lifestyles, and their impulsivity overtakes them in seeking something new.

Their constant paranoid thoughts pull them away from positive and healthy factors in life as they overthink even the most minute of incidences, struggling to distinguish between reality and imagination.

It's no wonder why Borderline Personality Disorder has one of the highest rates of suicide compared to all other mental illnesses, with over 75% of borderliners attempting suicide at least once in their lifetimes, and approximately 3-10% of borderliners completing suicide, exponentially higher than the average population.

CHAPTER 8
THE CHAOS

Borderline Chaos

ONE QUIET MORNING, Steve and Becca went out to a diner for a hot cup of coffee and some waffles. They had been dating for a year and had been living together for 7 months after Becca gave Steve an ultimatum to either move in together or risk having her walk out of the relationship.

Becca never had an intention of leaving, but the fear of Steve potentially sleeping with other women when she wasn't around drove Becca to the point where she felt the need to keep tabs on her boyfriend at all costs, forcing Steve to give into her demands because she seemed "perfect" in every other way, and he did not want to risk losing her.

Moments after they were seated, more and more people began entering the diner on this bright Sunday morning. As the sound of the pans rattling and the noise of the customers chattering increased, Becca's mind started reminiscing, with constant flashbacks of her traumatic moments as a child when her mother threw dishes at her father while they endlessly argued and fought.

Becca's eyes began twitching, her hands began shaking, and she continued to mutter under her breath for several minutes before Steve noticed her unusual behavior. Just hours ago, they were in bed, laughing and holding each other like they were all each other needed.

"What's wrong, honey?" Steve asked, curious and concerned about Becca's reactions toward the noise in the diner.

"Nothing, just nothing," Becca whispered quietly, her eyes failing to meet her partner's.

Uninterested in pressing the issue further, Steve then reminded Becca that his parents' anniversary is approaching, and that he will be gone for several hours later that afternoon to attend their party. Unexpectedly, he was shocked at Becca's response.

"What?! You're leaving me!? You can't leave me! You're cheating on me! I knew it! I bet there's no party. You just wanted an excuse to break up with me! Fuck you, Steve! I hate you!! You're dead to me!" Becca exploded at him just seconds before getting down on her knees and kissing his brown loafer shoes, begging for forgiveness and pleading for him to not walk away as the entire diner stared at them.

From an outsider's perspective, Becca's sudden public outburst seemed chaotic, uncalled for, and downright abnormal and psychotic. However, for the 14 million people in the United States alone who are also suffering from Borderline Personality Disorder, her verbal and behavioral outbursts seem like any ordinary day.

Borderliners make up 2% of the general population, but over 20% of the population residing in psychiatric hospitals with women more commonly affected than men. Their unusual rollercoaster of emotions alienates them from the people around them who become ashamed and embarrassed for the association as they often respond to simple situations with explosive outbursts.

If we look at the word "borderline" in Borderline Personality Disorder, the word implies that someone is constantly on the edge, living a risky and impulsive life and never able to stabilize and stand their ground. Their mindsets become a tilting ship, tipping off the edge of a waterfall, unsure of whether to release or remain.

Like most mental illnesses, BPD is a disorder that is not well understood by those who have never experienced it. Borderliners often describe their disease as intense adrenaline rushes through their bodies that unconsciously make them act out in ways that go against their moral and logical beliefs to the point where they simply want to curl up in a corner and forget the actions they had done. One moment, they'll apply for law school, and the next, they'll dye their hair pink and become a groupie for a rock band, never truly being able to make up their minds.

Borderliners often jump to conclusions without taking a second to think through the consequences, and they become quick to assume that others have rejected and abandoned them even if it's all in their minds.

Despite the nonexistent evidence, borderliners are stubborn in standing by their perceived viewpoints, feeling hurt and betrayed when they believe others are walking out on them, even if they are just going into a different room, becoming fatally depressed and self-destructive when people leave them even for just a few hours, and becoming suicidal and psychotic when people do not pick up their phone calls on the first ring.

Surprisingly, borderliners are more comfortable during chaotic and stressful moments in relationships than in calm and stable situations because they know how to function in disarray. When relationships are stable, they become overly anxious and unsure of when their partners will leave them, often unprepared for the violence and disturbance that could potentially arise from the stillness before the storm.

On the other hand, when borderliners are amidst in chaos, their assumptions all come true, allowing them to confirm the fears they had since the beginning of the relationship. They are used to emotional turmoil as they thrive on manipulating situations from playing out the way they're supposed to and feeling like they are in control even when they are not.

They continue to persist the deterioration of romantic relationships until they have solidified that their initial beliefs were correct, refusing to stop until they have worn the other person down.

According to Otto Kernberg, one of the first psychiatrists to define the borderline personality, BPD arises from the direct experience of physical and/or emotional violence by those around them, paired with biological abnormalities that cause the minds of borderliners to divide into "positive and negative buckets" where they separate positive experiences to avoid them becoming contaminated by the negative ones, such as individuals holding onto the positive memories of their partners despite their partners abusing and abandoning them.

Studies have found exceptionally heightened activity in the amygdala, a brain structure that forms part of the limbic system and regulates both memory and sense of emotional reactiveness, where the reactivity generates a hair-trigger temperature.

Furthermore, several borderline patients have a common short serotonin transporter variant, or 5-HTT gene. It affects the amount of neurotransmitters accessible to nerve cells, and the short allele has been associated with nervous, aggressive, and impulsive conduct.

Borderliners have a warped perception of time when it comes to dealing with traumatic events and uncertainties, seeing life and the events in them as chapters rather than as a chronological sequence of events where one moment drastically affects the sequential moments that succeed it.

PART TWO

CHAPTER 9
CONTROLLED BY EMOTIONS

Human Beings are Controlled by Their Emotions

WE ARE all controlled by our emotions. Human beings behave in different, and sometimes complex, manners because we frequently allow our emotions to drive our behaviors and influence the decisions we make that concern our lives.

The external stimuli that we encounter on a day-to-day basis stimulate our internal senses, releasing neurotransmitters that create the emotions that travel with each experiencing thought. This is why we experience similar emotions when similar situations to those of our past's occur as our emotions are tied to the way we process our thoughts.

Human emotions drive our decision-making more than logic and common sense. It is difficult for people to objectively make conscious decisions without allowing their feelings to impact them. The decisions we make when we feel angry versus when we feel sad versus when we feel happy will always be different regardless of whether the situations are the same.

Our emotions drive over 80% of our day to day lives while rationality only influences 20%. Therefore, most of us experience moments where we feel like we have messed up and failed, or where we experience regret because we feel like we made the wrong decisions. This is because we allow our emotions to get inside our heads and control the actions we would have made differently under different circumstances.

Our emotions also cause us to favor our bias toward decisions based on feelings of safety, security, and comfort rather than based on cognitive thinking. Have you ever found yourself thinking, "This doesn't feel right," which in turn, deters you from making a certain decision?

We go against making decisions we don't feel right about despite whether it's the best decision for us because when we encounter familiar situations that have turned us off before, our emotions trigger our memories and prevent us from experiencing the same "bad feeling" we had experienced in the past. Our brains are designed to make us feel safe so we avoid repeating an act or being in a situation that has made us feel "bad" in the past despite all the facts and logic supporting it otherwise.

Different emotions affect our decisions in various ways. When we feel dejected, we are more inclined to settle for decisions that go against our favor due to a of lack of motivation and drive to think logically through the consequences.

Emotions are the strong drivers of decision-making

because they provide information about our circumstances in the quickest and simplest ways that do not require cognitive skills. We view our emotions as our "default brain" because we tend to trust our instincts more than we trust our knowledge.

Research has shown that the human brain comprises of two parts: the logical part and the emotional part. The logical part of the brain is slow, rational, and allows us to think objectively. This part of the brain lets us deliberate methodically through a list of pros and cons before coming to a conclusion about any given decision.

On the flip side, the emotional part of the brain is more impulsive and instinctive. It drives us to perform actions and behaviors that we are not always aware of performing, creating unconscious awareness in most of our decision-making.

In fact, most of our emotional lives are lived unconsciously. Because our emotional mind has more influence on our subconscious, as opposed to our logical, mind, it drives our current behaviors to fit a pattern that we already had experience with and trust, and we are more likely to act upon imprints on our subconscious minds rather than reflect and reason with our rational selves.

Humans falsely believe that they abide their lives based on thoughts and decisions controlled by the logical brain, allowing us to feel more enabled and powerful. Truth is, our emotional brains are what really control our lives.

Think about it, we enact decisions based on our thoughts, but our thoughts are often driven by how we feel rather than what we know because our thoughts are often associated with memories and what we know we do or do not like based on past experiences.

For example, people who have experienced trauma in their pasts change their decisions and behaviors based on their thoughts of these past traumatic memories and the adverse feelings they have felt as a result of them as opposed to their current knowledge about said situations.

All the knowledge in the world cannot protect us unless we understand and have lived the experiences of what we can potentially expect.

Emotional intelligence, or our ability to understand, evaluate, and manage the emotions we experience, has been shown to play a more vital role in decision-making than our brains.

Researchers have found that people suffering brain damage, who have lost their ability to experience emotions, often experience a decreased ability in making beneficial decisions as they have not dealt with the painful feelings that are often paired with poor decision-making.

Our emotions can also influence our attitudes and judgments, which can drastically change the choices we make. Intense sadness can either prevent the self from taking initiative, or it can prevent the self from engaging in impulsive decisions.

Fear of rejection can either prevent the self from stepping outside the comfort zones, or it can prevent the self from contacting potential pain. Despite this, our success largely depends on our ability to understand and interpret how we feel before making quick judgments.

CHAPTER 10
EMOTIONAL PRISONERS

We are Prisoners of Our Own Emotions

WE ALL HAVE an unlimited amount of emotions that travel within our thoughts. However, sometimes the thoughts that course through our minds are not always for our own benefits and can sometimes even harm us.

Despite what we think we know about fleeting and ever-changing emotions, we still follow the "gut instincts" that go against our well-beings, and we become imprisoned to them.

We continue to let our minds construct thoughts and mind-sets that disturb our inner peace.

We are prisoners of our own thoughts, whether these thoughts are positive or negative. When these thoughts are positive, they align with our general beliefs that following our "gut instincts" lead to positive results. But when these thoughts are negative and sometimes even distracting, vague, or confusing, we listen to them anyway because we still believe our "gut instincts" know best even as they lead us to our demise. This creates a vicious cycle of dysfunctional behaviors due to destructive thoughts that we continuously try to talk ourselves into by falsely believing that "this time will be different."

Human thoughts come from past conditioning. Our minds and our brains are made up of different components. Our minds are made up of our environmental surroundings, the thoughts that come and go, as well as how much we absorb these thoughts whereas our brains are created based on our genetic makeup.

The thoughts that we experience daily are due to "conditioning." If we carefully dissect and observe our thoughts, we realize that this "noise" is actually comments, explanations, judgments, projections, fantasies, and dreams coming from our minds, all of which are based completely on our own "unique" conditioning.

There is also no such thing as "original thought." The ideas and beliefs that we have acquired and learned growing up act as a base on which newly-conditioned thoughts are added daily and subconsciously.

This is why overthinking situations never actually solve any of our problems. It only serves to give us the illusion that our problems are being resolved and that we are actively working through our issues when in actuality, it serves no purpose. We will always act based on our past conditioning over our current and learned knowledge because experiences are far more powerful.

There is a substantial difference between what we think and what happens in reality. We are all trapped in our own perceptions, which become the only way we interact with the world because that is the only way we can see it.

We are also imprisoned by the circumstances and environment around us, including our bodies, our parents, our cultures, our geography, our technology, our economy, our politics, our influences, our education, and our interactions.

While our memories and our experiences help us maintain a sense of continuity in life, they also hold us captive as we use them to build walls that surround us, imprisoning our open-mindedness and forcing us to see life only through a small-tinted window.

We can never truly experience reality for what it is. Instead, we perceive reality through memories from past experiences and worries about future experiences, creating a distorted version of the present tense. Eventually, we end up living in a cell that defines how we will feel and how we will react to any given event or circumstance.

If something fits into our perceptions of life, we feel happy and satisfied, and if it does not, we become hostile, anxious, and depressed. Most people live their entire lives in mental prison cells, confined to the dictators that are their own minds. We think that by locking ourselves within the confines of our own core beliefs without the flexibility to branch out, then we are in control of ourselves.

However, the solace that we foolishly believe we have placed ourselves in is actually causing more harm to us as we remain trapped in only what we already know, with no additional knowledge on how to handle situations that we have not already experienced. Because of this, our minds channel all efforts into protecting our survival rather than allowing us to feel truly free and happy.

Buddha once referred to living inside our own minds,

where we constantly avoid the unwanted and become attached to the wanted, as living in suffering rather than living in peace, a constant state of conflict between the "I" and life.

We experience brief moments of relaxation and enjoyment, but because of its automatic nature, our minds quickly return to a state known as the "Monkey Mind," jumping back and forth between the past and the future, taking our focus away and distracting us between what's real and what's only a figment of our imaginations. Time after time, we fail to recognize that life does not always play out the way we want it to, and that it is meant to have constant ups and downs.

We are all presented with situations that either play out as stepping stones to higher levels of consciousness, or we stumble on them and fall. When we perceive our circumstances as stepping stones, we transcend and associate these situations and situations like them with "goodness" and something we would engage in again.

On the contrary, when we fail to "win" in situations that are presented to us, we associate similar situations with fear, terrified of encountering these situations again as they have destroyed us once before. Living in fear inside our own minds prevents us from exploring and seeking the "Eternal Truth," hindering us from opening our minds and preventing us from accepting that the true meaning of life cannot be discovered through limited logic.

CHAPTER 11
TORTURED BY SILENCE

We are Tortured by Our Silence

HAVE you ever been in a situation where the words and thoughts are inside your mind but struggle to come out when you try to vocalize them?

However, even during this silence, these thoughts are still expressed subconsciously through feelings and emotions, however, often coming into awareness when it is too late. Our emotions allow us to express ourselves in ways where we are unable to filter ourselves for fears of shame or embarrassment.

Our sensations allow us to portray the words we wish we could say to others without the fear of judgment. Our emotions help us overcome the phenomenon we experience known as the "Paralytic Effect," where we allow our painful and shameful memories of the past to silence us from using words to express the thoughts we experience, allowing our emotions to help us overcome this mental paralysis.

We are not used to living in a society where silence is acceptable and welcomed. Our society forces us to associate silence with depression, a torture of the mind, whereas being vocal and expressive is often associated with signs of happiness and optimism.

When we experience a failure in being able to express ourselves the ways we want, we become mentally blockaded by our anxieties of not being heard or understood.

We feel trapped in the abyss of our own minds where we feel like no one could possibly help or understand us, where no one can truly see us for who we are while we continue to stay confined in our self-destructive and vicious cycle of feeling like we are not good enough and should just remain silent. This paralysis results in the loss of individuality the more we feed into our silence, and we begin to feel depersonalized and forgotten.

Despite using our emotions over 80% of the time to express how we are, human beings are still, to this day, afraid of allowing others to see how they really feel, attempting to push all their reactions down even as they are reaching their breaking points.

Why are we so afraid of expressing simple sensations that everyone also experiences, sensations that can help save our very lives? Some of us have the fear of allowing our emotions to clash with the opinions or emotions of others, wanting to avoid rather than stir up conflict.

Unless it's our own emotions, not a lot of people are mature enough to handle the passions of others without taking it personally or feeling uncomfortable. Therefore, we avoid showing our true feelings to avoid relationship divergences caused by possible dismissals of us if we opt to be honest.

Similar to this, there are those who reject the idea of having emotions at all. To them, emotions are associated with imperfections and flaws, leaving the person feeling defenseless, powerless, and vulnerable for the attack of predators if they let their guards down. They fear that emotions give others reasons to dismiss them as weak and frail if they shed one tear or throw one punch.

Our reservations of being dismissed or disregarded by others if we show even a hint of vulnerability drive us to hide our emotions for life to avoid any types of rejection or disapproval.

We literally set ourselves up for a lifetime of misery and agony just to satisfy our inordinate needs to please those we don't even know and to avoid making them feel miserable and agonized.

Sometimes, we end up holding in our true feelings for so long that we no longer accept that it is worth expressing anything about ourselves, pulling us into this black abyss where our self-esteem become so low that we are convinced that our lives will never be worth pursuing and that our relationships will never make us happy, leading us down a cycle of hopelessness.

As a result, we begin to accept that our lives remain stagnant and that if we're not happy or satisfied by this point in our lives, then we never will be. However, it's not the truth in the matter that causes us to remain stuck in our patterns of ineptness; it's the constant mindset we possess where we have told ourselves so many times that we are not allowed to express how we feel or what we want that these beliefs turn into reality.

Others, however, repress their emotions for more active than passive reasons of trepidation. They believe they can use their emotions as a way of manipulating the feelings of others into doing what they want, such as using sadness to drive others to pity them or using anger to cause others to fear them.

They sometimes also believe that those close to them, or even not close to them, should automatically know what and how they feel even without them needing to express themselves. This belief that the self is the center of attention rings true for many as they often expect others to simply give them what they want without them needing to ask for it.

Some people also act as martyrs when it comes to emotions, refusing to accept that they have any kinds of emotions other than happiness and joy, always trying to please others and refusing to acknowledge self-pain.

They invest wholeheartedly in controlling their feelings so when they experience anger or hatred, they do not know how to react. They often race to avoid as a way of solving their issues rather than dealing with them head on and disclosing their feelings as the fear of judgment and criticism is always right around the corner.

It takes a lot of courage and effort for people to be able to express how they feel and to share their opinions. Doing so puts them in vulnerable positions where they will either thrive or perish, and it's that anxiety, that unknown, that keeps people from wanting to self-express, weighing the costs over the benefits, and ultimately bottling up their feelings inside.

CHAPTER 12
NORMOPATHY

Emotions are the Key Drivers of Normopathy

CHRISTOPHER BOLLAS once described normopathy as the "state of being obsessed with fitting in with society, to the point where individuals completely lose their personalities."

Normopaths often pursue to conform to the beings and lifestyles of others in attempts to gain society's approval at the expense of their basic need to express their own individualities, their survivals depending more on social approval and validation than on self-approval and authentication.

This constant preoccupation with trying to be "normal" and blend in with everyone else is often used as a defense mechanism in attempts to hide behaviors that normopaths believe others will condemn, thus, causing them to become extremely self-conscious, intensely focusing on how they appear to others and the constant need to impress them.

Unfortunately, normopathy is a socially-accepted reality that represents our collective and neurotic denial of our true selves to protect our bodies and our minds from emotional injuries.

Although it isn't necessarily a flaw or a danger to ourselves to develop this belief of being like everyone else, it only becomes a problem when our neurotic thoughts cause anxiety and anger that begin to interfere with our daily functioning.

Normopaths can become so out of touch with reality that they begin to live in an imaginary world where their pursuits to "fit in" and "belong" impair their personal performance, personal identification, individual well-being, personal success, and ultimately, their entire beings.

But what causes seemingly normal individuals to become normopaths? What causes someone to have such a strong desire to fit in that they willingly throw themselves away? Normopaths are usually sprouted during childhood, where children have tried to express their voices just to be shot down time after time or have tried to dress in a way that they preferred just to be teased and ridiculed, causing them to associate "having opinions" and "being different" with "hatred" and "isolation."

They soon develop this core belief that they must blend in with the rest of society in order to avoid more hatred and isolation even at the expense of completely losing themselves, leaving them vulnerable to others and blindly following misrepresented words even if they do not agree.

Thus, normopaths are left feeling crippled and paralyzed,

unable to speak or think unless given permission to do so, and they develop intense social anxiety, avoiding new situations and even new people for the fear of further mockery.

Another disadvantage for normopaths is that individuals who suffer from normopathy often become acutely aware of those who do act out of the norm and outside of the constant patterns. Seeing someone in an outrageous outfit or hearing someone speak against the "rules" triggers a reaction in normopaths that can range from discomfort to rage to disgust.

They speak out erratically and spontaneously when they see others going against societal standards in attempts to relieve themselves from their own discomforts, sometimes even at the cost of their careers or relationships.

When we spend decades and decades hiding our true emotions, we end up wearing our masks permanently to hide our secrets and protect our fragile egos from the pain of rejection.

We eventually become psychologically dead and emotionally drained, unable to feel our own emotions and constantly taking on the emotions of those around us. We flee from potential emotional terror and into the arms of social conformity and self-destruction as we shut ourselves off from the pain of lost and betrayal, living an inauthentic life on the face of the Earth like an imprint of another individual trying to achieve perfectionism and giving up ourselves.

But who's to say what's right or wrong? Who's to say which are the correct "rules" we follow? The ones who hold the most power are always the ones who hold the most confidence and refuse to bow down to the injustice of others.

Normopaths become who they are because their insecurities cause them to doubt their own judgments and beliefs, and they resort to obeying the judgments and beliefs of others because they think they're "better."

Human beings want to fit in so much that they lose their

sense of self-worth by engaging in actions they don't even enjoy just to avoid feeling like outcasts. We give up on acknowledging our greatness, and we refuse to overachieve because then, we would be seen as "different" and "weird."

We are so desperate to please others and become what's considered "normal" that we dissociate ourselves from our inner beings, leaving us in a pathological, borderline, and eventual diabolical state.

When we no longer recognize who we are or what we want, what happens when we can no longer hold in our raging instinctual emotions? What happens when we finally feel like we have to express ourselves or risk mental explosion?

We become volatile and unstable, going back and forth between extreme and impulsive decisions because we are unsure of the goals we aim for as we become lost and forgotten in a world that only strives to promote the goodness of themselves.

CHAPTER 13
INCAPABLE OF SYMPATHY

Human Beings are Incapable of True Sympathy

CONTRARY TO EMPATHY, where we pretend to put ourselves in the shoes of others to understand their woes and sorrows, sympathy is a directed feeling of care and concern toward others with the desire for their well-beings and happiness. Sympathy usually implies a sense of shared similarities with others, promoting personal engagement.

However, unlike empathy, sympathy does not imply

shared perspective or shared emotions as sympathizing with someone is not the same as feeling concern for someone.

When we sympathize, we fool ourselves into believing that we are internalizing the feelings and emotions of others, understanding them. However, we can never truly feel sympathy toward someone else's pain because, in truth, we don't actually care about others, how they're feeling, or what they're going through.

We pretend to sympathize with others because we have been taught to care about others when in reality, we are self-absorbed, only listening enough to relieve ourselves from our guilt and never truly understanding the pain of others.

However, we are also unable to truly sympathize with others because of our own emotional blocks such as anger and envy.

When someone close to us is in agony, rather than getting our heads out of our asses to help them, we remain stuck in our closed mindsets, feeling anger toward the person for not listening to us in the first place or for committing acts we believe are stupid and idiotic, and instead of being there for the victim, we become disdained and detached from the present tense, unable to feel sorrow for someone who we believe behaved foolishly.

We also become detached from being able to express true sympathy because sometimes the pain of others forces us to reminisce about our own pain, the very same pain we have spent years avoiding and creating an emotional barrier toward.

We become selfish, and we perceive the victim as a trigger for our own emotional agony rather than as an innocent individual who needs our help. Because of this, we do everything we can to protect ourselves, acting in ways we wouldn't otherwise because we feel the need to prevent ourselves from pain at all costs, even if it means losing relationships because we cannot stand the suffering of others.

We find it easier to abandon and ghost people than be there for them in their time of need. This often happens when we are unable to separate emotions from personal pasts, absorbing the feelings of others as our own rather than seeing them as something external to us.

Like empathy, sympathy is an innate and learned skill that is often affected by how our environments and lifestyles have shaped us. In order to experience these skills, we would have had to have been taught how to separate our pain from the pain of others and be open and honest with ourselves enough to avoid triggering repressed feelings when we experience the feelings of others.

We lack these skills because, for so long, we have been condemned for having feelings and taught to shut them down whenever they arise at all costs, making us incapable of relating to or experiencing the feelings of others without taking offense.

As a result of not being able to portray compassion toward others, we end up lacking compassion toward ourselves, leaving us disconnected from our authentic selves and incapable of sympathizing with ourselves when we truly need it.

We use this disconnection with ourselves and others as a form of defense mechanism for our egos because we feel that if we sympathize, we open ourselves to the potential of taking in the pain of others, and many of us have tried to avoid pain for so long that we are not mentally prepared to even come into contact with the pain of others.

Because of this disconnection and fear of vulnerability, we resort to reacting selfishly with zero concern for the sensations of others, focusing more on status and benefit toward ourselves that we would rather lose others than attempt to understand them.

We have the tendency to behave selfishly, only looking out for what's best for us, that we lose the ability to hesitate when it comes to banishing the needs of others.

Don't get me wrong, it's not like human beings are completely incapable of sympathizing with others; it is in our inherent natures to want to help those around us. However, for so long, we have trained our brains to not care that apathy becomes almost instinctual as if we don't even notice when we dismiss others.

CHAPTER 14
HUMANS ARE IMPULSIVE

We React Toward Life Situations Based on Impulsivity and Fleeting Feelings

MOST OF US believe that the way we behave is based on pure logic and common sense. However, what we continue to live in denial about is that our behaviors are often driven by our raw emotions rather than our intellects.

This goes back to how we find it difficult to separate our logical selves from our emotional selves, actively pushing aside our emotional brains to prevent them from overpowering our logical brains when it is almost impossible to do so.

We often don't realize what we're doing until we are in the midst of doing it, constantly acting on impulses and sudden shifts in emotion, a dangerous pattern we all face. However, despite how much we realize this is happening, we STILL find difficulty preventing our emotions from taking over; that's because we can't.

Our emotions are a permanent and constant part of us, a subjective state of mind that behaves as a reaction to our internal or external stimuli such as our memories or surroundings.

However, emotions themselves are not always considered "good" or "bad"; they are simply an expression of our reactions to events occurring around us, impacting our decisions toward certain situations at any given time. Our emotions always play a key role in our daily lives despite how much we believe our decisions are based on lucidity and rationality.

The concept of "Emotional Intelligence" is our ability to understand and manage our emotions rather than letting them roam free impulsively and spontaneously. However, managing our emotions differs greatly from suppressing them. When we ignore our feelings, pushing away the pain we are meant to feel, we are neglecting our mind's way of telling us that something is wrong and needs to be dealt with.

Ignoring our feelings doesn't automatically make the pain go away; it just further pushes down feeling after feeling until the pain becomes so great that we are no longer able to manage the emotions effectively and as a result, we let them run rogue and negatively impact our decision-making, such as turning toward unhealthy coping mechanisms.

In contrast, there are also those who prevent the suppression of their feelings altogether, letting their emotions take charge of their lives at all times, acting impulsively and wildly without keeping their emotions in check and scanning their surroundings to ensure the appropriate situations.

These individuals tend to lack emotional intelligence and instead, behave like animals, living solely off their instincts and acting on temporary emotions rather than recognizing which emotions should be released and which should be quelled.

Temporary emotions include wanting to smash a car out of anger that someone instigated, wanting to eat everything in sight even when on a diet, or wanting to blurt hurtful words without considering the feelings of others. Individuals with Borderline Personality Disorder often act out solely based on temporary emotions, which in the long run, can lead to dangerous and fatal consequences.

Because Borderline Personality Disorder is most commonly characterized by impulsive reactions and emotional outbursts toward situations that are out of their control, it's no wonder that BPD victims have a negative correlation with emotional intelligence.

Impulsivity is a characteristic where those experiencing it fail to take the time to reflect on their feelings before acting upon them. They let their emotions run wild despite the situation and costs of the situation. Once borderliners decide they want something or have a temporary goal in mind, their emotions are ready to be unleashed, regardless of who they hurt in doing so.

Many people without personality disorders suppress their emotions, taking in and observing their surrounding situations and circumstances before unleashing the beasts inside their minds. Individuals suffering from BPD, however, fail to possess this ability to quell their overwhelming feelings, causing them to not realize the consequences of their emotions until the damages are too great.

While emotions are seen as a method of self-expression when verbal words have become silenced for most individuals, borderliners view emotions as their entire beings, relying on them wholeheartedly to help them respond to life and to grab hold of what they desire, trusting solely on their natural and raw instincts rather than their common sense.

According to a study by Gardner and colleagues in 2009, 523 adults were measured on four features of Borderline Personality Disorder: affective instability, identity disturbance, negative relationships, and self-harm using the Mayer-Salovey-Caruso Emotional Intelligence Test (MSCEIT) and the Schutte Emotional Intelligence Scale (SEIS). As predicted, they found a negative correlation between measures of emotional intelligence and borderline personality traits, especially in the ability to manage emotions, confirming the emotional dysregulation of this disorder.

Willpower often refers to how our minds are able to handle the influx of emotions our bodies experience, and the efforts we make in attempts to control our impulsive behaviors when they arise.

There are three components to every emotion: the subjective, the physiological, and the expressive. The subjective component refers to how an individual experiences a given emotion caused by a given situation. Some individuals are more prone to certain types of emotions, like anger or sadness, than others, some of whom experience indifference toward situations that would normally negatively impact others.

The physiological component refers to how an individual's body reacts to said emotion, such as the feeling of tensing up or experiencing heart palpitations. Finally, the expressive component refers to how an individual behaves in response to the emotion being experienced, either choosing to act upon it and create havoc on those around, suppress it and create fatal consequences on their own mind, or dissect it and figure out why they are experiencing the feeling and how to rationally handle it in a healthy manner.

Those who tend to behave more impulsively in response to their emotions are often those who have been drained of their emotional strengths and willpower to deal with the constant arising situations, giving into their urges and desires because self-control has been too difficult and painful.

There are several factors that can lead to a depletion of emotional strength, including ego depletion and cognitive load. Ego depletion refers to constantly having to deal with situations where the mind conflicts with the emotions, a constant battle between wanting and not being able to have, trying but grasping onto the last straw in attempts to succeed.

This constant back and forth ultimately leads to a loss of motivation and determination, causing individuals to give into their urges as a way to end the war.

Cognitive load, such as having to deal with overwhelming stress, is often a gateway for people to behave impulsively, dealing with so many emotions and situations at once that they run out of space in their logical thinking to react rationally to the uprising emotion, forgetting how to react other than with instinctual impulse because their convoluted minds no longer have space to store the influx of feelings.

CHAPTER 15
STRUGGLE TO SEE BEYOND

We Struggle to See Beyond Our Current Emotions and Life Circumstances

THE HUMAN MIND knows no limit. Some say the mind is a sanctuary, a heavenly place where we can imagine ourselves and let ourselves grow and develop into beautiful and strong individuals.

Others, however, perceive the human mind as a burning fire of hell, closed doors where we trap ourselves behind when we are ready to relinquish and die. Although neither perception is completely right, all of us have experienced both ideals at one point or another in our lives.

Most of us understand the struggle and grit it takes to feel like we're literally walking from one of those places to the other, the agony we all strive to avoid by preventing our minds from wandering altogether.

However, what we don't realize is that many of us are already living behind closed doors in the burning fires of hell, living comfortably in it as we become blind-sighted by how our refusals to express ourselves means that we are already mentally near death. We become blinded by the smoke that arises from our burning emotions struggling to escape, clouding our perceptions and inflicting pain upon ourselves when we are unsure as to why.

Eventually, we give up on trying to keep this fog from overpowering us that, rather than accepting that this smoke is just our emotions trying to roam free, we drive ourselves crazy trying to continue to push this smoke aside, seeing no way out, and turning to suicide as the ultimate way out of our miseries.

However, we have only come to this point because society has told us that expressing our emotions, especially the negative ones, can wreak havoc on us and cause the world to lock us in isolation for being outcasts. We live in a world where sharing our true feelings with each other warrant criticisms and laughter, forcing us to literally lock ourselves away or suppress our emotions from public eyes.

Because of this, some of us would rather remain stuck in the hell inside our minds, securely holding onto the emotions and refusing to let them loose, than live freely in a place where our minds are no longer convoluted.

We all crave to be individuals, but at the same time, we loathe ourselves for not being able to fit in with the standards of others, causing us to remain stuck in a cage where we constantly crave something we cannot have.

Suicidal thoughts are not uncommon when we remain stuck in our own minds with the refusal to accept that our emotions are not meant to be held inside under lock and key. These thoughts often strike when we feel hopeless that our situations will ever change, when we feel like we no longer have control over our lives and begin to lose meaning and purpose, or when we feel like we must bow down to the biased rules of others in order to stay alive in this messed up modern world.

We experience suicidal thoughts when we feel like we have fought the fight but end up losing every single time, struggling to hold something together as it breaks apart in our palms.

However, we only remain trapped in this suicidal mindset because we allow ourselves to be. By locking our emotions inside our heads, we're basically giving victory to those around us who may or may not even know what they're talking about and allowing them to cause obliteration to ourselves.

We are the only ones who can put ourselves in danger's way, just like we are the only ones who can take ourselves out of our suicidal miseries and see that we are the only ones forcing ourselves to live in a world we do not want.

We are trapped and encased by how we are taught to see the world, seeing our lives as a reflection of the lives of society and incapable of perceiving ourselves beyond the delinquents and degenerates we have falsely convinced ourselves to be.

CHAPTER 16
OBJECTIVELY IMPOSSIBLE

Thinking Objectively is Almost Impossible

MANY OF US foolishly believe that we are truly capable of thinking and perceiving the world in an objective manner, where we are able to take all the components of a situation and piece them together without allowing our own biases to get in the way. False.

We, as human beings, are only able to perceive the world subjectively, where we always, subconsciously or not, allow our biased views and opinions to affect the way we perceive any given situation.

For example, if we perceive a fight between a man and a woman in the middle of the street, depending on our preconceived notion about the male and female genders, we will automatically and biasedly choose one side over the other, claiming "facts" such as "he must have instigated the argument first" or "she probably deserved it" without fully understanding the entire story.

No one is able to perceive a situation 100% objectively as we have opinions of our own that will always entice our favorability toward one side or the other.

When we observe situations, we will always observe them based on our past experiences because we don't know any other way. We also cannot truly fact check the reality of given situations because even if we question the perpetrators at the scene of the crime, their subjective answers will in turn skew our subjective beliefs, never truly knowing which to accept as truth.

Even if we try to view a situation as independent of ourselves, there will always be a gap between how a situation appears on the outside and what's really going on in the situation behind the scene.

For example, take the man and the woman arguing. On the outside, it may look like a couple quarreling due to some sort of disagreement or domestic instability. However, for all we know, that "couple" could just be strangers who were in some kind of accident moments before or friends exclaiming in loud tones that come off as disputes.

We tend to focus our beliefs and judgments based solely on what we "see," never truly getting down to the points that transcend external appearances, never being able to make a conclusion based on the ENTIRE story, and therefore, making it difficult for us to truly perceive any given situation objectively.

CHAPTER 17
STUCK INSIDE MIND

We Remain Stuck Inside our Own Minds, Creating a Myriad of Internal Problems and Complications

OUR BRAINS ARE incredible and ever-functioning organs that constantly work their gears to ensure our survivals. They make it almost impossible to truly stop thinking because our brains like to acknowledge and assess all circumstances and scenarios that are occurring around us even when we are not facing a conflict.

Have you ever tried to sit down to meditate, only to find

your mind wandering and distracted less than a minute later? Our brains are regularly moving, sometimes even to our demise. This happens when we often overthink. Overthinking an external situation or an internal flaw can become detrimental when we focus our brains on these negative circumstances.

Our brains do not understand how to filter good situations from bad so when we overthink how flawed our appearances are, our brains become obsessive in those thoughts, eventually spiraling into low self-esteem of not being good enough and feeling a lack of self-love due to feeling unloved by others.

Our brains are designed to worry, always seeking the next big thing to "fix" or "update." This component, although can create failure to our self-esteem, can help us create the greatest of creations by allowing us the chance at imagination.

Our minds weren't built to keep us optimistic and blissful all the time. We aren't meant to be upbeat and positive individuals; our brains were created to allow us to feel content in any given situation by allowing us to solve the problems around us to live stable lives.

However, when we overthink, our perceptions become occluded where we are only able to see the world from one perspective, such as the one perspective of not feeling good enough, not being valued enough, or not feeling loved enough, where our brains begin to convince us that these self-generated thoughts are truths, creating a lifetime of traumatic and psychological complications.

When we train our brains to focus on one aspect of our thoughts, they do, turning toward unnecessary and toxic thoughts and away from productive and efficient mindsets that we need to possess to survive in this world. Fortunately, our brains also possess a skill known as "Neuroplasticity," where they have the capacity to change patterns of thinking over the course of a person's lifetime depending on which direction they are being directed toward.

Human beings love living inside their own heads, where the thoughts and surroundings are familiar, safe, and comfortable. This way, we can avoid stressing over the anxieties of "what if" and fearing for the potential unknown despite whether our current mindsets are self-destructive because living in discomfort triumphs living in fear.

We find comfort in staying in our problems because we know what to expect. Our familiar enigmas make us feel like we're beating life because no one is meant to go through life without experiencing some sort of problem or issue. When we live in tension and mayhem, that is, when we feel like we are alive, we are only alive in anguish. This has been especially true over the last decade or so, where social media has idealized struggles and depressing thoughts as the "norm," to the point where if we don't experience depressive thoughts, then we are not living life "well-enough."

The social media world has caused us to become trapped inside our own emotions because an indication of emotional expression is usually met with criticism and hate from Internet trolls. The sole purpose of Internet trolls is to demote our self-esteem as they find value in bringing others down.

Internet platforms such as Facebook and Instagram drown their users with subliminal messages that cause them to go against themselves and their true values. Authentic posts on Instagram about true happiness or true sadness are often met with hateful comments telling users to go kill themselves because they're "too fat to deserve happiness" or they "should just die instead of posting about their misery."

Because of this constant negativity, social media platform users have turned away from posting about their true feelings, and instead, turn to monotonous emotions and boastful bragging of materialistic things and accomplishments because they can still gain all the attention and fame without all the crushing emotional pain.

Thus, we find ourselves imprisoned inside our own gruesome emotions, emotions that continue to pile on top of each other, and we lock ourselves in beneath them as we have lost our outlet to escape from our own minds. Because we have lost this escape toward freedom, we eventually become mindfucked and explode when we find that we are no longer able to hold in our volatile feelings of anguish.

The human mind is designed to constantly evolve and survive not just to get by on chance or live based on the ideals of others. When we suffer, it is because we have given up on trying to achieve greatness not because we are finally living life.

Suffering and depressive thoughts cause us to remain stuck in the past, incessantly ruminating on events that had already happened instead of focusing on changing current events, causing us to remain stuck in our preconceived philosophies. This inevitably causes us to live in monotony, accepting defeat and torment as the norm rather than the exception.

We end up becoming powerless in our own lives, enduring endless distress as everyday life. Circumstances around us are neither good nor bad, neither destructive nor prominent; it's our reactions to them and how we choose to connect with those circumstances that dictate how our lives will turn out.

When we choose to give our powers away to our surroundings, we are actively choosing to give our lives away to those we don't even know. When we hold our emotions in and shelter them from the world, we are telling everyone around us that our lives matter that much less than theirs.